Born to Learn

Born to Learn

A Transactional Analysis of Human Learning

Richard John Stapleton

Effective Learning Publications

Statesboro, Georgia, United States

EFFECTIVE LEARNING PUBLICATIONS
Statesboro, Georgia, United States

ISBN: 0692584331
ISBN 13: 9780692584330
Library of Congress Control Number: 2015919443
Effective Learning Publications, Statesboro, GA

For information, contact
Effective Learning Publications
PO Box 2265
Statesboro, Georgia 30459
E-mail: rjstapleton@bulloch.net
Website: www.effectivelearning.net

**To my descendants, students, teachers,
coaches, healers, mentors,
and colleagues**

Preface

From the moment of birth, humans transact with others to get their needs met. Some are naturally better at it than others, and some are born luckier than others because they have better parents. Their early experiences can have lasting effects.

Back in the mid-1970s when I started learning transactional analysis (TA), I thought TA might become a psychological equivalent of a Salk vaccine for polio, if children as early as possible were inoculated in TA 101 courses to prevent them from suffering unnecessary emotional and mental distress caused by the irrational Parent and Child script messages of adults around them, opening their young Adult eyes enough to enable them to see what was generally going on psychologically with their parents and the other giants populating their worlds, some over six feet tall, to enable them to grow up feeling OK as princesses and princes, rather than grow up feeling not-OK as frogs.

Consequently I decided in 1976 to add a transactional analysis credential, what is now called a CTA, certified transactional analyst, in education and organizational consulting to the three degrees I already had from Texas Tech University, a BS in economics in 1962, an MBA in organizational behavior in 1966, and a PhD in management science in 1969. After receiving the CTA in 1978, called a Special Fields Membership back in those days, I used TA in my management courses in the Georgia Southern University business school, plus I taught TA in night continuing education courses at Georgia Southern for adults in the community for several years after 1978. I also used TA doing organizational development work with several businesses. I was active with this TA work during 1978-1982, but it slacked off after that as TA began to wane in influence and consumer acceptance in the US. On the other hand, I continued to use TA in my business school management courses throughout my tenure as a teacher, spinning the spinner of the Classroom De-Gamer to start the case discussion in every class, up to when I retired from teaching in 2005.

Most of the writing in this book, in the first ten chapters, is a revision and reprinting of material in my book *De-Gaming Teaching and Learning: How to Motivate Learners and Invite OKness,* which I published through my imprint, Effective Learning Publications in 1979, and some of the writing in this book was published in my book *Business Voyages: Mental Maps, Scripts, Schemata and Tools for Discovering and Co-Constructing Your Own Business Worlds* published by Effective Learning Publications in 2011. Some of the material in *Business Voyages* was included in my earlier books *Managing Creatively: Action Learning in Action* (1976) and *The Entrepreneur: Concepts and Cases* (1985), both published by University Press of America.

I used the case method procedures in this book in my business courses at Georgia Southern University from 1970 to 2005, publishing the original idea for the de-Gaming process in 1979 in an article in the *Transactional Analysis Journal* titled "The Classroom De-Gamer."

To my knowledge, this is the first book to apply transactional analysis to the total learning process—which includes not only interpersonal relations among teachers and students but also factors such as learning contracts, classroom layouts, teaching methods, testing and grading procedures, discipline, course content, and administration.

This book content can be applied to learning processes in all organizations and groups, including families, businesses, and governments, providing insights and models for understanding how learning happens automatically through experience. The book shows how to increase the quality and quantity of learning and unlearning by changing the physical structure of the environment and the transactions of the process. In many cases, in order for productive new scripts, concepts and processes to be learned, previously learned scripts, concepts and processes must be unlearned, suppressed, let go of, or gotten rid of.

I have included in this book explanations of transactional analysis concepts and models with a view showing how they relate to learning processes: Parent, Adult, and Child ego states, contracts, strokes, transactions, Games, the Drama Triangle, discounting, rackets, the OK Corral, injunctions, scripts, and miniscripts. You may be familiar with these concepts and models from reading books on TA or from didactic or experiential training in TA workshops or training sessions. On the other hand, even if you have had no exposure to TA, you will be able to read, understand, and assimilate the TA material in this book.

Invented by psychiatrist Eric Berne, MD, TA has been around since the early 1960s, resulting in the creation of the International Transactional Analysis Association (ITAA) in 1964. The ITAA has published since then the *Transactional Analysis Journal,* conducted conferences, and provided training and certification programs, offering internationally through the years various levels of certification for professionals in diverse fields, including practitioners in medicine, psychology, social work, teaching, management consulting, law, counseling, and religion.

There were two broad types of certification in clinical and special fields: clinical certifications for practitioners offering psychotherapeutic services to clients and special fields certifications for nontherapists. I received what is now called a Certified Transactional Analyst (CTA) for the application of transactional analysis in education and organizations in 1978.

By around 1980, the ITAA had grown to about ten thousand members around the world including regular members and certified members. Regular members were not certified but participated in workshops and conferences and subscribed to the *Transactional Analysis Journal.* Certified members were allowed to advertise themselves as TA professionals and use TA charging fees with clients. In 2015, the ITAA had about nine hundred members, mostly certified professional members. No one seems to know for sure what caused interest in TA to wane, especially in the United States. Part of it was probably caused by cultural change. The 1960s and early 1970s in the United States were times of hippies, free love, and flower power; by 1980, US culture had become more authoritarian and conservative. In TA terms, more people cathected, energized, or "turned on" Free Child energy in their transactions in the 1960s and 1970s than they did after 1980, as the culture began to require more Critical Parent and Adapted Child energy.

For whatever it's worth, I still think TA works. The only problem is getting people to use it.

When people communicate, they "transact" with one another, buying and selling all sorts of social and psychological goods and services. They trade facts, favors, ideas, feelings, attitudes, and "strokes." Strokes are words, feelings, thoughts and deeds that affirm existence, called by transactional analysts "units of recognition." Strokes can be positive or negative. They are used in schools and in all organizations by people day in and day out, much like money is used in business markets. Some people are rich in strokes, and some are impoverished. I hope you can get richer in good strokes by reading this book. If you do, you will become happier and more satisfied. Conditional strokes are recognition you have to earn, such as grades in school. Unconditional strokes are freely given because someone likes and appreciates someone or something.

You don't have to have a PhD in psychology to recognize an ego state, a transaction, a Game, a racket, or script behavior or know when you've been stroked, positively or negatively.

I have spelled the word *Game* in this book with a capital *G* to emphasize that I am writing about psychological Games and not about games such as football, basketball, baseball, soccer, bridge, poker, or computer simulations. People playing these games may use psychological Games as tactics to help win the game, but Games and games are different. In games such as football, basketball, soccer, bridge, poker, or computer simulations, the goal is overt and known to everyone: the objective is to defeat your opponent, to be more OK than your opponent, and to beat your opponent. Psychological Games are covert and devious. These Games entail people beating up on others in varying degrees while pretending to be something other than a competitor or adversary—such as a good friend, a wise judge, a concerned parent, a righteous enforcer of rules, a helpless child, or an entertaining clown.

Transactional analysis became popular with the American public in the early 1970s, largely due to the success of Eric Berne's books. His most popular book was *Games People Play*, first published in 1964. Over two million copies of this book have been sold, and the book is still being sold in bookstores. *I'm OK—You're OK*, by Thomas Harris, MD, is another best-selling TA book. *Born to Win* by Muriel James is another. Another of Berne's best-selling books (his best in my opinion) was *What Do You Say After You Say Hello? The Psychology of Human Destiny*.

Since the early 1960s, hundreds of books and articles explaining, developing, using, and applying TA theory have been published by authors in various fields. Many of these books and articles are used as reference material in this book. TA has been applied by thousands of medical doctors, psychiatrists, social workers, ministers, teachers, management consultants, school administrators, managers, and other professionals. The International Transactional Analysis Association has published the *Transactional Analysis Journal (TAJ)* quarterly since 1972. Articles published in the *TAJ* are refereed in a blind-review process.

Many countries now have their own TA associations, and TA is being taught and used in many countries around Earth, including Mexico, Peru,

Japan, India, China and Russia. In recent years, TA usage has grown outside the United States, while the number of people belonging to the ITAA in the United States has declined.

My particular de-Gaming procedures for learning situations were developed from my experience as a human being, student, and teacher and from my general knowledge of TA.

Transactional analysis enables us to see more of the beauty, pathos, and complexity of human existence. Phenomena such as Parent, Adult, and Child ego states and Games are as relevant to teaching and learning as matter and energy are to physics. The major value of TA terms, models, and diagrams is that they make it easier for people to understand complex psychological processes.

I worked my way through the Texas Tech University doctoral program in business in 1966–1969, teaching two courses of Economics 133, American Economic History, a required introductory course for all business majors during the fall and spring semesters, for which I was paid $3,000 per academic year. Still single, I could live on that in those days. Back when there were plenty of good students, and Texas Tech prided itself on flunking students out, my Economics 133 coordinator told me to go into class, assume students were appendages to the desks, and then bombard and inundate them with facts and ideas for detailed, lengthy, true-false, multiple-choice, short-answer tests to weed some of them out of the business school. This was one the most challenging intellectual experiences of my life, having never taught a course at any level in any kind of school, but it caused me to learn a good bit about American economic history. I prepared and delivered hour-long lectures on the subject for college students on Monday, Wednesday, and Friday each fall and spring semester for three years. I taught the same course twelve times over three years, while taking a full load of doctoral courses on all business subjects and writing my doctoral dissertation.

Hopefully, reading this book will give you a better understanding of how human life is shaped and controlled by both social and psychological messages, transmitted to all humans throughout life from the moment of birth, social messages being overt and spoken, psychological messages being covert and silent.

Richard John Stapleton
Statesboro, Georgia, United States
January 1, 2016

Contents

LIST OF FIGURES

APPENDIX I

Appendix I is a PDF copy of "Optimizing the Fairness of Student Evaluations: A Study of Correlations Between Instructor Excellence, Study Production, Learning Production and Expected Grades," by Richard John Stapleton and Gene Murkison, a colleague of the author at Georgia Southern University, published in the *Journal of Management Education* in 2001 presenting a metric I (Richard) invented, the CITP, the composite indicator of teaching productivity, for fairly evaluating the teaching productivity of teachers, causing *learning* to occur in students, not disseminating canned content to help students score high enough on standardized tests. This is the most successful article I have written, which has by now in 2015 been cited as a reference in sixty refereed journal articles in several disciplines. The article has been cited in the professional literature several times in the last two years, proving it is still being read and used by serious educators at major universities. Read a PDF copy of "Optimizing the Fairness of Student Evaluations" at http://www.sagepub.com/holt/articles/Stapleton.pdf.

One

Transactional Analysis: A Way Of Looking At Learning

In the late 1950s, Eric Berne, MD, invented a new way of describing the structure and functioning of the human personality. I became fascinated with what he called ego states and what he called transactional analysis while reading his Book of the Month Club selection I received in 1969, *What Do You Say After You Say Hello: The Psychology of Human Destiny.*

Berne grew up in Montreal, Canada, the son of a medical doctor father and a writer mother. He became a medical doctor specializing in psychiatry and developed an extensive and successful writing career, publishing scores of scholarly and scientific articles and several best-selling books. His most popular book was *Games People Play*, first published in 1964. His writing was based on empirical observations treating his psychiatric patients and clients and on his study and reading in disciplines in the physical and social sciences. He asserted that transactional analysis was a science harder than economics but softer than physics—hard in this sense being that propositions are verifiable and predictive. This assertion has been contested in the TA literature and elsewhere through the years, with critics asserting that because TA propositions have not been tested with scientific methods, TA is not a science. On the other hand, some observers (including this writer) assert that TA variables such as ego states and transactions, although metaphorical, are observable as people communicate; therefore, TA is scientific in the sense it is based on empirical observation.

Some of Berne's major assumptions were based on the scientific work and writings of Wilder Penfield, MD (1891–1976), a neurosurgeon and fellow Canadian. Penfield, sometimes called a cartographer or mapmaker of the brain, was able to elicit various responses in patients undergoing brain surgery by touching an electrode to certain parts of the brain. Berne theorized that transactional analysis variables such as ego states were stored in neurons and neural networks in the brain, much like information is stored on silicon chips in computers.

In 1957, Berne published an article titled "Ego States in Psychotherapy" in the *American Journal of Psychotherapy* in which he presented his invention of three stacked circles modeling the three basic ego states of the human personality.

The top circle represents the Parent part of the personality, the middle circle represents the Adult part, and the bottom circle represents the Child part, as shown in Figure 1.

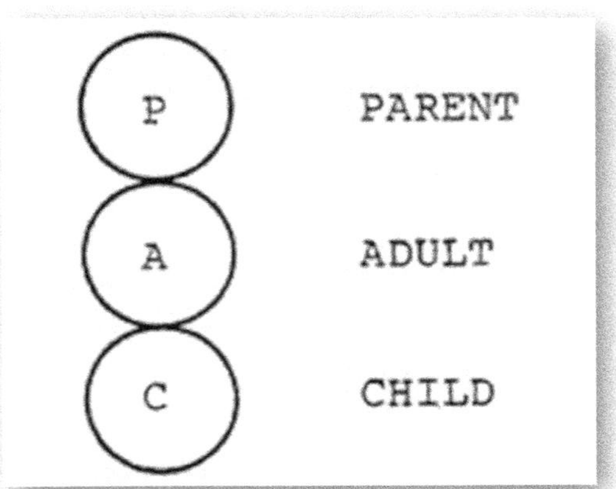

Figure 1. Eric Berne's Three Stacked Circles.

The Parent Ego State

People gradually develop their personalities as they grow up. It's no secret that people tend to become similar to their biological or foster parents in various aspects of their personalities. When someone says, "You're acting just like your mother or father," chances are, that individual is right. At times, people do act just like their parents. At such times, they are acting, feeling, or thinking from the Parent ego state.

People copy the gestures, thinking patterns, beliefs, irrationalities, and skills of their parents. Children at early ages tend to believe that everything about their parents is true, real, and moral, and they incorporate in their own personalities what they see, feel, and hear.

The human brain in the early years operates much like a videotape machine. In his or her head, the child videotapes the parents' behavior in living color with sound. These films serve as basic guidelines and policies for how to think, feel, and behave in various situations throughout life.

If the videotaped lessons were good ones, if the behavior, thinking and feeling of the biological or surrogate parents were appropriate, then the person carrying them around in his or her head will tend to do, feel, and think appropriately in school and life. Unfortunately, if what was videotaped was inappropriate or crazy, the person carrying these tapes around will tend to do, think, or feel inappropriately at times.

The major lottery in in life and prelife, in which people win or lose, is the evolutionary lottery that determines parents for children and children for parents. Some people are lucky enough to have parents who were good role models to videotape at an early age. Others were unlucky enough to have had parents who were models of poor behavior, thinking, and feeling and who were videotaped and copied as much as good parents. This is a fundamental injustice of human existence. No one can help but videotape what he or she is exposed to at an early age. What one videotapes helps determine one's success or failure or happiness or misery in life.

Those of us (the majority of mankind) born in families that produced offspring learning thinking, feeling, or doing patterns that are less than totally appropriate must watch our Parent ego states. Blindly following the impulses and urges of the Parent ego state may produce failure, not success.

People having inadequate Parent ego states should become aware of why and in what ways the Parent is inadequate and develop means of controlling detrimental effects. In general, in order for significant changes for control to be developed, the help of a skilled therapist is required. It is almost impossible for a human being to be really objective about his or her Parent.

It is often easy to see people operating from their Parent ego state. They look like parents. They are pointing with their index fingers; they are looking down their noses with their heads tilted back; they are saying things like "never do this again," "make sure you always do this," and "if I've told you once, I've told you a thousand times." They have stereotypical ways of saying things, frowning, smiling, and wrinkling their eyebrows and foreheads; and they have stereotypical ways of pursing their lips, jutting their chin out, flexing their jaw muscles, clenching their teeth, or holding their shoulders and hips.

You can see yourself in your Parent ego state by looking in a mirror or hearing yourself on a tape recorder. If you think about it, you can internally see, feel, and hear yourself in your parent—doing, feeling, or talking just like your father or mother. You can even hear yourself using the same clichés your parents used.

Being in the Parent ego state is not necessarily related to age. Kindergarten students can be spotted in their Parent ego states.

The Adult Ego State

The Adult ego state is the logical, rational, businesslike part of a person. The Adult is the here-and-now data gatherer and processor. The Adult identifies alternatives for problems and opportunities and assigns probabilities to possible consequences of alternatives. In general, the better people can predict the consequences of possible actions, the more effective they are in life.

The Adult ego state makes decisions on the basis of facts, data, logic, and probabilities in the here and now. People form representations of what life is like in their minds based on facts, data, imagination, past teachings, and various forms of information. The more these representations approximate what really exists in the real world, the better a person's decisions will be. What people refer to as "common sense" and "good judgment" is produced by the Adult ego state.

Using the Adult ego state, decisions are not based on platitudes, ideologies, or theories. Adult decisions are based on appropriate facts, given stated goals and objectives, taking into account the probabilities of the consequences of choices.

In that small fraction of human decisions where the best choice can be proved using mathematical models, it is Adult to use mathematical models. In the vast majority of human decisions, however, the facts are so untidy and unusual that they will not fit standard mathematical models. In these cases, humans have to use common sense, taking all the facts into account with the Adult ego state. It is an unfortunate that with hindsight, all humans will frequently think they would have been better off had they made different choices. Chances are the Adult ego state will make better decisions than the Parent ego state or the Child ego state, but many mistakes will still be made. The world is too large and complex, and human minds are too small for any human to always make good decisions.

The Adult ego state in the brain of the human being is more sophisticated than any computer. A computer makes decisions only according to preprogrammed rules and procedures—past learning. Current data can be processed by a computer only according to programs, which have previously been read in the computer. These programs constitute the "Parent" of the computer. Computers can't decide to reprogram their own Parent programs because of current data being read in. Computers can't decide to improve their programming because of reading a new book of ideas or models. Humans can.

If humans are skilled, knowledgeable, or "autonomous" enough, they can decide which Parent tapes or programs to use, change, or create to process current data, based on an online, real-time reading of data. Computers can be programmed to select among alternative programs based on incoming data, but there must be an algorithm programmed in for this; that is, another Parent tape must exist to simulate real autonomy. Computers cannot arbitrarily create or change their programs. Perhaps the real difference between the human Adult ego state and the computer is that the human Adult can change Parent tapes based on new incoming data and information in the here and now. But it's not easy, as we shall see.

Humans are rarely, if ever, truly autonomous or truly arbitrary. Most, if not all, of what they do, think, and feel is due to past programming, learning, and conditioning. Success, for many people, depends more upon forgetting or "letting go of" past programming and conditioning that was inappropriate than it does upon learning new knowledge or skills. Being able to use the Adult is not necessarily a function of age. Young and old people have Adult ego states, which can be cathected—that is, energized, or turned on.

The Child Ego State

The Child ego state is generally more complex and powerful than the Parent or Adult.

The Child ego state contains not only the natural feelings and instincts of uninhibited, uncontaminated, uneducated, "natural" human beings; the Child also contains unnatural Parent feelings, behaviors, and beliefs introjected from biological parents and other parent figures in early life.

Introject is a fancy word for taking in, or absorbing, from parents and other influential people, energy and direction, much like a plant takes in energy from the soil and sun through osmosis, automatically.

The Child ego state contains the Parent, Adult, and Child of the biological or surrogate parents as perceived and videotaped by the person of concern before he or she was seven or eight years old.

The Child, therefore, contains the natural part of the personality, which may be suppressed, and it contains the adapted part of the personality, which is what the parents, rightly or wrongly, in conjunction with the child's correct and incorrect perceptions, caused to be learned.

Thus, we have the Natural Child and the Adapted Child. The Natural Child naturally feels mad, sad, glad, and scared when it seems appropriate. The Natural Child does what it wants to do because it wants to do it. The Adapted Child, on the other hand, is thinking, feeling, or doing what the parents have taught, consciously or unconsciously, verbally and nonverbally.

Early messages heard and videotaped from parent figures become lodged in the Child ego state, and, thus, people have a Parent in the Child. This Parent in the Child, which contains videotapes of all three Parent, Adult, and Child ego states of the father and mother, is the most significant ego state.

People rarely ignore their parents' teachings. Even if they decide to always do the opposite of what their parents have taught them, they are still letting their parents run their lives. The person decides not to think, feel, or do naturally for himself or herself. Doing what the Parent dictates is OK if the individual can be successful doing it. Harming the self or others by obeying the Parent, however, is not OK.

Functions of The Ego States

The human personality can be looked at from the standpoint of the functions it performs or from the standpoint of what it is and where it comes from.

The functions of the personality are drawn in TA modeling, as shown in Figure 2.

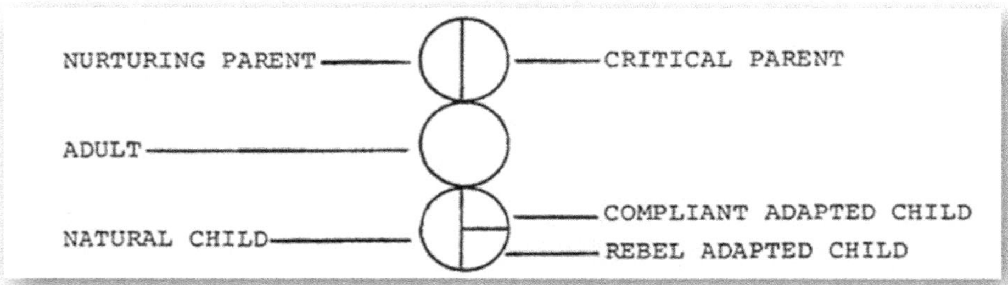

Figure 2. Functions of the Ego States.

There are six basic personality functions performed by six ego states:

1. The Nurturing Parent ego state is the part that cheers, encourages, and protects.
2. The Critical Parent ego state sets limits, criticizes, judges, and evaluates.
3. The Adult ego state processes real data in the environment in word and number form, thinks logically, delineates alternatives for problems and opportunities, and assigns probabilities to the consequences of alternatives.

4. The Compliant Adapted Child ego state is the part that always obeys Parent messages—the agreeable, nonthinking, cooperative part of the personality.
5. The Rebel Adapted Child ego state is developed by many people for automatically rebelling against parents and authority in general.
6. The Natural Child ego state is the fun-loving, Game-free, spontaneous part of the personality that "naturally" does, feels, and thinks.

We all need some of these functions in our personalities. Unfortunately, some people overdevelop some of the functions and underdevelop others.

The most productive and creative classrooms and organizations are heavily endowed with Natural Child, Adult, and Nurturing Parent.

Structure of the Ego States

The structure of the personality is modeled in Figure 3.

The C_2, the second-order Child ego state, contains the three ego states a person develops before the age of seven or so—the first-order C_1, A_1, and P_1. The C_1 is the original "natural" Child that existed at birth—the natural feelings and instincts.

The A_1 is sometimes called the "Little Professor," an illogical thinking device developed at an early age that relies primarily on intuition.

The P_1, sometimes referred to as the "electrode," or the "Pig Parent" (Steiner, 1974), contains accurate and inaccurate messages received and interpreted from parents or parent figures prior to the age of six or seven. Many of these messages are negative and will be discussed in more detail in the section on scripts.

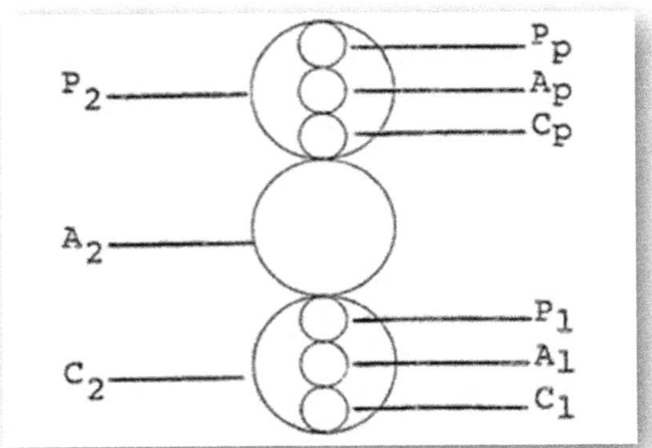

Figure 3. Structure of the Ego States.

Within the P_1 are contained the Parent, Adult, and Child ego states of parent figures as accurately and inaccurately videotaped by the person of concern before the age of seven or so.

The A_2 is the Adult ego state developed after age seven or so, which thinks more logically and businesslike.

The P_2 is the Parent ego state developed after the age of seven or so and includes the rules, regulations, words of wisdom, and videotapes of parent figures exposed to. The P_2 is continually updated. I am updating your P_2 right now. The three circles inside the P_2 are the Parent, Adult, and Child ego states of persons exposed to after age seven or so.

People are thus composed of Child feelings, messages, and ideas that they never forget; an Adult part, which is capable of using logical judgment based on current facts; and a Parent part, that makes decisions based on rules, models, formulas, theories, and precedents discovered and laid down by others.

Whether someone feels, thinks, decides, and acts appropriately in the here and now depends not only on which ego state he or she uses but also on the quality of the content of the ego states.

Strokes

A stroke is a unit of human recognition. It may be positive or negative. It may be verbal or nonverbal. It may be a greeting or a response. A stroke can be a physical touch or a hug. A stroke may be a thought, a feeling, or an impression. A stroke may be a compliment or a criticism.

Strokes are to transactional analysis what money is to economics and atoms are to physics. They are the basic power, building block, and medium of exchange of the field of knowledge.

In order for a stroke to exist, a human being must somehow be "touched." In most cases, one person must be touched by another in some way in order to be stroked. Although not as potent as person-to-person stroking, self-stroking exists.

Plastic strokes are make-believe, untrue compliments that people give, usually to manipulate. Target strokes are strokes that relate to reality and are those the receiver appreciates.

Positive strokes are positive compliments and feedback. Negative strokes carry negative feedback and discouragement.

Conditional strokes, which can be negative or positive, are given to people for meeting or not meeting standards through a Parent ego state; unconditional strokes are given from a Child ego state because someone is liked for being himself or herself.

The right target stroke, given at the right moment by the right person, can have a profound and lasting effect upon someone's life. The effect may be positive or negative. In group TA work, especially when Gestalt therapy techniques are used, people sometimes "explode" emotionally when the right stroke hits its mark.

The nucleus of the human personality contains the P_1. The P_1 contains early parental messages, which are sometimes called "witch" or "ogre" messages (Steiner 1974). Such messages tell a person to do, think, or feel something that is harmful to him or her.

P_1 messages enter the young child via verbal and nonverbal means like radiation entering Earth's atmosphere. The energy thus absorbed remains trapped in the P_1. The absorption and storing of P_1 messages comes about in the struggle to secure enough strokes to stay alive. If the strokes flying about the environment of the young child are crooked, plastic, cold, negative, or almost non-nonexistent, negative emotions and beliefs, grief, anger, and negative opinions about self and others will be trapped in the P_1.

P_1 messages and energy can be released through various modes of therapy. A powerful stroke from another human being is probably required to release the trapped negativity. These good strokes are sometimes premeditated, created, and delivered by people with sufficient genius to see what is almost unseeable. More often, these potent strokes naturally emanate from genuinely loving people, and one hits its mark randomly. Being fortunate enough to be around stroke-rich people is the best kind of luck.

Society represses the free giving and receiving of strokes (Steiner 1971). We learn at early ages what stroking is and is not socially acceptable. What is acceptable and not acceptable varies greatly from family to family. Some families are relatively free in stroking, and others are extremely repressive. Some are stroke rich; others are stroke impoverished.

In general, we are not supposed to "hug" other people in public. In most school systems and businesses, if we were to go around hugging our students, employees, and fellow faculty members and managers, we would probably be looked upon with more than mild disapproval.

I don't go around always hugging people. I can see and have experienced and felt the satisfying effects of good hugs from hundreds of OK people at TA conferences, TA workshops, and other places. I think the world would indeed be better off if we could go around hugging people all the time and never get hurt. But, given the way many people are, I don't think going around always hugging people is the thing to do. If this is your practice, and it works for you, great, keep it up. Unfortunately, people sometimes consider Natural Child and Nurturing Parent hugging to be sleazy and Gamey. And hugging can become so ritualized that its value is diminished.

Get stroke rich, and give valuable strokes away profusely, but use your Adult in deciding on the transactions necessary to do it.

The world is richer in stroke production and consumption now than it was in the Victorian nineteenth century. I think we will continue to get richer and richer in strokes.

Good strokes are the best thing in life, and, so far as I can tell, they are the only medicine that helps emotionally disturbed people.

You don't have to be emotionally disturbed to need strokes. In fact, the reason you are not emotionally disturbed in the first place is that you have had plenty of good strokes. Cut off your supply of good strokes, and you might catch a good case of emotional illness.

The Analysis of Transactions

Transactional analysis as the term is used in the TA occupation is a trade name that includes the analysis of transactions and several other kinds of analysis, such as Game analysis, script analysis, functional analysis, structural analysis, and relationship analysis.

Transactional analysis as a subset of "Transactional Analysis" is the analysis of transactions between two or more people.

What is a transaction? A transaction is a transfer or a trade of feelings, thoughts, attitudes, and strokes through communication from one ego state to another.

Transactional analysts are not necessarily interested in seeing how people trade, spend, save, and invest their money; they are mainly interested in seeing how people transact with, save, and invest their strokes.

People gain and lose in transactions. They feel better or they feel worse after transacting. They have increased self-esteem or decreased self-esteem. They have more useful knowledge or are more confused.

When two or more people communicate, there are a minimum of six personalities involved, as there are three in each person—the Parent, Adult, and Child ego states, as shown in Figure 4.

In Figure 4, I have diagrammed the most common transactions: Adult to Adult, Parent to Parent, Parent to Child, Child to Parent, and Child to Child.

All of the transactions diagrammed in Figure 4 are complementary. In all, there are nine basic complementary transactions. Transactions are complementary if the stimulus-response vectors are parallel between any pairing of ego states.

Complementary Transactions

A complementary transaction is a transaction in which all parties respond from the appropriate ego state. The appropriate ego state is the one the stimulator was aiming for when he or she started the communication process.

When you decide to communicate with someone, whether verbally or nonverbally, you somehow decide, consciously or unconsciously, which ego state you want to use, or "come from." You decide to "come on" parentlike, adultlike, or childlike.

Let's say you decide to come on from your Parent ego state, and assume you are stimulating, or causing, the transaction.

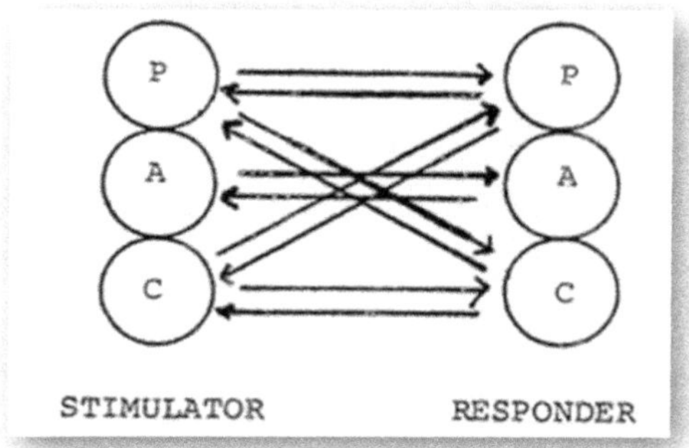

Figure 4. Complementary Transactions.

The first thing you do is select the thought or words to use; you next decide on posture, voice tone, facial expression, and body language. You might plan this consciously with your A_2, or your C_2 might do it for you.

Coming on Parent, you tend to use words like "always," "never," and so on—dogmatic-like expressions. Your voice probably changes tone, becoming firmer and more emphatic; and your body probably stiffens somewhat. You may beam your stimulus vector, your line of communication, at the Child ego state in your responder, as shown in Figure 5.

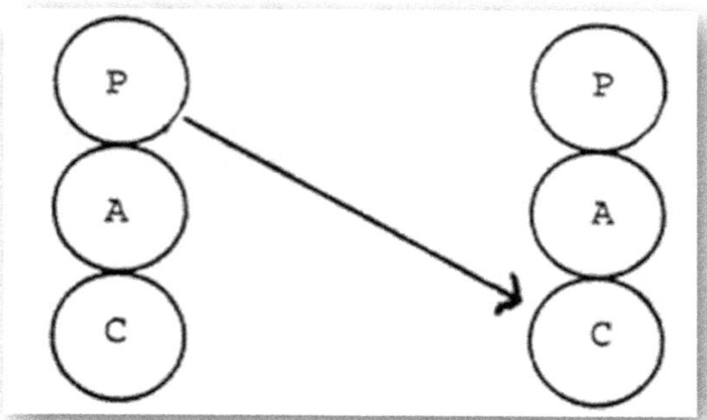

Figure 5. A Parent-Child Transaction.

Assuming you indeed set the above up, and assuming you get back what you want in the way of response, the other person will "come back" Child. He or she will turn on the Child ego state to respond, as shown in Figure 6.

The transactions in Figures 5 and 6 are complementary. A complementary transaction is one in which stimulus-response vectors, or lines of communication, are parallel. If the stimulus-response vectors are parallel, this means the responder used the appropriate ego state in responding, the ego state the communication stimulator tried to plug into in the first place. The responder satisfied the stimulator.

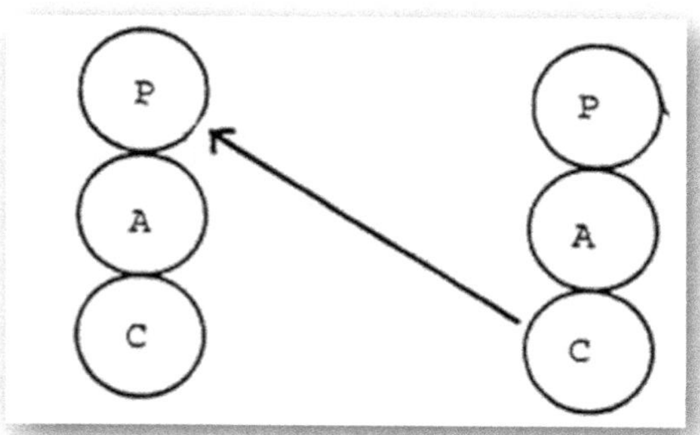

Figure 6. A Child-Parent Transaction.

You may be thinking (here I go mind reading again) you don't decide which ego state to use—you just act naturally—and that if you did decide which ego state to use to get along better, you would be manipulating yourself and others, and to heck with this whole TA process. I have observed several people respond like this when learning about controlling ego states and transactions.

My view is that you consciously or unconsciously decide which ego state to use in communicating, even if you have not learned the terminology for ego states.

Would you like to draw them in the matrix in Figure 7?

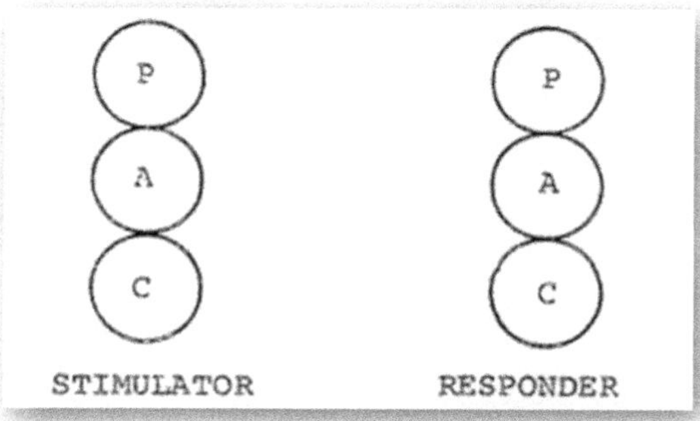

Figure 7. A Blank Transactional Matrix.

Crossed Transactions

Crossed transactions often emanate from "cross" adults or children. People sometimes cross transactions for the sheer devilment of "ticking" someone off. A crossed transaction is one that involves nonparallel stimulus-response vectors, as shown in Figure 8.

Crossed transactions can occur in any number of combinations. They result in bad vibrations between people, and communication tends to cease when they occur.

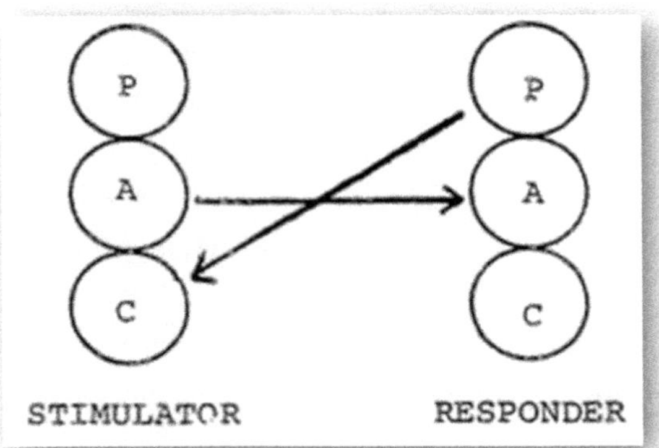

Figure 8. A Crossed Transaction.

Sometimes it is a good idea to deliberately cross transactions to get away from someone who is "locking" you into repetitive, over-and-over-again transactions in which you come out the loser (Karpman 1971).

Ulterior Transactions

An ulterior transaction is a silent, covert transaction in which you tell someone something without putting it in words. You use body language and verbal cues of various kinds. This occurs in various combinations. A sample ulterior transaction is drawn in Figure 9. The actual ulterior, or "psychological," transaction is normally drawn with a dotted line.

The above transaction is also known as a duplex transaction. Duplex transactions involve double messages or "talking out of both sides of your mouth at once." Triplex messages also exist.

It is possible for two sets of ulterior, or duplex, transactions to be going on simultaneously in a communication episode between people. Two people may be sending and receiving double messages, as shown in Figure 10.

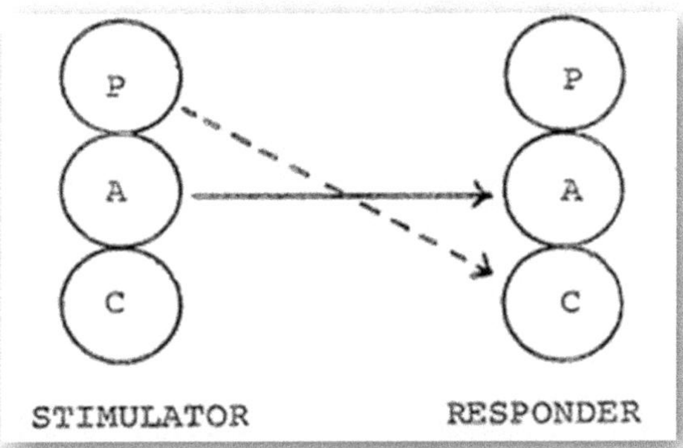

Figure 9. A Duplex Transaction.

Most people are not consciously aware of ego states as they communicate with others. Ego states in people can shift rapidly. What is most noticeable is someone operating for several minutes or hours using the same ego state. This sometimes happens with individuals who are acting out what they understand to be their proper role. Most people have far more options for transacting than they think.

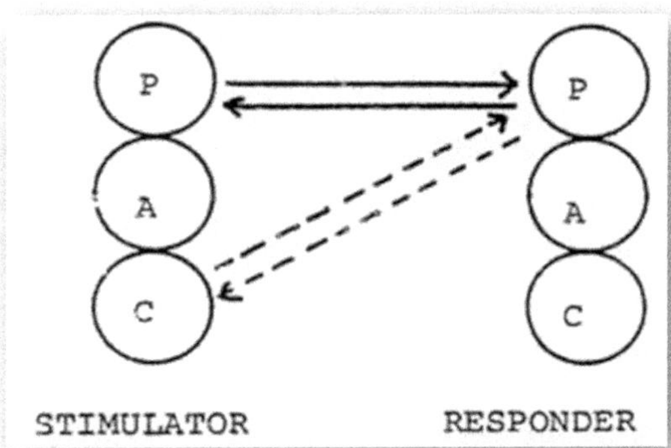

Figure 10. Simultaneous, Complementary Duplex Transactions.

Two

Psychological Games And Rackets

Eric Berne achieved fame with his best-selling book, *Games People Play*. In it, he defines a Game as follows:

> An ongoing series of complementary ulterior transactions progressing to a well-defined, predictable outcome. Descriptively, it is a recurring set of transactions, often repetitious, superficially plausible, with a concealed motivation; or, more colloquially, a series of moves with a snare, or "gimmick." Games are clearly differentiated from procedures, rituals, and pastimes by two chief characteristics: (1) their ulterior quality and (2) the payoff. Procedures may be successful, rituals effective, and sometimes profitable, but all of them are by definition candid; they may involve contest, but not conflict, and the ending may be sensational, but is not dramatic. Every game, on the other hand, is basically dishonest, and the outcome has a dramatic, as distinct from merely exciting quality. (Berne 1964)

Why Play Games?

Games are socially acceptable forms of war wherein the participants are aware of the ground rules and fight one another on a fair, level playing field. The rules are not overt, and the behaviors are not straightforward when people play psychological Games. In a psychological Game, the players beat up on one another in varying ways and degrees while pretending to be something other than a competitor or adversary, such as a clown, a concerned parent, a helpless child, or an entertaining conversationalist. Psychological Games entail covert, ulterior, unspoken, crooked messages.

People play Games to get needs met. Games start in the Adapted Child ego state. People have expectations regarding what is about to happen, based on past experience. According to Harry Boyd (1976), there are two basic expectations people have when they play Games: one is a *catastrophic* expectation, and the other is an *anastrophic* expectation. Both relate to basic needs for love and acceptance.

Behind the catastrophic expectation is the fear that basic needs will be discounted, unrecognized, or unmet. Behind the anastrophic expectation is the hope that at last, basic needs for good parenting will be met. So, despite the ulterior, devious, and disingenuous quality of Games, and despite the fact their existence normally causes bad feelings, the Game player is still searching for a basically positive outcome.

In addition to the above, there are three general reasons why people play Games: to satisfy stimulus hunger, recognition hunger, and structure hunger (Berne 1964).

If basic needs are not met in direct, logical ways, psychological Game playing becomes a substitute, or compensation, for the unmet needs.

Growing up, many people did not learn how to acquire strokes in direct ways. These people later in life play Games to get strokes and create stimulation, recognition, and structure for themselves.

Students, employees, and others want to be noticed; they want to be praised and loved. Students, family members, and employees who play Games may actually look upon the teacher or manager as a "good parent" who can provide what they need or want in their Adapted Child ego states. They may expect the teacher or manager to meet Child needs rather than Adult needs for more competence, knowledge, or productivity.

They want attention.

Structure hunger is more complex. As people learn and grow up, they begin to look upon themselves in various ways—as the good guy or gal, the shady lady, a hero, or whatever. They develop favorite feelings. They develop role preferences. They may see themselves as Rescuers, Persecutors, or Victims. Later on, they play Games to put or keep themselves in the structure they have partially learned and partially imagined. It's comfortable this way, despite the negative consequences that result.

The Drama Triangle

Stephen Karpman, MD, won the Eric Berne Memorial Scientific Award in 1972 for one of the most useful diagrams ever developed—the Drama Triangle (Karpman 1968).

Karpman is a psychiatrist and a viewer of football and stage drama. He is also a thinker and inventor. Once upon a time, he was in England watching a stage play and rummaging around in his head, which was filled with football plays, medical books, TA theory, and novels that he had absorbed, and all of a sudden, he conceived and set up a formation of persecutors, rescuers, and victims, previously recognized by Berne as necessary for a Game. He jotted down some scribblings that finally resulted in the Drama Triangle formulation, sometimes known as the Karpman Drama Triangle (Karpman 1973). He published his formulation in an article titled "Fairy Tales and Script Drama Analysis" (1968).

All plays, fairy tales, and day-in-and-day-out soap operas, if they are dramatic, have a Persecutor, a Rescuer, and a Victim. You can check this out for yourself just by thinking about it.

The more dramatic the play, the heavier and more serious the Persecuting, Rescuing, and Victimizing. The faster the action, the greater the number of switches between roles as the Games progress.

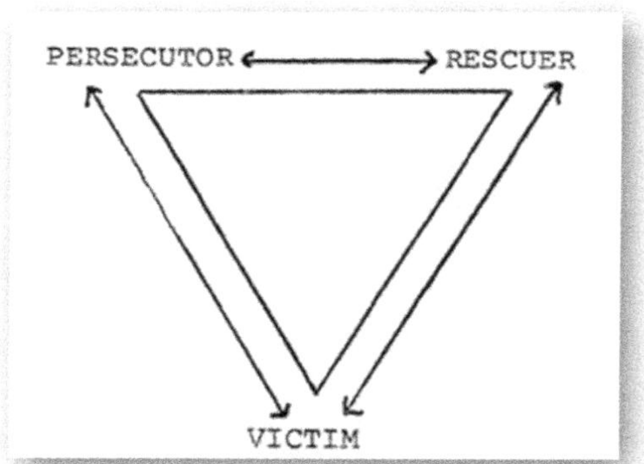

Figure 11. The Drama Triangle.

Ordinary structure hunger causes some people to want to be a Persecutor, a Rescuer, or a Victim. They create their own dramas to create the illusion that life is continuing on as usual. How did they learn to like to be Persecutors, Rescuers, or Victims in the first place? They came upon it more or less accidentally, given the circumstances they grew up in. It may be that they copied their favorite roles from an influential parent figure. It may be they were forced into one of the roles by the way parent figures treated them. It may be they were more or less required to act out one of the roles at an early age. It might be they just took on their favorite roles while playing with and competing with siblings and friends at an early age. It might be they decided to act out one of the roles as a reaction to what they perceived to be negative requirements from parent figures.

The Drama Triangle is the best Game detector there is. If you or people around you are acting very dramatic in one or more of the above roles, you can generally rest assured they or you are playing Games.

The Pervasiveness of Games

Most people play Games to some extent. Games are a compensation for a failure to get emotional needs met in direct ways. They also compensate for lack of competence and an inability to achieve stated goals. And they compensate for lack of courage.

Games are also sometimes called "the bridge to intimacy." Real intimacy—total honesty and sharing among people—is, of course, very rare. People are afraid they will be embarrassed if they are intimate. They are afraid they will be taken advantage of in some way if they are intimate. Sometimes, these fears are well grounded.

It would be better to be intimate without first playing Games, but if no intimacy would otherwise exist, Games do have a positive quality. On the other hand, some people play Games relatively frequently and rarely achieve intimacy. While Games may be a bridge to intimacy for some people, they are not such a bridge for all people.

Scores of Games have been described and categorized. The first book on the subject was Berne's *Games People Play* (1964). Ken Ernst published *Games Students Play* in 1972 (1972). The dynamics of specific Games have been published in various issues of the *Transactional Analysis Bulletin* and the *Transactional Analysis Journal* since 1962.

A handy listing of Games was provided in a chart called Game Matrix, compiled by Paul and Sally Edwards, published by PAA Publications of Kansas City, Missouri. The chart contained detailed descriptions of twenty-three of the most common Games, plus related and complementary Games. Included in the chart are the theses behind the Games, the Game payoff, players' roles, and social and clinical interventions. It was possible to scan the chart and see Games in which you have been involved. Most likely, the chart is no longer sold, but it was a handy one.

The Games have names such as "courtroom"; "cops and robbers"; "rapo"; "kick me"; "stupid"; ""; "schliemazl"; "poor me"; "ain't it awful"; "I'm only trying to help you"; "if it weren't for you"; "uproar"; "now I've got you, you SOB" (NIGYSOB); "harried"; and "why don't you—yes, but."

"Courtroom" involves a Persecutor trying to convict a Victim of some crime or infraction; "cops and robbers" involves a Persecutor doing something wrong so as to arouse a Persecutor, who will make a Victim out of the wrongdoer when caught; "rapo" involves a Victim sexy object parading around a Persecutor Wolf, who will be turned into a Victim if moves are made on the sexy object; "kick me" involves a Persecutor who wants to become a Victim when sufficiently irritating moves are made to infuriate a Victim, who becomes a Persecutor when the kick is administered; "stupid" involves a Victim acting more stupid than is the case to get a Persecutor to label the Stupid player stupid; "schliemiel" involves a Persecutor masquerading as a Victim, making messes and tearing things up to get attention and turn a Victim into a Persecutor; "schliemazl" carries "schliemiel" one step further by the mess maker demanding an apology and Persecuting the victim of the mess for having the gall to get angry at the mess maker for making the mess in the first place; "Poor me" involves a Victim taking up a Rescuer's time; Ain't It Awful involves a Victim or Persecutor constantly talking to a Rescuer, Victim, or Persecutor about how awful things are; "I'm only trying to help you," involves a Rescuer pretending to help a Victim; "why don't you—yes, but" involves a Victim soliciting but ignoring advice from a Rescuer; "if it weren't for you" involves a Persecutor pretending to be a Victim telling a Persecutor (who is really a Victim) that life would be fine if the Victim weren't around; "uproar" entails a Persecutor (who may be a Victim) roaring and yelling at a Victim or Persecutor about perceived abominations; NIGYSOB entails a Persecutor who thinks he or she is a Victim telling a Victim who is thought to be a Persecutor that enough is enough and that this is the last straw; "harried" entails a Victim who is really a Persecutor deliberately putting things off so long that he or she has to make messes hurrying up, and Persecuting Victims are caught up in the make-believe whirlwind.

All Games involve tricky, devious, ulterior, complicated, unstraightforward, antisocial, dishonest behavior. They create not-OK situations in any social system.

A particular teacher, parent, or manager may be skilled at playing two or three Games. In addition, given even a small class or work group, several students or workers will be skilled at several Games. Therefore, the potential number of different, specific Games that may exist in a classroom or workplace is generally in excess of ten.

Games usually involve switches of roles. The Game starter may start out as Persecutor or Rescuer and wind up a Victim, with the initial Victim coming out as Persecutor or Rescuer.

I think you can detect Games in your classes, workgroups, or social systems simply by virtue of having read about the Drama Triangle and thinking about whether and for whom the shoe fits.

There are apparently some groups in existence that are relatively Game-free. Some of your students, children, or workers may be Game-free. You may be Game-free. This is not likely, but it is possible.

Game Analysis

Berne pointed out in *Games People Play* that Games are repetitive, and they appear superficially straight; but an ulterior hook exists at a covert, deeper level. This is shown in Figure 12.

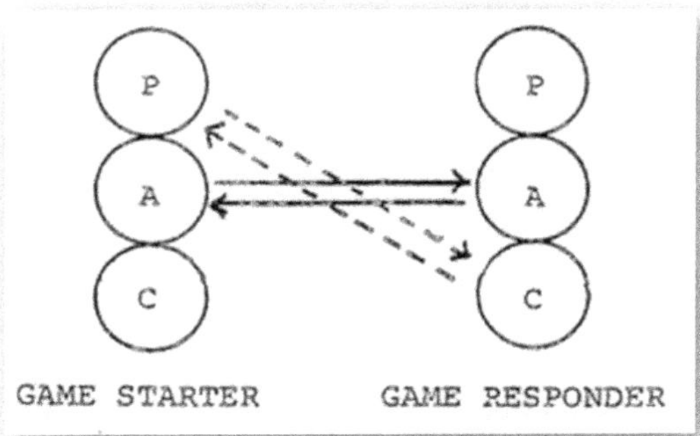

Figure 12. The Opening Transactions of a NIGYSOB Game.

The basic formula (Berne 1970) for Games is this:

Con + Gimmick = Response → Switch → Cross → Payoff.

Two sets of complementary transactions are going on at once—a social-level, spoken, overt set and a psychological level, nonverbal, covert set.

In general, Games "take place outside the awareness of the Adult," which unfortunately means that Game players do not realize they are playing Games. They have been playing Games for so long that they think their Game playing is "just natural."

The con is an invitation the Game starter throws out; the gimmick is some artifice designed to appeal to a particular weak spot or vulnerability in the responder that causes her or him (sometimes referred at as the "mark") to respond and get hooked, just like a trout rising to take a fisherman's artificial fly.

Once the responder is hooked, after a series of transactions—which may require a minute or so or several days or perhaps months or years—surprises will occur.

The Game starter will then begin to cross transactions, as shown in Figure 13.

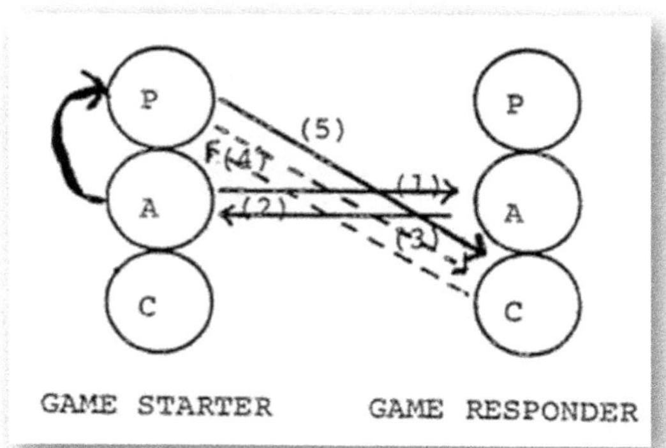

Figure 13. The Crossed Transactions of a NIGYSOB Game.

Before (or perhaps after) the crossed transaction, in most Games, the starter and responder will switch roles—Persecutor, Rescuer, or Victim—from whatever role they started with to a different role.

Figure 13 depicts the Game of NIGYSOB, which is a very common Game. Move 1 has to do with some Adult-sounding faults, mistakes, or deficiencies the Game starter has found in the Game responder. At move 1, the starter says something to the effect that such and such is not up to par, which may be true. At move 2, the responder then asks what is wrong, and so on. Several transactions may occur at the Adult level, dealing with what appears to be Adult data and information along the paths of vectors (1) and (2).

At the same time transactions (1) and (2) are going on at the Adult, social level, transactions (3) and (4) are going on Parent to Child at the psychological, ulterior level. The Parent-Child message is an angry variant of "you're not up to par, kid." The Child-Parent message is a variant of "don't give me a spanking," "who cares?" and so on.

After a few minutes (or perhaps days or weeks), the starter will decide the responder has been securely hooked, and now it's time to go for the payoff.

What the starter will do at the payoff is switch the social-level message away from the data, the issue, or the problem and move into Parent. At move (5) at the social level, the starter will cross the responder at (2) with the message, "Now I've got you, you SOB" (or some variant of it).

The payoff for a NIGYSOB player is a feeling of triumph or being "one up." One of the main reasons NIGYSOB players play NIGYSOB is to feel justified in venting their anger, which they have pent up inside themselves. The payoff for the Game responder in the above example, perhaps a "kick me" player, will be to feel humiliated, dejected, and perhaps rejected.

Some people go through these antics on an over-and-over-again basis. I think many people assume that all people are NIGYSOB players, since one-upmanship Game playing is so widespread. While most people tend to get caught up occasionally in one-upmanship Games in organizations, some people are much more heavily invested in playing NIGYSOB than others, depending on their training and learning in early childhood.

Whether someone is criticizing someone else to actually improve things or merely to satisfy a Game hunger can be determined by seeing whether the drama thus created or the issue is more important to the criticizer.

It is easier to see why people play NIGYSOB than "kick me" or some of the other self-debasing Games. In the Game of "kick me," people seek out literal or verbal "kicks" as payoffs. Games like "stupid" or "schliemiel" also result in punishment and rejection payoffs.

In the above NIGYSOB Game, the starter starts at the social level as a Victim of the responder's mistakes, insults, or deficiencies. The responder comes across initially at the social level as Persecutor. The starter starts at the psychological level as Persecutor, and the responder starts at the psychological level as a Victim. At the payoff, the starter switches at the social level from Victim to heavy Persecutor, and the responder switches to the Victim position at the social level.

As will be pointed out more fully later, there are degrees of Games. Most Game players are not out to really hurt anyone. They play Games out of fear or out of hope for something good. There are some Game players—sociopaths—who have given up on getting anything good from people and who do intend harm. Teachers and managers will encounter relatively few sociopaths in their work. On the other hand, school-system teachers and managers do sometimes encounter heavy, negative Game players among students. This will probably be in the lower grades, since these Game players generally don't stay in school very long.

Not allowing students or employees to play Games in classrooms and businesses can have various consequences. Some students and employees will get fewer Adapted Child needs met than previously. The group as a whole may become more Adult, however, and more energy will be spent learning the subject matter. Also, the teacher or manager may have to create OK child fun for strokes.

Discounting

A "discount" is some act, statement, gesture, or feeling that has the effect of reducing the significance of a person, problem, or existence itself (Schiff and Schiff 1971).

When someone is discounted, his or her value as a contributing, capable, entitled human being is reduced. The reason I am using *his or her, he or she,* and so on in this book is to avoid discounting either gender in my writing.

Much so-called "kidding" is really serious discounting. When people "pick on" one another, they are discounting. While some kidding, picking on, and insulting is "only in fun," it still hurts. Much so-called kidding is actually vicious discounting, which has real consequences.

Anytime a person sees and defines someone (himself or herself included) as less significant than he or she really is, a discount exists.

According to the writings of Jacqui and Aaron Schiff (1971), there are four modes of discounts: existence, significance, change abilities, and personal abilities. The Schiffs also postulated there were three types of discounts: stimuli, problems, and options.

Discounting the existence of stimuli is the most serious discount. This can drive people crazy or dead. For example, if I discount the existence of this computer keyboard I am typing on, I will immediately become nonfunctional as a writer, and if I discount a sixteen-wheel truck in the wrong lane heading right for me at seventy miles per hour, I won't be around very long on this Earth.

Discounts such as chiding someone about his or her ability or appearance also result in the loss of some functionality.

Discounting—that is, seeing or defining the existence, significance, change abilities, and personal abilities of people, problems, and options to be less relevant or significant than they really are—is always present when Games are being played.

Discounts are another Game detector.

Who is "cutting" or "knocking" whom or what? It is not in fun, and, most likely, the cutter is playing Games to rip off strokes and avoid her or his own deficiencies.

Degrees of Games

Games vary in terms of seriousness. Most Games do not have lasting consequences, but some do. There are three degrees of Games identified by Eric Berne (1964):

* First Degree Games. These Games involve minor discounts such "cuts" and "kidding." Although people generally feel worse than they otherwise would when the Game culminates in the payoff, there is no serious damage.

* Second Degree Games. The negative stroking and discounting is harder than in first Degree Games. Violent emotional outbursts exist at the Game payoff, complete with name-calling, shouting, and heavy red and gray stamp collecting (stamps are explained shortly).

* Third Degree Games. These Games result in people being socially and physically harmed. Berne called these Games tissue-tearing Games. People wind up in the hospital, morgue, fired, flunked out of school, or divorced at payoff time.

Perspective

In most organizations, if simple no-discount contracts could be established among members, efficiency, productivity, and creativity would increase. If you could get each member of the organization—student, faculty member, administrator, manager, worker, child, or parent—to agree not to discount himself or herself or others, more learning, work, happiness, satisfaction, and so on would take place. In some cases, this can be accomplished by merely teaching people what discounts are and asking them not to produce them.

Rackets versus Real Feelings

Rackets, like Games, involve contrived, manipulative behavior on the part of people, unrelated to the Adult here and now.

In her article, "The Substitution Factor: Rackets and Real Feelings" (1971), Fanita English states,

> It is not hard to recognize what T.A. practitioners call a "racket" when it manifests itself in, say, a patient, student, or friend. The expression of feeling seems artificial, repetitive and stereotyped. One wonders: Is this genuine regret, or a "guilt racket"? Genuine sadness, or a "depression racket"? Genuine friendliness or a "sweetness racket"? Surely this person could become more authentic.
>
> But it is not that easy to intervene successfully in regard to some's racket, even under a treatment contract. Pointing it out does not change it; sometimes this only reinforces the racket. However artificial his feelings may appear to the outsider, the patient holds on tightly to his racket, saying: Don't you want me to express how I feel?"
>
> For, behind each racket, however phony it may seem, there are real feelings or perceptions of another kind which the individual is not allowing himself to be aware of in the present because they were prohibited in the past.
>
> Rackets substitute, within a feeling category that was permitted in the past, other feelings which would appear now had not this category of potential real feelings or perceptions been suppressed when the person was growing up.

According to English (1972), rackets are precursors of Games. Rackets develop in the personalities of people at an earlier age than Games.

Whereas different Games lead to certain well-defined payoffs in transactions with others, rackets largely exist within the head of the individual possessed with one. Certain people want to feel certain feelings, regardless of what is taking place in reality.

There are four basic real feelings: mad, sad, glad, and scared. Other feelings are compounds of these.

What do you do with the employee or student who appears sad all the time, mad all time, or scared most of the time? Usually no amount of cheerfulness will cheer up a sadness racketeer.

The "racket" part of the racket concept comes about because of the falseness and unstraightness of the presented feeling, which was not caused by events in the current reality.

The employee or student who appears to be sad all the time is not really sad about what he or she appears to be sad about. His or her racket is that you are supposed to believe he or she is sad and stroke the sadness, when what he or she is really feeling is something else. It may be that the student or employee has to appear to feel sad, because he or she was never allowed to feel glad. Unfair, you say? Yes, indeed. But this seems to be reality for some people. Do some family and work systems not allow their members to feel glad and express joy? Yes, it would seem so, however irrational this might be. Feeling rackets involve magical thinking and what are known as confluent contracts. The deal is that if you feel sad enough, you will eventually be rewarded for it by the universe or some other force, even if you do nothing or produce nothing in the here and now.

Why are some people possessed with feeling rackets?

As with Games, people learn at an early age that they are "supposed" to feel and not feel certain things. If they felt and expressed forbidden feelings (perhaps even gladness), they were punished one way or the other—through physical spanks, perhaps; through nonverbal means such as being isolated or by having their supply of love and strokes cut off, reduced, or withdrawn; or by Critical Parent looks, glares, stares, frowns, grimaces, and the like. So in order to be protected and feel secure at an early age, they had to learn to fake their real feelings and feel what parent figures wanted them to feel.

This faking became habitual, and when these people grew up, they had to keep on faking their feelings in order to feel "comfortable" or "protected" inside their own heads. Unbelievable, you say? Well, no. It's believable, say transactional analysts.

Teachers, students, parents, children, managers, employees, or anyone may be contaminated with rackets. As a parent figure, do you not allow your students or employees to feel certain feelings? Have you noticed that some of your students or employees seem to feel mad, sad, scared, or glad most of the time, regardless of the grades or wages or salaries they receive or what you do or don't do?

There is no easy formula for getting someone out of his or her racket. This sort of thing is not easy to change. Probably the best thing you can do in the business or classroom or family is to realize that rackets exist and see them for what they are in you and your employees or students or children. And, while pointing out to the racketeer that you are aware of the racket and think it should be changed, be prepared to exercise much patience waiting for it to happen.

If you become aware that you have a racket, you need to watch yourself so that you do not impose it on your employees or students or children. It works out that most people possessed with rackets are not fully comfortable unless people around them are feeling what they say they are feeling. Therefore, if you have a gladness, sadness, scaredness, or anger racket, there will be a tendency for you to invite others around you to feel the same thing.

Given that a manager, teacher, or parent is relatively racket-free (i.e., that he or she is capable of naturally feeling and expressing all feelings from appropriate ego states), much understanding and patience are required to cope with the rackets of others.

The expression of extreme anger, scaredness, sadness, and gladness is generally inappropriate when work activities are being conducted in classrooms and organizations. But some expression of all four basic feelings, when appropriate, is not only permissible but desirable in order to maximize learning, production, happiness, satisfaction, and so on.

What many parents, managers, employees, teachers, and students need to learn most is how to deal with real feelings.

Payoffs and Trading Stamps

Both Games and rackets are means of keeping life predictable and under control. Rather than experience life as it really is, the Game player and the racketeer attempt to manipulate people to fit their predetermined hungers, perceptions, programming, decisions, and frames of reference.

Rackets generally lead to Games, and Games lead to various payoffs. Rackets, Games, and payoffs are part of the life script, which is treated in the following chapter.

When someone manipulates himself or herself into the position of feeling justified in feeling whatever they feel at the end of a Game, they tend to "collect" or "save" the feelings, just like some people save trading stamps (Berne 1964). The same goes for whatever they do to justify the racket feelings.

Game players and racketeers stick their favorite feeling payoffs, figuratively, in their trading-stamp books. Various "prizes," of course, can be obtained for various numbers of completed books when traded in.

Various colors are used to describe various feelings—gray for depression or sadness, white for scaredness, red for anger, and gold for gladness.

If someone is an anger racketeer, he or she is a red-stamp collector; sad-feeling payoff manipulators collect gray stamps; scared-feeling manipulators collect white stamps; and glad-feeling manipulators collect gold stamps.

You might argue that it is OK to collect gold stamps. Good grades might be considered gold stamps, and poor grades might be considered gray stamps.

Where I am, if gold stamps are collected through unstraight, devious means, gold stamp collecting is still basically not OK.

Teachers, managers, employees, parents, students, and administrators sometimes collect stamps over the course of a year, semester, quarter, or other time period, and whenever they think they have enough books full, they cash them in. The "prizes" they sometimes cash them in for include quitting school, going on drugs, getting drunk, committing acts of vandalism, threatening the teacher with bodily harm, having a nervous breakdown, quitting a job, divorcing someone, or firing someone.

It is a good idea to be aware of whom you are collecting stamps from and who is collecting stamps from you, in order to do something about problems before they get serious.

Three

Life Scripts

According to transactional analysts, young children make some significant decisions about themselves and the world they may believe and use for a long time. According to Berne (1970),

> Each person decides in early childhood how he will live and how he will die, and that plan, which he carries in his head wherever he goes, is called his script. His trivial behavior may be decided by reason, but his important decisions are already made: what kind of a person he will marry, how many children he will have, what kind of a bed he will die in, and who will be there when he does. It may not be what he wants, but it is what he wants it to be.

A person's script may be partially determined even before birth, according to Lois Johnson (1978), who states that mothers transmit nonverbal messages to babies in the womb electrochemically, thereby possibly predisposing the baby to feel certain feelings that are peculiar to the mother during pregnancy. According to sources cited by Johnson (1978), the imprinting a baby receives shortly after birth also helps determine the nature of her script.

The ego states, transactions, rackets, and Games that people introject early in life also become incorporated into the script. You may think you autonomously decided to develop the ego states, transactional patterns, rackets, and Games you use, but if you check on yourself, chances are you will find that these patterns were passed on to you by your family. Most of us are not nearly as original as we think we are regarding the creation of our personalities and scripts.

According to script theory, most students, teachers, administrators, and parents have already made their important life decisions by the time you encounter them in school. Assuming this theory is true, it follows that most teachers do not significantly affect the lives of their students. The teaching of reading, writing, arithmetic, and other subjects will probably not affect the early decisions that determined the life script. Since the script is generally completed by about age seven, it follows that nursery-school and first-grade teachers may have more of an impact on the final destiny of students than teachers of other grade levels. It may be that they are the most significant teachers of all by virtue of what is taking place within the minds of their students at this age.

The finishing touches are put on scripts, according to Berne (1972) during adolescence, when students generally decide on some specific job, vocation, trade, or profession.

There are three kinds of scripts according to Berne (1972): winner scripts, loser scripts, and banal scripts. Winners are people who achieve their stated goals; losers do not. Banal scripts result in colorless, humdrum outcomes.

Some scripts call for people to almost, never, always, or repeatedly do certain things over and over—almost achieve something, never feel good about themselves, always make it and feel good about themselves, or try and fail and retry over and over again.

There are many specific themes for scripts that call for particular characters, activities, Games, and dialogue. Scripts interlock. People you are relatively intimate with are normally selected in the first place on the basis of whether they fit your script. Whether someone wants to be your close friend or spouse may depend upon whether he or she wants to act out a particular "slot" or "part" that you have written in your script. At the same time, you decide whether you want to interlock with someone else's script using the same criteria. In other words, in order to be a close friend or spouse of someone, what sort of "part" would you have to act out on the stage of life with that person?

Teachers and administrators who get along harmoniously for long periods probably have relatively complementary scripts.

Since ego states were passed to parents by their parents, who had them passed on by their parents, and so on back into history, no one single generation or individual is totally responsible for his or her ego state applications in social affairs. In some respects, the transmitting of ego states is analogous to the transmitting of genes. One difference in degree is that there are fewer ego states to pass down to offspring than genes, and, therefore, it is easier to predict what script an offspring will have than physical characteristics.

Through scripting, ancestors are reincarnated, or not allowed to fully die; some of their ego states are kept alive from one generation to another by parents breeding and conditioning children, like runners passing the baton in a relay race.

According to Berne, the parent of the opposite sex generally has a greater impact on an offspring's script than the parent of the same sex, due to heterosexual attraction. A mother will tend to recreate her father's script in her male children, and a father will tend to recreate his mother's script in his female children. The parent of the opposite sex will subconsciously train his or her offspring of the opposite sex to be like his or her parent of the opposite sex.

The Script Matrix

The script-transferring, transplanting matrix is shown in Figure 14.

The script proper is contained in C_2.

C_2 contains the Parent, Adult, and Child ego states that a person develops before the age of seven or so.

A_2, the more grown-up Adult that the person usually develops after age seven or so, is capable of processing abstract data such as words and concepts, numbers, and musical notes, using logic and grammar, mathematical rules and formulas, and other abstract structures.

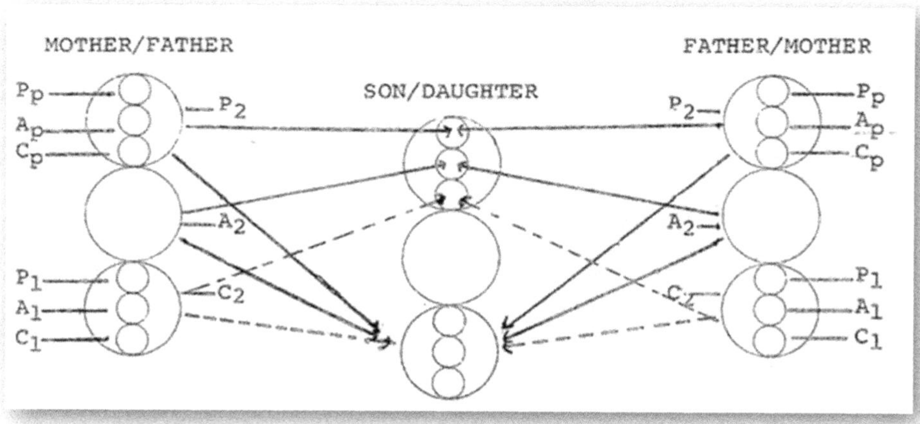

Figure 14. The Life Script Matrix.

P_2, by the same token, contains the Parent, Adult, and Child ego states and data assimilated into the personality from parent figures after age seven. P_2 contains more overt rules and programming than P_1. Much of the programming of P_1 was accomplished through nonverbal, covert, psychological, ulterior means.

P_2 is where you and I come in as teachers, managers, and latter-day parents. Some children, students, employees, and perhaps fellow parents, managers, or teachers may copy some of our ego states as well as learn or not learn our subject material and skills. We might be used as role models. Since no teacher, manager, or parent is perfect, it is wise to discourage people from copying many of our ego states and script controls.

In general, P_1 in C_2 is the most potent, significant ego state. This ego state contains the script messages passed down in the family of origin.

These messages are transmitted from the Child of the parent to the Child of the child at an early age. They are prohibitions called injunctions. They are stored in the P_1 of parent figures.

According to Bob and Mary Goulding (1976), there are about fourteen of these injunctions that are commonly transmitted in family scripting:

Don't be
Don't be you (the sex you are)
Don't be a child
Don't grow
Don't make it
Don't
Don't be important
Don't be close
Don't belong
Don't be well (or sane)
Don't think about X (forbidden subject)
Don't think what you think, think what I think
Don't feel
Don't feel X (mad, sad, glad, scared, etc.)
Don't feel what you feel; feel what I feel

These injunctions are transmitted largely nonverbally. Rarely would any good parent verbally communicate any of the above socially to a child, for these messages are negative, limiting, and ridiculous. People obeying these injunctions would be crippled. Their chances for happy and satisfying living would be relatively low. Unfortunately, such messages are transmitted psychologically, secretly, and covertly, and while most people subjected to them or transmitting them may be vaguely aware of the messages, they learn to act as if they were not, keep up a brave face, and act as if it never happened. And on and on it goes.

The main way parents, managers, and teachers tell children, students, and other subordinates "don't be successful," "don't be powerful," "don't feel what you feel," and so on is by what they do when their subordinates are successful or powerful or mad, sad, glad, or scared.

If mother, father, manager, or teacher gets unhappy when subordinates become glad about being successful or powerful, he or she in effect tells them psychologically, "don't be successful," or "don't be powerful," by the emotional response, the attitude shown, and the physical gestures and looks used, without a word being spoken. If the subordinate is adaptive enough and is exposed to these messages long enough, that person may decide he or she really is not supposed to be successful and powerful, and that person may stop being successful and powerful. Once a belief of this nature is committed to and is incorporated in the ongoing behavior of an individual, its effects are difficult to change.

The looks, gestures, and emotions displayed by and emanating from a person, in many (perhaps most) cases, are more truthful than audible words. According to Fritz Perls, MD (1972), the founder of Gestalt therapy, "most talking is a lie."

Unfortunately and fortunately, most people eventually "get the message" about what you really think and feel about them and what you really want them to think, feel, say, and do. Your Child will let it out one way or the other.

Many families are handicapped with one or more injunctions. The specific injunctions may be replicas or variations of those listed above.

There can be a positive side to injunctions in that they may forbid someone to do, feel, or think something, which then gives the person more time and energy to do something else in which he or she specializes and at which he or she develops exceptional skill or expertise. Some people wind up doing what they do because of what they can't do rather than because of what they can do.

After children get older, usually around age six, parents, teachers, and others begin to verbally tell them what to do in order for the parents or teachers to be proud of them at the P_2 level.

Messages transmitted from the P_2 level are explicit: "study hard," "strive for perfection," "grow up and make something of yourself," "be polite," "mind your manners," "clean those fingernails." These are the things that will cause most parents to be proud of their kids.

The Parent-Parent messages contradict the Child-Child messages. Therefore, these P_2 to P_2 messages are called counterinjunctions. They comprise the counterscript.

How Hard Is Script Theory?

It is obvious families and parent figures exert much influence on children at early ages, which can have a programming effect. But are the messages and the outcomes to the messages as precise as TA theory indicates?

It is also obvious that all children in a particular family, of the same sex or otherwise, do not grow up the same and do not have the same scripts. Some families produce both winners and losers. A particular family may produce a priest and a lawless derelict. Did the priest receive different messages as a child, or did he decide to be a priest irrespective of script messages? Or did the derelict decide to be a derelict irrespective of script messages that should have produced a priest?

Many TA theorists purport the existence of an antiscript. That is, the child decides to do the opposite of what the script messages indicate, which can account for phenomena such as the one above. On the other hand, some TA theorists purport that children make decisions based on everything they observe in their environments and make decisions that determine their life course that are not determined by messages passed on to them by their ancestors. Younger children observe the older children and can see what happened to the older children because of what the older children decided. If the older children did not get their needs met (perhaps as a result of rebellion), the younger child may see that this won't work and may become quite compliant and adapted.

In any event, children at the earliest ages have some power to make decisions using the A_1. Claude Steiner has indicated that parental pressure is the main determinant, however, since children are small and cannot resist their parents.

According to Steiner,

> The first and foremost concept, in my belief, which Berne introduced to psychiatry is embodied in the aphorism: "People are born princes and princesses, until their parents turn them into frogs." Eric Berne presented many of his most radical ideas in the form of aphorisms which were veiled statements that disguised the implications of his thoughts from the minds of those who heard them in order to soften the blow of their meaning. Stated in this oblique way, the notion that people are born OK and that the seeds of emotional disturbance, unhappiness, and madness are not in them but in their parents who pass it on to them is made palatable to those who, faced with the full meaning of the assertion, would almost surely reject it. (Steiner 1974)

Dealing with Scripts

I think it is relatively certain that most students, employees, children, and trainees have decided their life scripts, for whatever reasons and because of whatever influences, by the time they enter the second grade. They will decide what to study to fulfill their scripts later in adolescence, and they will make various decisions throughout life that may or may not be script bound—that is, determined by the script.

It is the job of psychotherapists to help people change their scripts, if, for whatever reason, individuals decide their scripts should be changed. Some psychotherapists, no doubt, have better track records in this regard than others. On the other hand, ingrained behavior, such as script behavior, is difficult to change, even with the use of professional help.

It is the teacher's job to teach whatever his or her subject is or whatever concepts or skills the consumer wants to learn. On the other hand, teachers must deal with the scripts of students. Teachers who have students who do not have permission to learn or be successful will likely be frustrated if they measure their success in terms of how much their students learn. Teachers should do what they can to give their students permission to do whatever it is the irrational injunctions forbid, even though the probability of success in this endeavor would be relatively low.

Managers and supervisors generally must simply teach the employee to do the job. If the employee's script prevents the employee from doing the job, if the employee cannot or is unwilling to change the script, the employee over time will probably be sluiced out of the business. Businesses and other productive organizations over time wash out employees who are not willing or able to conform to the organization's technical job requirements and the organization script. The gold that is not sluiced out are the employees who can satisfactorily do the job and fit the script—those who can and/or will conform to all the requirements of the organizational culture.

Parents in general cannot fire or sluice out their children, and all sorts of dynamics can happen in family systems. It is not uncommon for parents to criticize (with their P_2 behavior) their own children for what they themselves caused by the injunctions they unconsciously transmitted to their children through their P_1 states. It's possible that if parents like this accidentally encounter this writing in this book, they might seriously analyze their own injunctions and do their best not to transmit them to their children, which should improve the family functioning from then on. If the parents become aware of their children's injunctions that they caused and have been reinforcing for years, they should do their best to cease such reinforcement and do their best to give their children psychological permission to violate the injunctions. In my opinion, the best thing a good parent could do about this sort of thing would be to find a good family therapist to work on the problem with group sessions involving the whole family.

Games and rackets that are a part of the script can cause a teacher, manager, supervisor, parent, or trainer to teach or train less effectively than he or she might otherwise. Games played by students and employees for script reasons can cause other students and employees to learn less than they would otherwise. Therefore, in order for the teacher or trainer to do a good job, he or she must do something about the Game (and indirectly the script) of a particular student. This can be accomplished to some degree by stroking winner behavior and refusing to play Games with students.

The teacher or trainer should check to see if he or she transmits injunctions in the classroom, home, or business. Since Games are generally played outside the Adult awareness of Game players, considerable self-monitoring is required to avoid being enmeshed in Games.

Scripts and Folktales

One way of getting insight into your script is to think back to your favorite fairy tale or hero or heroine in childhood. Did you identify with Cinderella or

Little Red Riding Hood or the wolf? Were you Grandmother or the evil witch who lived deep in the forest? Were you Sir Galahad, Robin Hood, Superman, Richard the Lionheart, Batman, or Robin? Who were you in fairy-tale land?

Your favorite folk hero or heroine may tell you something about your script and the character you decided to be. Originally, tales about folk heroes were not fantasies. People existed who lived lives that became stories passed on orally from generation to generation. Folktales don't die out, as do most stories, because many people identify with them. People identify with the folktale characters because they have acquired scripts similar to the ones possessed by the folktale characters. Robin Hood never dies out, because the downtrodden always need a hero to rescue them from evil sheriffs and politicians.

It seems the human race keeps much the same characters generation after generation in the comedy and drama of life. The characters have the same scripts, which are acted out in the same plots. This accounts for the fact that the human race keeps about the same percentage of the population in various roles—such as saint and sinner, criminal and creative genius—generation after generation (Berne 1972). It also accounts for the wars and other disastrous activities conducted generation after generation by supposedly intelligent human beings.

As a teacher or manager, you might improve your effectiveness simply by realizing that your students or employees are not alike in many ways. Their scripts differ. The minds of your students and employees are permeated by various fantasies, messages, and beliefs regarding the nature of the world and themselves, based logically and illogically on the distorted, accurate, and incomplete data they were immersed in during early childhood.

The more you understand scripts, the more you can understand the behavior of your students or employees and deal with them more appropriately.

Students or employees cannot be molded to fit your script. You will naturally like some of your students or employees more than others based on how well they agree with your P_1 requirements (i.e., your injunctions and script needs and problems), but this should not affect your teaching or supervision.

Because of scripts, people are sometimes rewarded on the basis of P_1 standards in schools and organizations rather than on the basis of Adult A_2 contract performance. In my view, this is unfair and immoral.

The Miniscript

The 1978 Eric Berne Memorial Scientific Award was awarded to Taibi Kahler, PhD, for his formulation, which he called the miniscript.

The miniscript was first presented in an article by Kahler and Hedges Capers entitled "The Miniscript," published in the *Transactional Analysis Journal* (1974).

The miniscript interrelates some of the above-presented script material in a different format. According to Kahler, people can experience a version of their life script in a matter of seconds or minutes. Kahler focuses primarily on Parent-Parent messages, as opposed to Child-Child messages. He begins with the counterscript rather than the script.

People have OK and not-OK miniscripts, according to Kahler.

The not-OK miniscript unfolds according to a repetitive sequence, from driver to stopper to Vengeful Child to payoff. Someone with a not-OK miniscript will hear or feel a message in his or her Parent ego state that tells the person:

Hurry up

Please me

Try hard

Be perfect

Be strong.

Drivers are messages transmitted from the Parent of the parent to the Parent of the child that attempt to drive or motivate the child toward certain behaviors; stoppers are injunctions that prevent the achievement of certain goals; the Vengeful Child are angry feelings caused by the process.

These messages are counterscript messages that were or are commands issued over and over again by parents, teachers, managers and other parent figures to children, students, or parents to do things to make the parent, teacher, or manager feel proud of the child, student, or employee.

The next step in the sequence is for the driven person to feel energy and script injunction messages in the Child ego state. Kahler refers to these messages as Stoppers, because they stop people from doing things that are generally OK to do. These messages are transmitted from the Child of the parent to the Child of the child.

The driven person then shifts energy from the Adapted Child to what Kahler calls the Vengeful Child. This is the part of the Child that became angry at parent figures because of the script injunctions that were laid on him or her. At this step, passive-aggressive behavior, Games, and other forms of not-OK behavior are produced.

Much of the not-OK behavior of students and employees in classrooms and businesses is the payoff of not-OK miniscript sequences. The sequences can be triggered by anything that reminds the student or employee of episodes with past scripting parent figures. If a student or employee consciously or subconsciously associates a teacher or manager with past parent figures who commanded the student or employee to hurry up, please the parent figure, be strong, and so forth, not-OK miniscript behavior can be triggered in the student or employee in the present.

In a class or thirty or so students, it seems I always have one or two students who for some reason do not like me, my personality, or what I say and do, while the majority of my students think I am OK. No matter what I say, it seems the same students always react negatively. In most cases, I am sure the basic cause of this reaction is a not-OK miniscript. Somehow, I remind the student of someone in the past who aroused hostility in the student. Something about me stirs something up in the student. This reaction is much the same as what psychiatrists have called transference phenomena. Transference, in psychoanalytic terms, means that a patient transfers feelings that were felt in the past with a significant other to the therapist in the present. Students and employees can do the same thing with teachers and managers.

There is no easy cure for miniscript or transference reactions in the classroom or work group. I certainly have not discovered any easy cure for my students who react negatively to me because of miniscript issues. I think my knowing or thinking I know the cause of this behavior enables me to react less negatively than I did before I knew about miniscript behavior. When I first started teaching, I used to get bent out of shape when students reacted to me in this manner. I thought the students were juvenile delinquents out to do harm in the classroom just for the hell of it. The ideal solution for problems of this nature would be to give the students permission to do what their injunctions preclude, but life in classrooms and work groups is not ideal for this. It is one thing for teachers and supervisors to understand the causes of this behavior; it is another matter for teachers and employees to be able to change miniscript behavior. Sometimes, the best thing to do is simply ignore the miniscript behavior or the student or worker. Sometimes, it is best to call the student or worker into the office for a private talk about the observed behavior. The teacher or manager can tell the student or employee what he or she sees and hears that is offensive to him or her and ask the student or employee to please refrain from producing the behavior. Sometimes this will work. Some students can and will control themselves for an hour or so during a class if they know the teacher knows what he or she is doing.

We can model what goes on inside our head with the diagram shown in Figure 15.

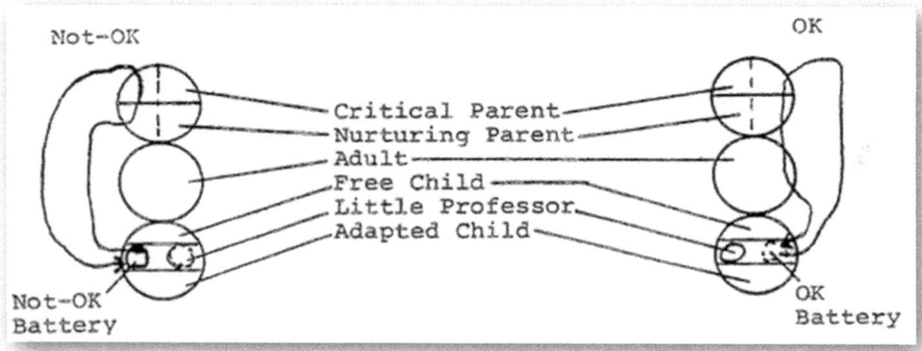

Figure 15. The OK and Not OK Miniscript Batteries.

The final step in the not-OK miniscript sequence is rejection, punishment, feeling hopeless, feeling unloved, feeling powerless, feeling unsuccessful, or feeling whatever the negative payoff feeling of the specific person might be.

A whole childhood of programming can be acted out in the present in a few seconds, according to Kahler. The relevance of this to teachers and employees is that from time to time, not-OK miniscript sequences will take place in classrooms and workplaces. The teacher or manager should be aware that it is not he or she or other students or workers who are "causing" the not-OK miniscript behavior.

When someone has a not-OK miniscript, he or she sometimes responds to internal dialogues. Most people talk to themselves inside their heads. We make up and hear voices in our heads. Many people are visual internally and can see pictures inside their heads with their eyes open. Consequently, a lot of what people say and do is in response to what they are saying, hearing, and seeing inside their own skulls.

On the left side of the diagram in Figure 15 are internal transactions between the not-OK battery in the Little Professor and the not-OK Parent. On the right side of the diagram is the converse. Kahler and Capers state that people in early childhood develop OK or not-OK batteries in the Little Professor as survival mechanisms. The batteries help the child become self-sustaining. If he or she is given ample positive strokes by parent figures, he or she will develop an OK battery instead of a not-OK battery.

The not-OK miniscript sequence is between a not-OK Nurturing Parent and a not-OK battery in the Little Professor.

The OK miniscript sequence is between an OK Nurturing Parent and an OK battery in the Little Professor, with Adult awareness.

Teachers and managers can teach or train themselves to give appropriate messages to students and employees who have not-OK miniscripts.

Miniscripts are disclosed through body language. There are some body-language signals disclosing not-OK miniscripts and some suggested messages teachers can use for reducing the effects of not-OK miniscripts.

If one of your students or employees frequently drums his or her fingers on a desk or pumps a leg up and down in nervous, rapid jerks, chances are he or she has a "hurry up" driver. Without knowing the injunctions at the Child level, you can improve your relation with the student or employee by transacting with the "hurry up" driver in such a way as to let the person know that "it's OK to slow down and take your time."

The "try hard" driver is identified by frequent frowns, a strained voice, head on hands, tense gestures, and an overall message of "it's tough." "Try hard" students and employees, one way or the other, need to be told and learn that "it's OK to do it."

"Be perfect" drivers are identified by haughty, superior, and virtuous facial expressions; an aloof, proper, overbearing voice tone; a stiff, straight posture; grandiose, pretentious gestures; and slogan-like, patent words. "Be perfect" students and employees need to be taught and learn that "it's OK to be yourself."

"Please me" drivers constantly watch for approval; they often sound insecure or insincere, and they use many polite, Adapted Child words. "Please me" students and employees need to be taught and learn that "it's OK to consider and respect yourself."

"Be strong" drivers are identified by stony, stoic facial expressions; by firm, monotone, expressionless voice tone; by stiff, erect posture; by tense or no gestures; and by an impervious, "it doesn't bother me" attitude. You can help "be strong" students or employees if one way or the other you can get the message across that "it's OK to be open and take care of your own needs."

The ideal thing to do is set up an OK miniscript sequence with your students and employees. This sequence is as follows:

Allower → Goer → Affirming Free Child → Wower.

Allowers are messages that give people permission to succeed, goers are strokes that support the process, the affirming free child accepts the messages, and wowers are feelings of joy at the end of the miniscript sequence.

The OK miniscript sequence involves the Adult and Nurturing Parent giving messages that encourage the Adult and Natural Child to act appropriately and joyfully in order to achieve success.

In most classrooms and businesses, teachers and managers supply most of the Nurturing Parent messages and energy, and students and employees supply most of the Natural Child energy. On the other hand, it is desirable for teachers and managers to get in Natural Child occasionally, and there is nothing wrong with students and employees supplying some Nurturing Parent energy. All people in ideal situations can use all three ego states of their personalities. This produces success, satisfaction, and happiness for all involved.

The more OK miniscript sequences there are in your classes and meetings, the better your classes and meetings will be. Students, employees, teachers, and managers hampered by various miniscript drivers will have to be given permission to ignore them in a powerful way, either by repeated messages or by an especially timely target stroke, in order for the miniscript driver behavior to be significantly reduced. While this type of behavior does not change overnight, it can be changed given persistence and perseverance.

Don't be alarmed if your foot pumpers and finger drummers keep it up despite your having given them permission that "it's OK to slow down and take your time" once or twice. Don't be alarmed if they keep it up all semester—or all year, for that matter. Their early parent figures told them to "hurry up" hundreds or thousands of times in their early years. There is no way you can easily enable your "hurry up" driver students or employees to stop listening to this message playing in their heads.

Many of the ideas for the above discussion of miniscript behavior were taken from "Understanding the Miniscript," by Kenneth M. Sowers, published in *Managing Creatively: Action Learning in Action* (Stapleton 1976).

Time Structuring

Not only do people play Games and impose rackets, they also have other favorite ways of structuring or "spending" time.

For many people, deciding what to do with their time is a problem. Avoiding loneliness and boredom can be a problem for many people.

From the earliest days parents teach their children how to spend their time. Once the pattern is established it is difficult to change. In general offspring introject time structuring patterns similar to those of their parents and grandparents, but variations occur among siblings, especially if variations existed among parents and grandparents.

According to Eric Berne, there are six ways people can structure time, in ascending order of stroke productiveness:

(1) Withdrawal—physically or mentally leaving the scene and removing contact with others. This can occur by people staying alone or by daydreaming when with others, as in classrooms. This is the least stroke productive way to structure time,

(2) Rituals—people can spend time doing responsive reading, taking the roll in prescribed ways, memorizing and reciting, having meetings that have the same words and phrases time after time,

(3) Pastimes—people can spend their time gossiping about the weather, sports, martinis, errant husbands, or wives or children, students or teachers, cars, and other tidbit, chitchat topics,
(4) Activities—people can spend time doing things, such as learning assigned material, building houses, performing heart surgery, and the like,
(5) Games—people can spend their time playing Games. Games yield a lot of strokes, even if they are primarily negative strokes,
(6) Intimacy—Game-free closeness and sharing—feeling life as it is, experiencing life as it is, seeing it for what it is, telling it like it is, being totally honest. This is the most stroke productive way of structuring time.

Due to the programming of early life and later life, people become programmed to structure their time in repetitive ways. Given sixteen awake hours per day, some people will spend various percentages of their time in the above categories. Some spend much more time playing Games than others. Some unfortunately are afraid of intimacy and are incapable of entering into intimate relationships. Some people withdraw much more than others. Some must be constantly involved in activities, busy-work perhaps.

An individual's time structuring pattern depends on what he or she has experienced over and over again within the confines of the script.

If you have certain students who withdraw a lot in your classes, you are probably not the cause. Your withdrawing students have probably been conditioned to withdraw by the most influential teachers they will have, their parents.

If you become aware of the nature of time structuring, as it relates to the scripting process, you will be able to see differences in your students in the way they structure their time and deal with those differences more appropriately.

One of the main tasks of a teacher is to structure the time of classes. How much time do you spend on withdrawal, rituals, pastimes, activities, Games, and intimacy? Are you spending an appropriate percentage of your time in each? What needs to be cut down on? Increased?

Given your current class time structuring pattern, was this pattern established somewhat subconsciously, or did you use your Adult in deciding how to structure your class time?

Four

OKness

Regarding the self and others, an individual at any point in time is feeling and thinking that he or she and others are OK or not OK.

OK does not mean perfect. OK means things are generally satisfactory. OKness concerns not only performance but also personal characteristics of the self and others—general appearance, ethnic background, level of intelligence, social position, economic position, and personality factors, such as cleverness, seriousness, meekness, assertiveness, social dominance, and obsequiousness.

A person sees himself or herself and others as OK or not OK based on various criteria. Depending on the level of perfection required and the criteria used, it is easy or almost impossible for anyone to be OK.

OKness varies from person to person.

Regardless of current events, people feel OK or not in various combinations. The reason for this is that people generally decide at an early age whether they and others are OK or not and stick with this decision regardless of new data received later on. According to Berne (1962), this decision is made between the ages of three and seven. According to Berne, there are four basic positions a person can take regarding OKness of self and others:

I. I'm OK—you're OK
II. I'm OK—you're not OK
III. I'm not—OK, you're OK
IV. I'm not—OK, you're not OK

Franklin Ernst, MD, points out in his article "The OK Corral: The Grid for Get On With" (1971) that people live in a corral with respect to the above four positions. You must be in one position or the other with people. Ernst sets the four positions up in a four-quadrant graph (to which I added numerical calibrations), as shown in Figure 16.

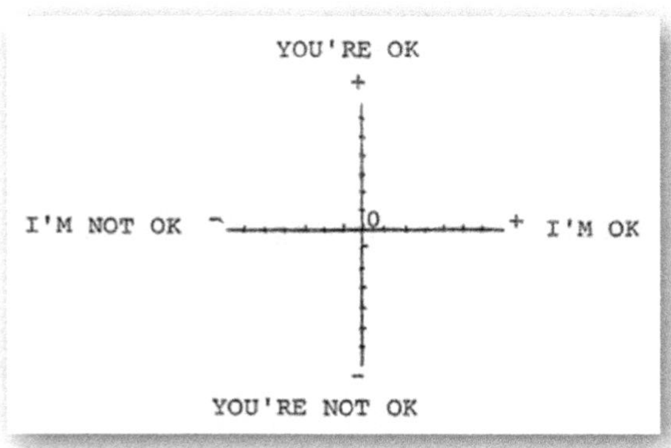

Figure 16. The Four OK Quadrants.

The ++ quadrant of the math scale is the space of the I'm OK—you're OK position, the +- quadrant is the I'm OK—you're not OK position, the --quadrant is the I'm not OK—you're not OK position, and the -+ quadrant is the I'm not OK—you're OK position.

Where would you place points on the above graph for your position with each of your students? Your employees? Your children? Your faculty members? Your supervisors? Your family members?

Would you be 10, 10 with each person? That is, would your coordinate points be in the upper right-hand space of the graph? Or are you –10, –10 with some people? Or would your points be spread out all over the graph, showing that you vary greatly in relation to various people?

What accounts for your positions? If your OK position with a particular student or employee is heavily I'm OK—you're not OK, what are your criteria for deciding the student is Not OK? Is it the employee's performance of job duties that determines his or her position with you, or is it that you feel his or her appearance, manners, or social or ethnic position is not OK?

Where we are with ourselves and others is largely a function of what we have decided at early ages. In order for many of us to get OK in the here and now, we must redecide in our Child ego states that we and others are OK.

One way to determine where you are in the OK Corral is to keep track of yourself after each encounter or conversation you have with others.

Most people want to be winners. A winner in the OK Corral is a person who can conduct himself or herself in such a way as to stay I'm OK—you're OK most of the time when dealing with people. This is not always easy. Sometimes other people are really not OK. Sometimes we are really not OK, and no amount of rationalizing or excusing will change the fact.

The realistic thing is not to strive for an undefeated season but to strive to develop a winning season. If you can come out of more than 50 percent of your encounters I'm OK—you're OK, you have had a winning season. If you can emerge from 90 percent of your encounters a winner, so much the better. What is your won-lost record? As in sports, it is possible to keep statistics on how well you are doing.

An OK Corral won-lost record can be kept by marking down on a sheet of paper where you are after each of your encounters with others. An encounter can be a short conversation, a meeting, a class, a work session, a family dinner, or any means of spending time with people. A simple frequency tabulation is sufficient to paint you a picture of where you are.

I'm OK—you're OK ++
I'm OK—you're not OK +-
I'm not OK—you're not OK --
I'm not OK—you're OK -+

Mark a checkmark beside each of the above possibilities every time you think of checking on yourself to see where you are at that moment with others. After some period of time has elapsed, say a week or month, add up the checkmarks for each possibility, and then divide the total checkmarks for each possibility by the total of checkmarks for all of the possibilities. This will tell you the approximate percentage of your total encounters with others for each of the possibilities.

If, after keeping won-lost statistics, you find you are losing more than you like, you can probably think up some things to do or stop doing to improve your record.

If you find you are dissatisfied with your record and can't seem to do much about it on your own, you can decide to find a therapist to help you.

Whether you win or lose with people depends on staying I'm OK—you're OK. According to Ernst (1971), changing just a small percentage of encounters to ++ from otherwise can result in changing a nonwinner script into a winner script.

The Total OKness Spectrum

Martin Groder, MD, developed a 5-OK Diagram (1977), which makes it possible to analyze whether and how OK you are with respect to (1) yourself,

(2) the other person, (3) your group, (4) the other group ("they"), and (5) the system, society, the world, or universe ("it").

A diagram developed in Groder's schema is based on a determination where a person is considering his or her position regarding the degree to which

I am or am not OK,
you are or are not OK,
we are or are not OK,
they are or are not OK, and
it is or is not OK.

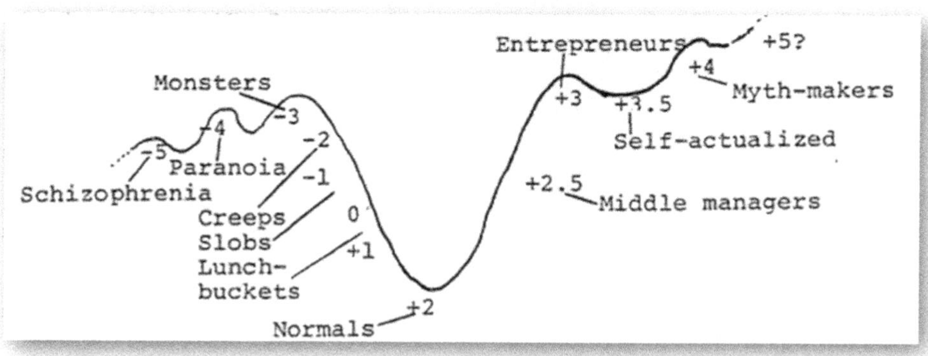

Figure 17. Martin Groder's People Map.

To be fully OK using Groder's framework, you must be OK with yourself, the other person, your group, the other group, and the world or universe. He measures how OK you are in terms of -1 (least OK) to +1 (most OK).

Adding up where someone is, from -1 to +1, on each of the five OK dimensions develops an overall OKness factor. OK ratings for specific people can vary from -5 to +5.

According to Groder, -5 people are generally labeled schizophrenic. He calls +4 people "myth-makers." These are the top winners, the cultural heroes.

He doesn't know what to call +5 people, since they are so rare. Normal people have a +2 rating. Middle managers have a +2.5 rating. Entrepreneurs have a +3 rating.

Groder also makes the observation that the energy a person releases into the world is related to his or her OK position. He developed the curve shown in Figure 17 showing the energy release characteristic of various points in the OKness spectrum. Energy releases change the environment. High-energy people change their environments more than do most people. They leave more footprints in the sand than do low-energy people.

According to Groder, the higher the point on the curve in Figure 17, the greater the energy required to maintain a particular OKness position. Regarding the positions, Groder says,

> Up in the –3 peak area are the kings of the monsters, who are psychopathic leaders. Minus three (–3) is a very high energy state and has a very strong effect on the world from the position of "I'm OK, My buddy is OK, You're not-OK, We're not-OK, They're not-OK, It's not-OK, We are going to take the world with us." This position Eric Berne described as that of "I'm going to make the world pay."
>
> On this next plateau at +3, which is a long pull, are what I identify as entrepreneurs. Entrepreneurs are highly energetic, leader types who win the races their culture provides, especially if the culture is a competitive one. They win the race, they make the million dollars, or whatever it is. Entrepreneurs are quite different from normals. They're cunning and shifty, they cut corners, they're high energy people, they bowl people over. They do a whole lot of Machiavellian stuff. They invest a whole lot of energy in their goals and skills, and the only other people that look very much like them are the psychopathic leaders. The main difference between entrepreneurs and psychopaths is that

> the entrepreneurs are winner-survivors, and the psychopaths are loser-survivors, and sometimes you will see shifts between the two. Both the winner-survivor and loser-survivor have experienced childhood abandonment and reacted with decisions to survive—get revenge by "showing them," live for drama and excitement rather than for life itself. Often, later generations who "have it made" from birth do not invest the energy in surviving; they're mostly up here because the money keeps them up. If the money disappeared, they often couldn't make it up again. (Groder 1977)

Groder asserts the main difference between an entrepreneur and a myth-maker is that a myth-maker is supported by a column of people and has higher energy by virtue of converting people to his or her world view. Groder states that he can't describe +5 people, but "there are some people so described in famous ancient books" (1977).

Groder spent several years working with character-disordered people in federal prisons. His Askelepieion system is an effective therapeutic personality-behavior-changing system, and he used it at the federal prison at Marion, Illinois, with good success. The system uses a variety of treatment modalities. Groder states that it is easier to change a –3 monster into a +3 entrepreneur than it is to change a –3 monster into a +2 normal. Apparently, human energy levels do not change that much, so it is easier to shoot people across the arc horizontally from a negative-energy OK position to a positive-energy OK position than it is to move them down the curve.

Negative-OKness people in prisons generally have some of the most difficult-to-deal-with behavior, thinking, and emotional problems that exist. Managers, teachers, and administrators in businesses, classrooms, and principal's offices sometimes encounter students who have thinking, emotional, or behavioral problems that will cause them to eventually wind up in prison. Fortunately, these people constitute a small minority in businesses and schools.

Most classes and work groups are pretty much alike, but none are totally alike. The students and workers attracted to and placed in classes, work groups, and businesses have almost as much to do about the success of a group as the leader. True enough, the leader has some power to change those in his or her charge, but the basic OKness positions of subordinates have generally been predetermined.

The OKness of a class or business work group is a function of not only the OKness of the teacher or leader; the basic OKness of the students and employees significantly affects the group, regardless of what the formal leader does or does not do.

Many classroom and work-group problems are caused by teachers and managers not knowing what to do with high-energy students and employees. The +2 normals are relatively easy to deal with. They generally do what they are told. The –3 monsters and the +3 entrepreneurs—the ones who will really have an effect on the world later on—are the problems. They do not like to sit still and politely do what they are told. They find other things to do. Many high-energy people have to start their own businesses because they keep getting fired trying to work for someone else. Some people are much better teachers than they were students because teaching takes more energy (in general) than does being a student. Some students who want to take over the class really will make good teachers.

What do you do with the high-energy students and employees? Unless you force them to entertain themselves in their heads by withdrawing and daydreaming (or figuring out ways to undermine you), you must develop learning and work activities that require and utilize a good bit of energy. You must let these people take an active part in the learning and work activity. Mere passive absorption will not do the job. They have to be allowed to be serious participants in the overall process.

How to Move from Not OKness to OKness

Moving from not OK to OK depends on where someone is in the OK spectrum, how negative they are and how positive they want to get.

In the high negative positions, some form of psychotherapy will probably be required to move someone to a positive OK position. In many cases, lengthy, detailed discussions are required on each of the OKness dimensions described by Groder, in order for someone to change his or her understanding, beliefs, feelings, and behavior. Strokes and support over a period of time are normally required.

There are plenty of professional people in the world today who devote their lives to helping people move from negative positions to positive positions. As Stephen Karpman, MD, pointed out in his article "The Bias Box for Competing Psychotherapies" (1975), there were some ninety-eight competing types of therapy available in 1975. The main four, according to Karpman, were Gestalt therapy, transactional analysis, psychoanalysis, and behavior modification. This competition among psychotherapeutic approaches has not always been therapeutic.

According to Karpman (1975),

> With the exciting growth of psychotherapeutic approaches in the past 15 years there has existed an unexciting war among disciplines, one putting the other down, saying their way is right, the other way is wrong. For example:
>
> I'm OK—You're Unscientific
> I'm OK—You're Mechanical
> I'm OK—You're Superficial
> I'm OK—You're a Rip-off

I'm OK—You're Wild
I'm OK—You're Unstructured
I'm OK—You're a Head Trip
I'm OK—You're Incomplete

While differentiation and innovation probably produce more total theory, opinion, and methodology, they also increase uncertainty about what is best or correct. Innovation and differentiation also increase insecurity and conflict among various vested interest groups. No one school of therapy can "prove" it is right or any better than any other. Each has evidence that it produces results. On the other hand, according to the study "Measuring the Effectiveness of Transactional Analysis," conducted by Ted Novey in 2002, published in the *Transactional Analysis Journal,* TA was considered more effective than competing therapies in his sample.

What is the consumer desiring to change or improve to do? Go to the yellow pages and look under "Psychotherapy" and pick a psychotherapist at random? Or take the advice of someone who makes a referral? Who is to say the person making the referral knows what is best?

As I see it, people feeling the need to increase their OKness or the OKness of others through psychotherapy more or less accidentally fall into one or more of the various approaches. If the person experiences success with the approach, he or she becomes an advocate or practitioner of it. But this still does not mean the approach is right or best for everyone.

Where I am, the relevant thing is whether the approach works. As Karpman pointed out in his Bias Box article, the main determinant regarding the selection of an approach by a therapist is the personality of the therapist. If a therapist is by nature structured and mechanical, he or she will be inclined to select a structured approach, such as TA. On the other hand, a person who has high emotional affect will probably select an approach that places a high regard on high affect, such as Gestalt therapy.

As I see it, we are lucky we live in a society as relatively free as the United States. The uncertainty, conflict, innovation, and differentiation that we have in our psychotherapeutic industry are simply not tolerated in dictatorial societies. As Karpman points out in his bias box article, it really doesn't make that much difference who is right; the free market will eventually decide which works best, anyway. The more effective approaches will develop a large market share, and the least effective approaches will experience declining market shares and perhaps extinction.

This same problem and process exists in free societies regarding businesses and products and services. The same process is also at play in academic environments wherein various effective disciplines get more students, and the less effective ones have fewer students. The problem in academia is that administrators who are not free-market oriented often try to intervene in the process and rescue the disciplines or courses with declining enrollments. The presumption here is that they are smarter than the students. The students are presumed not to know what is good for them regarding courses to take and material to learn. Some administrators presume they know what is best for the students in their institutions and have a moral obligation to impose their opinions on people in their systems.

Russia decided in 1987 that Communism didn't work after a seventy-five-year-experiment. Based on this experiment it appears the free-market system is superior to Communism. Is there anything better than both Communism and the free-market system? If not, the world must learn to live indefinitely will a host of serious economic, environmental, political, and social problems. The free market has yet to produce an OK economic existence for all people.

Much so-called "advising" is little more than teachers and counselors telling students to take certain courses because the administrative process has determined that it is right and or best for the student to take and learn such and such. Much of this "advising" and "counseling" is actually dictating or high-pressure selling.

But in psychotherapeutic learning environments, there is little or no direction on what the patient/client/student should take or learn. No one has enough power to lay down arbitrary regulations. Where I am, this is a desirable situation. Let the consumer choose in a free market.

I have no way of knowing what method of psychotherapy is best. Apparently many psychotherapists do not either, as they use various methods of therapy with various clients. One approach is to seek out therapists who understand and use various methods of therapy.

Most people, seemingly incorrigible students, employees, managers, business owners, and convicts included, have more options for change than most people think.

Three Levels of OKness

As I see it, there are three types of human OKness:

1) Existential OKness—This is unconditional OKness. Everyone is OK by virtue of being born without asking to be. It's OK for everyone to be here. Most people are here for the same reason: their parents were gratifying themselves sexually, and the woman got pregnant. All people are basically OK. It's OK for all people to get what they want and need from life so long as they don't harm themselves or others. All people are equally entitled to the necessities and luxuries of life at birth.

2) Subjective OKness—Through early parental influence and illogical decision processes, children decide various things about their OKness, the OKness of others, the OKness of themselves and others in groups, the OKness of other groups, and the OKness of the world. These decisions, which are normally made before age seven, may be completely

inaccurate and inappropriate, but they become as significant as real facts and may stick with a person throughout life.

3) Objective OKness—By virtue of feelings, thoughts, and acts, people place themselves in relatively OK or not-OK positions, financially, socially, and physically. People in pain from illness, accidents, or poverty are, objectively speaking, in relatively not-OK positions. It is possible for people to be caught up in varying degrees of permanence in objective not OKness by virtue of negative trends and processes at play in the society in which they live. Some people, by the same token, are in relatively OK objective positions because of being lucky enough to be caught up in favorable societal or environmental trends and processes.

The major problems in classrooms, businesses, and everywhere else involve subjective and objective not OKness in various degrees. How do you convince people who have decided they and others are basically not OK that they and others are basically OK? How do you teach people how to feel, think, and act in such a way as to place and keep themselves in objectively OK positions? To what degree are psychotherapists able to help their clients increase subjective OKness? To what degree are teachers and managers able to help students and employees increase objective OKness?

I hope this book will help clarify some issues regarding OKness and help teachers and managers deal with and develop appropriate attitudes toward subjective and objective OKness in themselves, students, and employees.

Five

What Is In The Contract?

The first step in developing a Game-free classroom or business is to establish, as clearly as possible, from the outset of the year, course, or employment relationship, the contracts between teacher and administration, between manager and owner, between teacher or manager and students or employees, between students and administration, between employees and owners, and between students and employees.

I am using the word *contract* in a general way. A contract is an agreement to do something. Benefits and detriments are associated with fulfilling contracts. Contracts between people are of the order of "I will do such and such for you if you will do such and such for me."

Human relationships in general are based upon contracts. Many people are not aware of what all their contracts with others are, but the contracts exist nevertheless.

Contracts can be logical or psychological. They can be straight or crooked, useful or harmful. They can be overt or covert.

What are the contracts among people in classrooms and businesses?

The basic contract in the classroom is the learning contract. If the student learns such and such material, his or her grade will be such and such or he or she will earn such and such diploma or certificate. If the student does what the teacher says, he or she will learn such and such. If the teacher teaches such and such, he or she will be paid according to his or her employment contract with the school system.

The basic contract in a business is the employment contract between the employee and the business. If the employee produces so much according to the job description, he or she will receive so much in pay.

If the teacher or manager attends such and such meetings, he or she will have satisfied his or her administrative requirements for attending meetings. If the teacher or manager implements in the classroom or workplace required administrative procedures, he or she will have satisfied his or her administrative contract.

Classrooms exist for learning, and businesses exist for producing goods and services. If learning and production contracts were all that existed in classrooms and businesses, there would be no need for this book. There would be no psychological Games; everything would be straight.

Unfortunately, strictly learning contracts are not the only contracts in classrooms or businesses. Many students and employees contract to please the teacher and manager and get good grades or high pay by being extrapolite, nice, supportive, helpful, talkative, quiet, nicey-nice, humorous, precocious, and so on. In these types of contracts, which teacher's pets, apple-polishers, and others set up, the reward system is undermined by ulterior, unstraight manipulation. The student or employee may be rewarded not for learning or producing but for pleasing the teacher or manager. The teacher's pet or crony becomes the teacher or manager's object of manipulation. Or vice versa, the teacher or manager may become the student or worker's object of manipulation. The teacher or manager, rather than working to cause Adult learning and productivity to occur, may invest energy in pleasing, taking care of, playing Games with, or "politicking" with students and employees. Or the teacher or manager or student may be primarily investing his or her energy in playing Games with administrators, higher managers, or owners.

Manipulation, trickery, deception, unstraightness, and basic unfairness always exist when Games are going on. At the root of the matter, someone is trying to get something for nothing by ignoring the Adult contract and outwitting the system.

The straight, Game-free teacher or manager rewards students and employees based upon the Adult, overt learning and productivity contract that is established by mutual agreement between the Adults of all parties involved. The Child or Parent ego states are not used to manipulate unspoken, ulterior, covert, psychological contracts.

Eliminating unstraight, covert, psychological contracts eliminates much anxiety, fear, and confusion.

How to Establish a Straight Contract

The first step is to see the learning or work situation from an Adult perspective for what it is. Are you teaching first graders or students in medical school? Are you teaching history or calculus, chemistry or English, economics or physics, or metalworking or management? What kind of widgets or services are you producing in your business? Given realities such as these, certain Adult considerations regarding what is to be done, learned, produced, and so on become obvious. Given the obvious, what should be learned or produced? Secondly, how is the best way to cause that learning, production, or change to occur? Are these considerations obvious enough for everyone to see them? If disagreement exists as to what should be done, is the disagreement due to actual complexities of the situation, or is the disagreement due to Game playing, vested interests, or past conditioning? A good deal of thought and discussion should be conducted by relevant parties in classroom and work situations in order to get a good, clean, clearly spelled-out, overt, Adult learning and production contract established.

While most issues involved in establishing a good learning or work contract would be obvious to a hypothetical observer alien from some distant planet in outer space, they are often not obvious to the average human Earthian. This is caused by the tendency of education itself to create confusion and diversity of opinion. For example, many holders of training, degrees, and certificates of various sorts have psychological contracts with their previous trainers, teachers, managers, and programs to continue believing that "the way" taught by the previous teachers, managers, programs, and so on is really "the best."

Therefore, when teachers and managers get together, rather than use their Adult ego states in the here and now to establish good, useful, effective, appropriate learning and production contracts, they frequently refuse to enter new Adult contracts, because of the psychological contracts with past teachers and mentors they have been using as defenses in their professional lives. The basic psychological contract here is that if the teacher or manager always adheres to what and how his or her past teachers and mentors taught, he or she will be protected.

Another problem involved in setting good contracts, in addition to the past educational experiences of teachers, students, managers, employees, and administrators, is the problem of determining how to measure the results of the contracts.

Measuring specific content learned or production produced seems relatively straightforward. Students and employees are supposed to hear or read certain material and remember what they hear or read. Measurement then becomes a matter of constructing a test to see how much the student remembers relative to the total he or she was expected to learn or relative to what his or her peers remembered

I was never clear on this point. I never got it straight that 70, or 70 percent right, and thus a "C," resulted from learning 70 percent of the total knowledge of that particular subject or from learning 70 percent of what the teacher knew or whether the 70 meant much of anything. A 70 obviously means a student answered 70 percent of the questions right (assuming the teacher graded the test right), but what does this mean?

Grading in most businesses is even more subjective. Except where piecework systems are used, managers and employees rarely have an actual count of production produced that can be used to compare one employee against another. An employee's salary raise generally depends on the opinion of the supervisor regarding the quantity and quality of work produced, attitudes, and job knowledge, but rarely is there anything equivalent to a test in school to prove what one employee should receive relative to peers. In many businesses, employees are not allowed to compare or even disclose their "grades" (salaries) with other workers. This proves the business has no objective way of proving that fairness in grading exists.

I think the relevant point is that if you are going to use a percentage-based grading system, you should transmit to your students or employees what you think a 70 (or whatever) means and, if possible, get your students or employees to agree to abide by your definitions.

But what do you do if you establish teaching students and employees to communicate, create, and think as your overt purpose? What sort of test can you devise for this? I don't think a satisfactory written test can be developed for it. The only way a teacher or manager can grade this type of learning and production is to observe and listen closely to what students and employees say, think, and do and grade them relative to standards that are agreed upon. This can be the purely subjective judgment of the teacher or manager regarding where the student or employee is relative to other students and employees of the same age and job classification. This grading must be based on observation if it is to be valid and reliable. Read my book *Business Voyages* where I spent many pages on this problem, showing grading case analysis, communication, decision making, and leadership can be done and produces salutary results.

Despite the fact that the standards for grading the memorizing, thinking, doing, communicating, and so on of students or employees in your classes or business are arbitrary in nature, it's OK if you, your students or employees, and your superiors use the Adult ego state in creating logical and fair contracts necessary to govern the process.

All goals, objectives, and standards, worthwhile or not, involve arbitrary assumptions. Whether they are OK or not depends upon whether harm to the self or others results and whether manipulation is used to trick people into accepting them.

Even though the setting of standards involves an arbitrary process, once agreed upon through the Adult ego state, they should not be enforced arbitrarily. You should enforce them as you said you would enforce them.

Elements of a Learning Contract

A good learning/employment contract should include the following:

1. A general outlining of the subject matter, skills to be learned, and goods and services to be produced
2. The methods by which the subject matter and skills will be presented and taught
3. The testing and measurement procedures for determining grades and raises, if grades are to be assigned or raises given
4. The classroom/work layout(s) to be used

5. Policies for managing the classroom or work area, including the procedures and rules of the teacher or manager for governing the following:
   a. Tardiness and absences
   b. Permissible and impermissible behavior, such as sleeping, talking about non-subject-matter topics, chewing gum, throwing paper wads, smoking, etc.
6. The responsibilities of the teacher or manager as a supplier of additional information, discussion leader, problem solver, etc.
7. Rewards and penalties for students and employees for doing or not doing day in and day out what is in the contract
8. Some discussion of how the group time will be structured; i.e., how much time will be spent on withdrawal, rituals, pastimes, Games, activities, and intimacy
9. Some discussion of how the participants will know day in and day out whether the contract is being fulfilled
10. Some discussion of what participants sometimes do psychologically in order to sabotage the fulfilling of Adult contracts

Before you begin implementing your contract, you might inform your principal, department head, vice president, dean, or whatever your administrative superior is called of what is in your contract. If your authority structure (i.e., your principal, department head, supervisor, or whatever) and his or her superiors do not agree that your learning contract is valid, true, and moral, they can sabotage you. If disagreement exists, perhaps you can change their minds or your contract. Perhaps you will want to leave and teach or work somewhere else where your learning/work contracts will be honored.

Perspective

In the lower grades, teachers and managers must spend more time attending to the psychological needs of students and employees than at higher levels. Children are children, and, in varying degrees, children must be taken care of from the Parent ego state. But the main function of teachers and managers is to cause Adult learning and production to occur. Teachers and managers are secondarily babysitters and social workers. Students and employees should be encouraged to grow up and learn what is appropriate for their age and ability levels from the Adult ego state.

Psychological Straightness

Martin Groder (1975) pointed out that organizations are clean or dirty based on whether they actually do what the sign on the door says they are supposed to do.

The sign on your classroom or department door may say, "arithmetic teaching and learning," "social studies teaching and learning," "chemistry teaching and learning," "management teaching, training, learning," " law or medicine teaching and learning," "x-, y-, or z-widget production," "x, y, or z services provided," and so on.

Your classroom or business is clean if most of the energy in your classroom or business is invested in doing what the sign on your door says. Your classroom or business is psychologically dirty if you are investing most of your energy enhancing your personal power, proving you are right, proving you are smart, proving you are sexually attractive, or somehow misusing money.

Groder calls power, sex, money, smarts, and righteousness the five deadly organizational sins.

Sin is perhaps too strong a word. *Perversion* might be a better one. Many perversions of this nature go unquestioned. They are so common that most people don't think anything about them. Who doesn't occasionally do things to cause others to admire him or her sexually rather than technically stick to the knitting? How many people never do things to prove they are smart or right when they should be getting the work done?

It is no secret that these perversions are committed daily in various organizations. Secretaries are hired for being pretty and sexy rather than for how much work they can do. Managers act in such a way as to enhance their personal power at the expense of the good of the total organization. People are rewarded for supporting the power moves of administrators rather than for actually doing work. Funds are embezzled and misused. The list is lengthy.

Check to see if you ever set up psychological contracts with your students, employees, your bosses, and your fellow faculty members or workers in the areas of the five deadly organizational sins. If you establish contracts in these areas, you will be engaging in psychological Games and wasting much of the potentially productive, life-enhancing energy at your disposal.

Based on the above, it would be difficult for most teachers or managers to be "clean" with their contracts all the time in their classrooms and businesses.

Given human weaknesses, various teachers and managers commit some of the five organizational sins from time to time.

Probably the most compelling temptations for teachers and managers are power, smarts, and righteousness.

Many teachers and managers think it is part of their job requirements to be powerful, smart, and right all the time.

It is OK to be powerful, smart, and right, so long as being so does not get in the way of your doing what the sign on your door says you are supposed to do—cause learning to occur in your specific area of expertise and produce whatever you are supposed to produce.

Six

The Classroom Setup

In my lifetime, I have sat in approximately 110 formal, non-TA classrooms. Most (80 or 90) were row-and-column classrooms.

The rest were seminar classrooms, in which we sat around a seminar table.

As a professor at the University of Southwestern Louisiana, I taught in an amphitheater classroom.

The amphitheater classroom is a classroom in which the desks are positioned in a horseshoe fashion around a lectern in front, with each row of desks from the front to the back being raised a bit higher than the row immediately in front.

The circle classroom is a classroom in which students position their desks or chairs in a circle.

In my teaching at Georgia Southern University from 1970 to 2005, for about twenty years, I arranged my classes in either circle or horseshoe fashion. After the business school moved into its new building, I taught in an amphitheater classroom for about fifteen years. I did not stand behind the lectern in front at the bottom in this room, the best classroom in the business building, the same room for fifteen years. I sat wherever I felt like sitting every day among students in the amphitheater. I would spin the spinner of the Classroom De-Gamer and announce the number selected to start the case discussion. More about this later.

Virtually all the classrooms in the Georgia Southern School of Business were row-and-column classrooms when I arrived in 1970, requiring me to rearrange the desks in all my classrooms. This rearranging of desks from rows and columns to circles and back to rows and columns after my classes were over caused some inconvenience but not a serious problem. The biggest problem was the attitude problem that arose among my colleagues. It seems many of them thought students couldn't learn sitting in circles. Some of the faculty seemed threatened about desks being positioned in circles, as if it were a bad omen.

The accounting faculty seemed especially concerned about this, perhaps because they were used to adding and subtracting in rows and columns on their ledger sheets.

In most classrooms, desks are positioned in rows and columns for the sake of orderliness, discipline, and efficiency.

The next-most common classroom is probably the seminar classroom, in which students sit around a large table in chairs. I don't know what would come next: the amphitheater classroom or the circle classroom. My hunch is there are more amphitheater classrooms than circle classrooms in schools of business in colleges and universities. Outside of school or college classrooms, I think the favorite is the circle classroom.

I developed another way of setting up classrooms at one point in my career: I used the circle or horseshoe system but had students push their desks away from the walls of the classroom, giving me room to walk around the room behind them. I called this layout the Orbit Classroom because I was in orbit around the room when the learning was going on.

Another classroom layout procedure sometimes used, particularly in TA and management training in organizations, is to have people sit in several small groups, called dyads, triads, and so on. This system works particularly well in large classes of fifty to one hundred students. The students can be broken up in several small, circular groups of six to ten students each for learning. The teacher can walk around from group to group to supply information, participate, answer questions, or teach while the learning is going on.

Classroom Layouts and Transactional Analysis

All classroom layouts have advantages and disadvantages.

The Row-and-Column Layout. The main disadvantage of the row-and-column layout is that it sets up a Parent-Child pattern from teacher to students, especially if the teacher is standing behind a lectern on a podium. The persona of the teacher, standing tall and erect in front of the lower, seated students, comes across as basically Parent, as in a church. The student's persona is basically Child.

The row-and-column layout tends to engender an I'm OK—you're not OK position on the part of the teacher and an I'm not OK—you're OK position from students.

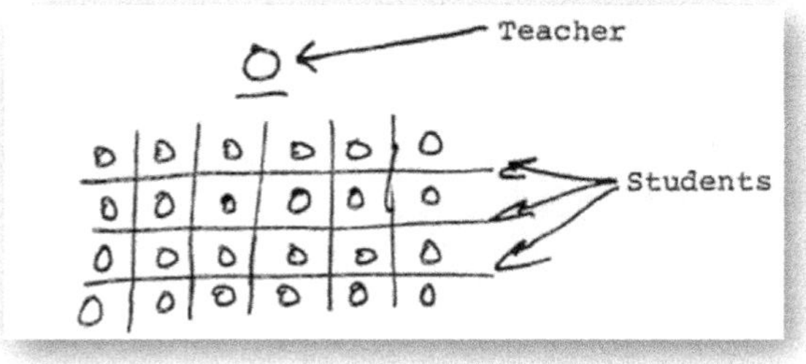

Teacher

Students

The physical structuring of the classroom tends to bring the above about, regardless of how friendly, helpful, or entertaining the teacher might be.

The main advantage of the row-and-column layout is that it lends itself to keeping order and is perhaps more efficient for disseminating information that requires little or no discussion. In teaching situations wherein students are not supposed to talk to one another (only to the teacher), the row-and-column Layout is probably most efficient.

The Seminar Layout. The seminar layout, with the teacher sitting at the head of the table can also become Parent to Child but is basically more Adult to Adult. While it can also be I'm OK—you're not OK, it tends to be more I'm OK—you're OK in the overall transactional patterns set up by its physical structuring.

One of the main advantages of the seminar layout is that everyone can be OK—and even a little Parent—assuming everyone is sitting at the same big table in the same types of chairs. The size and position of the chairs may not put anyone in a Child position from a physical standpoint.

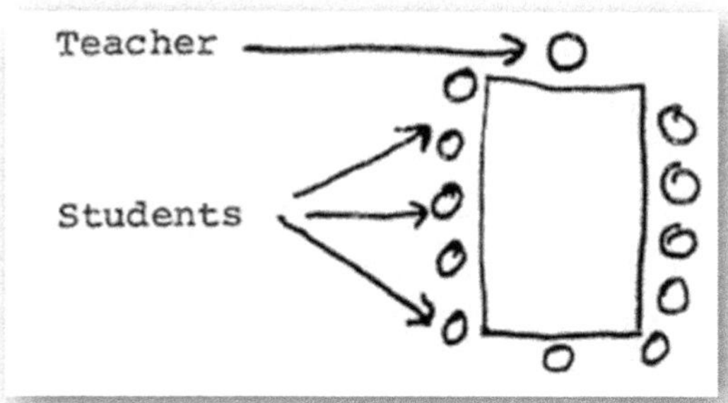

The Amphitheater Layout. One of the disadvantages of the amphitheater layout is that students sitting on the front row tend to be a little less OK than those at the top and a little more Child than the Parent types at the top. The teacher, since he or she is usually placed down in front, lower than everybody else, may actually be placed in an I'm not OK—you're OK Child position in an amphitheater classroom. I had this feeling when I taught from behind a lectern at the bottom of the room in an amphitheater layout.

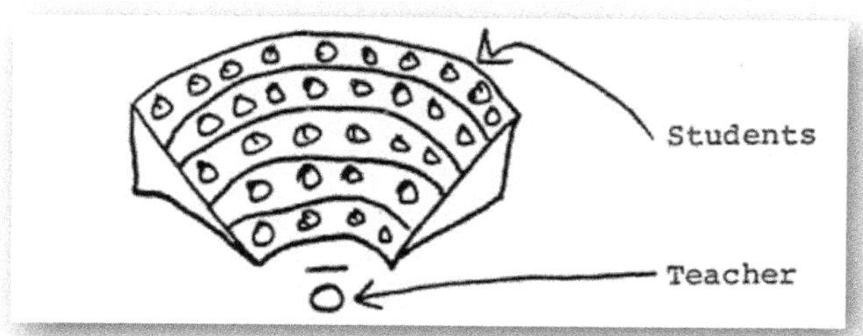

The amphitheater layout definitely tends to keep teachers out of Parent and students out of Child more than the other layouts if the teacher teaches from behind a lectern at the bottom of the room. One way this can be counteracted is for the teacher to sit on the top row and forget about the lectern, as I often did.

Probably the main advantage of the amphitheater layout is that more students can be crowded in a given space without having to look directly at the back of someone's head.

The Circle Layout. A disadvantage of the circle layout is that it is difficult to disseminate information from a chalkboard. Some students are always in a position wherein they can't see the chalkboard. A portable chalkboard is of little help. However, it is actually easier to pass out handouts, tests and the like in a Circle layout. All you have to do is hand the stack of paper to one student and send it around the room.

It is sometimes postulated that the circle layout requires small classes, since you can't get as many students in a room with the circle layout as with the row-and-column Layout. This is not fully true. You can position almost as many students in desks set around the perimeter of a room of given size as you can in a row-and-column Layout.

The main advantage of the circle layout is that the teacher, if he or she sits in the same type of desk or chair as the students, is placed in a more I'm OK—you're OK position and comes across as less Parent and more Adult or Child, engendering more OKness on the part of students.

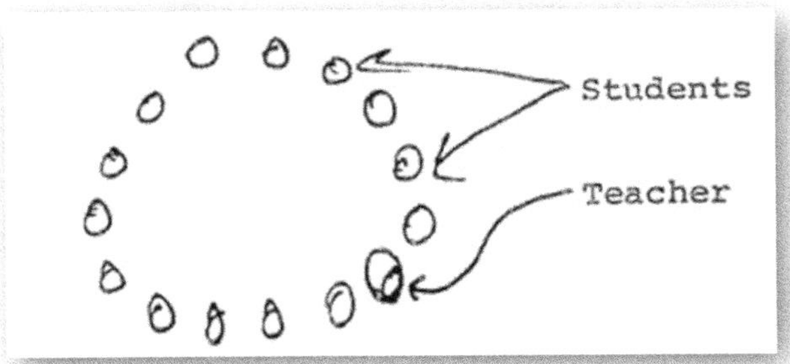

Another advantage of the circle layout is that by not having a table to block off the lower part of anyone's body, it is possible for more total verbal and nonverbal communication to take place. It is much easier in a circle layout for a "hurry up" driver to communicate that he or she is in a hurry by pumping a foot up and down for everyone to see, for example.

Also, the absence of the big table, as in the Seminar Layout, helps keep people out of Critical Parent and Adapted Child and more in Adult, Natural Child, and Nurturing Parent.

In classrooms in which the teacher encourages discussion of ideas among students, the circle layout is by far the most efficient from a time and motion study, engineering standpoint. Students don't have to waste time and energy turning their bodies or necks around to talk or listen to fellow students. Also, it could be that even if the teacher does most of the talking in class, students will still learn more in a circle classroom since they don't have to look at the back of someone's head and can't hide from the eye contact of the teacher.

The Horseshoe Layout. The horseshoe layout has many of the same advantages and disadvantages as the Circle Layout.

An advantage of the horseshoe layout is that the open end of the horseshoe can be facing the chalkboard, giving access to the board for teacher and students.

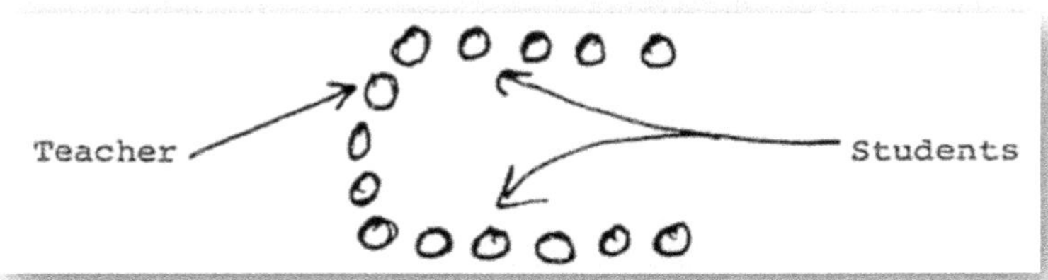

The Orbit Layout. A disadvantage of the orbit layout is that the teacher may come across as less I'm OK—you're OK than in the Circle Layout when he or she is up walking around the room, and the students are sitting down.

A major advantage of the orbit layout, however, is that when the teacher is up walking around the room, it's difficult for students to talk solely to the teacher in Child-Parent transactions. If the teacher notices students coming on to him or her Child to Parent, all he or she has to do is walk around the room and stand behind the student. The student must then talk out into the room to fellow students, thereby coming across as more Adult to Adult and I'm OK—you're OK.

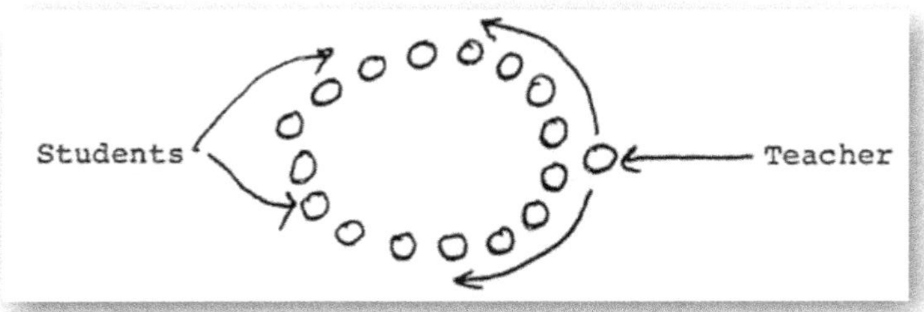

The Orbit Classroom, in general, has the same advantages and disadvantages as the Circle Layout, with a few exceptions.

Walking around the room in orbit, the teacher can pick up various bits of Adult data, showing how much students have prepared or how interested they are, by noting notes, underling in books, and body language. The teacher can also come down to earth at various times and places by lighting in various empty chairs or desks and getting more into Adult or Child.

The No-Clique Layout. Cliques, pods of cronies with political agendas, sometimes become a problem in classrooms. Three or four students will sit near one another with psychological contracts among themselves to always react in certain ways socially and psychologically when certain things are discussed or happen in classes. Sometimes, cliques in a classroom will compete with one another to see who can cause more disruption in the natural flow of the class and draw more attention to themselves than others.

The best thing to do in such classrooms (assuming you know the names and faces of all students in the class so that you can mark them absent if they do not show up for class) is bust up all cliques in the classroom. The best way to do this is to simply tell all students in the class that from then on in the course, they have to maximize the distance between themselves and the students they sat by last by sitting in different places in the room. In every classroom in which I inserted such a law, agitations created by the cliques were significantly reduced, if not entirely eliminated.

Teaching Methods and Transactional Analysis

The Lecture Method. The most common teaching method in colleges and universities is the lecture method. The teacher normally uses a Row-and-Column Layout and stands in the front of the room behind a lectern. Amphitheater Layouts are sometimes used.

In these classes, teachers normally do most of the talking; anywhere from 75 to 100 percent of the airtime is consumed by teachers.

Questions are sometimes asked and answered by teachers and students in discussions.

The overall transactional pattern is Parent to Child and I'm OK—you're not OK from teacher to students.

The lecture method is effective where the teacher is presenting new material that has not been published. The most efficient way of getting unpublished material across is with a monological lecture.

In many cases, the teacher lectures on material that is already in the assigned textbook, essentially repeating what is in the textbook. This procedure discounts the ability of students to learn by reading and may waste time.

The lecture method is effective for teaching material that has not been brought together in a good textbook. The teacher can present a good summary that is available through nontextbook sources unavailable to students.

This can be a Gamey method. It can work out that most of what is said in the lectures is readily available in the textbook and the class time could have been better spent discussing the material in the textbook, assuming the students had a textbook and read it

Games are kept to a minimum if few questions are asked by teachers or students.

The Reading/Arithmetic/Discussion Method. What I call the reading/arithmetic/discussion method involves teachers assigning overnight reading or math problems and having the class talk about it the next day. This was the most common method used by my high school teachers.

This can be a very Gamey method. It can work out that practically all the questions asked by teachers and students to talk about are for the purpose of Persecuting, Rescuing, or Victimizing.

In many cases, the teachers call on only the "bad guys" in order make them look bad, and they call on the "pets" to make them look good. At the same time, it sometimes works out that only the "pets" hold their hands up to volunteer to answer questions. And the "bad guys" ask mainly trick questions to make a fool out of the teacher.

The major advantage of the reading/arithmetic/discussion method is that it is efficient and does not waste the class's time by having the teacher repeat orally what has already supposedly been read.

The Case Method. The case method of business teaching, as developed in the early part of this century by the Harvard Business School, involves students reading and discussing "cases," rather than concepts, formulas, theory, or history. The case method is used extensively in law and other professional teaching.

Under the case method, students are supposed to read factual problem-laden cases overnight and analyze them for discussion in class.

Students are supposed to talk about problems, alternatives, and recommendations for the cases in class.

This method can be as Gamey as the reading/Arithmetic/Discussion Method if the teacher makes it that way, calling on only the "good guys" or the "bad guys."

A unique feature of the Case Method is that students in class are not evaluated on the basis of how well they remember the assigned material; they are evaluated on the basis of how well they can make sense out of the cases and defend their recommendations. Therefore, there is little wasting of anyone's time repeating in class what has already supposedly been learned.

The case method can be as Parent to Child or I'm OK—you're not OK as the lecture method. One of the worst things a teacher using cases can do is to sit and listen to what the students have to say until the end of the hour and then say, "All right, you dummies, here is the right answer."

In most cases, the "right" answer is the "answer" the teacher read in the instructor's manual, prepared by the casebook writers (although all good casebook instructor's manual writers state that they are only "suggested" answers to start with). The truth is that real cases do not have right answers. Some answers are definitely better than others, but in most cases, it's impossible to prove that an answer is "right."

The Learning-the-Book Method. The learning-the-textbook method is a fairly rare teaching method, but it is one I consider effective. In my college career, I had two professors who used this method, and I learned more in those courses than I did in most.

What this method amounts to is that the teacher requires students to learn what is in the book—no more and no less.

In both of the learning-the-textbook courses I had, the teacher asked questions from paragraphs of the text. Both courses were somewhat Gamey in that some Persecuting, Rescuing, and Victimizing went on when the professor asked particular students to explain various paragraphs or formulas. There was some "get the bad guy" and "give the pet a chance to shine" behavior going on.

Yet the students read and generally learned the text. The overall process was less Gamey than most of the other learning processes I was exposed to.

There was no attempt on the part of the professors to "snow" students with how much they knew or their cleverness in oration or conversation.

There was more pressure in these courses than in most of the courses I had. The tests generally came straight out of the book.

The What-Do-You-Want-to-Work-On Method. Psychiatrists, psychologists, and various therapists and freelance helpers and teachers primarily use the what-do-you-want-to-work-qn method.

What this method amounts to is that the student, patient, or client creates his or her own material to talk about. The teacher, helper, or therapist does little disseminating of information but primarily serves to reinforce and analyze whatever the student or client has already learned. Occasionally, the teacher or helper will make some "interventions" and tell the student or client something he or she did not already know.

This method can be the most or the least Gamey of the lot. In general, therapists, helpers, and social workers are seen as Rescuers of helpless Victims, which automatically sets up the Drama Triangle.

On the other hand, tests are generally not given in this type of teaching, and this tends to keep down Games. Therefore, this type of teaching can be less Gamey than methods that require tests.

As with the other methods, the degree of Game freeness or Game infestation depends to a large extent upon the personalities of the therapists, teachers, and so on.

Other Teaching Methods. Counting self-study courses, one-on-one tutoring methods, and various experiential methods, there are, of course, a large number of methods.

As far as I am concerned, the Lecture Method, the Reading/Arithmetic/Discussion Method, the Case Method, the Learning-the-Textbook Method, and the What-Do-You-Want-to-Work-On Method cover most of the bases.

Testing Methods and Transactional Analysis

The Multiple-Choice/True-False/Matching/Fill-in-the-Blank/Short-Answer Test. This is the most common type of test in schools.

One of its advantages is that it seems to be more objective than other test types. All the teacher has to do is add up the Xs, use whatever point system he or she uses, and assign As, Bs, and so on.

A problem with this test, as with all tests, is the problem of the teacher deciding on the questions to put on the test.

As is well known among the Adults of teachers, any student can be flunked in practically any subject. All the teacher has to do is ask increasingly obscure or irrelevant questions.

Therefore, it is difficult for a teacher to stay off the Drama Triangle when he or she makes up the test. Are the questions placed on the test for the purpose of seeing if the learning contract has been fulfilled from an Adult perspective or for the purpose of Persecuting or Rescuing students?

I would say that 90 percent or more of all students see themselves as Victims when they sit down to take tests, and I would be willing to bet that 75 percent or more of teachers see themselves as Persecutors when they police the room to keep down cheating when tests are going on.

The Solve-the-Problem Test. This test is used primarily in mathematics, statistics, and scientific-type courses. The students are supposed to solve the problem and get the right answer.

This test is probably more objective than the multiple-choice/true-false/matching/fill-in-the-blank/short-answer test, but the Drama Triangle may also be brought into play when tests are being made up, taken, and graded.

The Essay Test. With this test, the teacher asks a small number of open-ended questions, for which students write short essays as answers.

This test is, of course, more subjective than the preceding ones. I am not sure whether the Drama Triangle hangs heavier or lighter in general than with the other methods.

The Case-Write-Up Test. The case-write-up test is not really a test, but it is used as if it were a test.

The teacher passes out another case, which students read and write up during the exam period.

Since real cases do not have "right" answers, the students are graded on how well they diagnose problems and logically think about and write down alternatives, consequences, and decisions.

This method can also entail a heavy dose of the Drama Triangle.

The No-Test Test. The no-test grading procedure is the most subjective of all.

The teacher gives no written tests but grades students on the basis of class participation.

Peer ratings are often used to confirm or counterbalance the judgment of the teacher.

This method can be an absolute horror in the hands of a really Gamey teacher. I am convinced, however, that in classes conducted by relatively Game-free teachers, this can be a good method.

In most courses, when class discussions have been well conducted in a Game-free atmosphere, it is obvious to the Adults of everyone in the class what grade most students earned.

On Tests in General

Testing is the focal point of Games in schools. Testing is the most Game-infested activity in schools. Game-prone teachers and students have obvious ample opportunities for furthering their Game plans at test time.

Tests put teachers in a heavy I'm OK—you're not OK position with respect to students. Tests heavily put teachers in the Critical Parent ego state and students heavily in Adapted Child.

Perhaps the biggest consequence is that some students score well on the tests, and others score poorly. The high scorers become OK and winners; the low scorers become relatively not OK.

The advantage of tests is that they tend to motivate the winners who score high on them.

Is it an advantage for society to have a few honor students sufficient to offset the larger number of students who are placed in less-OK positions because of scoring low on tests?

There is no definite correlation between high grades in school and success in life. The grade losers often become the money and fame winners.

Another problem is the effect written tests have on the learning process. The biggest disadvantage here is that tests encourage students to think about and learn only what they think will show up on tests.

The Learning/Testing Bind

Most educators who know the definitions of *Nurturing Parent*, *Adult*, *Natural Child*, *Critical Parent*, and *Adapted Child* would agree that the best ego states for enhancing learning are the Nurturing Parent, Adult, and Natural Child.

Assuming you were to find some perfect teacher who motivated his or her students to the maximum with just the right blend of Nurturing Parent, Adult, and Natural Child in his or her classes, this teacher would have a high trust level among his or her students. The students in such a class would be more honest in saying what they really thought and felt. They would set up relatively few Games in class. Chances are these students would actually like their teacher, and their teacher would really like them.

But what happens if that teacher must give tests and grade his or her students?

In the first place, the teacher will be forced to move into the Critical Parent ego state. Rather than nurturing and encouraging all of his or her students, he or she will now be forced to criticize and put some of his or her students in less-OK positions, unless he or she gets Gamey and Rescues all the students by asking easy questions that don't sample the material.

A double bind exists in all classes that involve teachers grading their students. The double bind is that students are supposed to think and feel that teachers both like and don't like them.

While the teaching/learning is going on, the teacher is a helper; at test time, the teacher switches into a critical judge.

I sometimes told my students that in order for me to be fair and do my job right, I would be forced to turn into a werewolf at grading time. Whether I like the student or not is irrelevant at grading time. The student gets what he or she deserves based on performance in class.

Because of this double bind, and because of various confusions regarding being OK or not OK, many students never know for sure whether their teachers really like them. If the student does not have faith in and trust the teacher, he or she cannot learn as much as would have otherwise have been the case. People cannot learn well when they are emotionally distraught.

I regard grading as a necessary function in most formal educational processes, despite its disadvantages.

For various subjects, classroom layouts, and teaching methods, certain grading methods are less harmful (or better) than others from a Game standpoint.

The teacher should use the grading method that is least detrimental from a Game standpoint—that is, the one that seems to invite the least amount of Persecuting, Rescuing, and Victimizing while enforcing the Adult learning contract.

Thoughts on Grading

One procedure I would support is separating teaching and testing in some courses. Have teachers do nothing but teach; let a specialized group of testers do the testing.

Unfortunately (or fortunately), certain forms of skill and comprehension learning—such as case analysis, oral communication, general problem solving, and leadership—cannot be measured by written tests. This can be evaluated only by observation. A problem with grading this learning in individual students by an impartial observer is that the observer has no way of knowing what amount of the above learning he or she observes in a particular student was learned from a particular teacher. A student might be naturally gifted and perform better than other students without having learned anything from a particular teacher.

An impartial observer should be able to tell if a class as a whole was below, equal to, or above "average" for case analysis, communicating, general problem solving, leadership, and overall comprehension, and, thus, it should be possible to evaluate how well a teacher caused this learning to occur in his or her class as a whole.

.Grading students based on case analysis, communication, general problem solving, and comprehension in class participation is inherently subjective, requiring the teacher to make a judgment regarding the relative position of the student in the class. In memorization courses, on the other hand, the student's grade is based on the actual number achieved on the so-called objective tests, most using true-false, multiple-choice and short answer questions.

The problem is that some skills and comprehension cannot be fairly graded using the same procedures used to grade memorization. Since some skills and comprehension cannot be easily graded, most teachers don't attempt to grade skills such oral and nonverbal communication ability, leadership, and problem diagnosis. This has the effect of discounting these skills and increasing the importance of memorization. What is more important for success in life? Skill, comprehension, and thinking ability or memorized facts, theories, history, and so on?

What are we primarily causing to be learned in school? How to memorize or how to be successful human beings?

We need both types of learning. And both should be taught and graded.

Where to Sit in Class

In most classes, the teacher can learn the names and faces of all of his or her students by two weeks or so into the course. Therefore, there is no Adult reason that students should sit in the same desk every day, even if the roll is not called out aloud. The teacher can scan the room and see who is there and not there and make whatever recordings are necessary.

Students, for various reasons, pick out special physical places to sit in classrooms—in the front, in the back, in a particular corner, in the center of the room, or wherever.

Students often express where they are coming from—that is, whether I'm OK—you're OK or otherwise; Parent, Child, or Adult; or Persecutor, Victim, or Rescuer—by where they sit in the room. Some places are just naturally better for Persecuting, Rescuing, or Victimizing.

Therefore, if you establish a rule that your students must sit by different people in different parts of the room each day, you will be changing their Game plans. This will frustrate them somewhat, but they will play fewer Games and learn more.

I have established a rule in some of my classes that it's not OK to sit in the same desk or between the same two people on two consecutive days during the whole course. This rule busts up various cliques that inevitably form in classes.

If you set up an Orbit Layout, with students moving about each day, not sitting by the same students on consecutive days, you will add dynamism and remove Games from your classroom, all other things being equal.

Listening and Teaching from Ego States

It is possible to diagnose the ego states your students are coming from by reading their body language.

People don't have to talk for you to see what ego state they are coming from. People also *listen* from ego states (Ernst 1973).

If your students are sitting slouched down in their chairs or desks with their chins down on their necks, and they are looking up at you from their tilted-down heads, you can be almost sure they are in their Adapted Child ego states. It can be either Compliant Child or Rebel Child.

If your students are sitting fairly straight in their chairs with their heads pretty straight (both horizontally and vertically) and looking straight at you, blinking their eyes frequently, you can be almost certain they are in their Adult ego states.

If they are bending back in their chairs, with their heads tilted back, and they are looking down their noses at you, with their arms crossed over their chests, you can be almost sure they are in their Parent ego states.

If they are in ego states other than what you would like, you must determine what you might have done or said to bring this about. Was it something you said or the ego state from which you said it? Perhaps you need to shift your ego states to bring about a shift in theirs.

What percentage of your students are in the ego states you deem inappropriate? If only one or two (or a clique) are in the inappropriate ego states, chances are they are trying to start a Game with you, and you need to De-Game them by not getting hooked and reminding them of their Adult responsibilities for fulfilling the learning contract. You might need to remind them several times during the course that the Adult learning contract is what counts, and they will have to play their Games somewhere else.

Perspective

My theory is that the main reason that tests and grades are considered necessary in schools is that people think tests and grades are necessary to motivate students to learn.

While negative, fear-type motivation does work, positive recognition-type motivation also works.

Students will learn assigned material in order to receive day-in-and-day-out praise, recognition, positive strokes, and success as well as to avoid losing points.

Also, many people feel that a permanent record of how much a particular student learned relative to what other students learned is necessary. Tests and grades are generally considered necessary to derive a permanent record of arbitrarily defined achievement or failure.

Another problem is with insecure teachers and administrators. Feeling that higher authority or the public will criticize them for not teaching very much, many teachers and administrators use test scores to prove how good *they* are.

If their students score well on the tests, this line of reasoning goes, then it naturally follows that the teachers and administrators are doing good jobs and thus should be rewarded with higher funding, positions, and so on. The flaw in this line of reasoning, of course, is that a teacher can tell students, in various ways, what will be on the tests before they are taken. Thus, students don't learn what is not destined to show up on the tests. And, thus, they might learn less than they would if the tests were not administered.

Tests tend to channel behavior and energy into narrow channels if the students want to be considered good or excellent students, as most seem to want. Whether this good or bad for education is debatable. There are no easy answers for the problem of measuring the efficiency or effectiveness of teaching or learning.

The No Child Left Behind educational program of the last few years, entailing schools administering standardized tests nationally to grade the effectiveness of teachers and schools, has produced much controversy for the above reasons. Some states have now opted out of the program. In 2015 in my state of Georgia, insecure teachers and administrators have been sentenced to jail terms for changing the answers of students on the No Child Left Behind standardized tests to make teachers and schools appear more effective than they were at producing learning.

Seven

Classroom Games

In most classrooms, teachers are generally viewed psychologically as Persecutors or Rescuers, and students come across as not-OK Victims. Students come across as less OK than teachers because teachers know something students don't, and there's always the chance the student might "fail."

Classrooms are inherently Gamey because of the natural presumption that students need teachers to help them, which more or less creates a Drama Triangle situation. Also, part of the problem are cultural attitudes and expectations in learning environments. Part of the cultural problem has to do with "readin', writin', 'rithmetic, and the hickory stick," which spells out the historical attitude toward education. The real message behind "readin', writin', 'rithmetic, and hickory stick," from an Adult standpoint, is "education is dull and boring, and force is required to make lazy students learn."

This attitude discounts not only students but also teachers and learning. Many students dislike school because they have obediently learned from their teachers, in and out of school, that school and learning are boring, hard, uninteresting, and perhaps worthless.

If the teacher believes that learning and teaching should be hard and that students are lazy, then the teacher will almost inevitably come across as a Persecutor or Rescuer in class and start Games that self-fulfill his or her prophecy. On the other hand, if the teacher thinks learning is a trivial pursuit, he or she will probably Rescue students by oversimplifying or dumbing down the material so as to be entertaining in class and make the tests easy to pass for all students.

Some students believe that all teachers are worthless and useless and that learning is of little value. These students generally agitate in class as Persecutors or Victims, since they are being forced to be in class. They start Games and create their own self-fulfilling payoffs.

All Games that people play in general will be played in classrooms, including "NIGYSOB," "kick me," "I'm only trying to help you," "do me something," "blemish," and "stupid." A common classroom or training-room Game is "gee, you're wonderful, Professor." In this Game, the student pretends to be full of admiration for the teacher or trainer but is secretly looking for some flaw or mistake that will prove how stupid the teacher or trainer is. Students playing "if it weren't for you" would have you believe they might study if only the teacher were not so incompetent or obnoxious. "Why don't you—yes, but" students solicit help but reject all suggestions. No matter what, they can't solve their problems.

"I'm only trying to help you" teachers offer suggestions and help that are inappropriate in the context, which frustrates or irritates the students. When the students retaliate for this, the teacher lets them know how ungrateful the students are and may try to make them feel guilty.

As discussed in the section on Games in the TA material, all Games essentially result in passivity—that is, in people not doing things to solve real problems or achieve stated goals. In businesses and classrooms, Games waste time. The participants' energy is wasted playing Games instead of being used to learn skills and concepts and produce goods and services.

Two pervasive school Games I have observed and described are "isn't education wonderful?" and "so what?" "Isn't education wonderful?" is a cognate of "I'm only trying to help you," and "so what?" is a cognate of "do me something" (Berne 1964). Both Games contain elements of NIGYSOB, since, as will be shown, there is some attempt for both the teacher and students playing these Games to get "one up." Isn't education wonderful?" also invites the Game "gee, you're wonderful, Professor." (Berne 1964). I am sure there are probably some other Games that are related or complementary.

"Isn't Education Wonderful?"

"Isn't education wonderful?" is started by teachers who feel inherently insecure about their positions, their capabilities, or their subjects and who feel that the way to acquire security is to make everyone feel that education in general—and his or her subject in particular—is wonderful.

In this Game, the teacher initially comes across socially as a Rescuer of uneducated unfortunates. This Game usually starts in the classroom with the teacher telling students via verbal Adult transactions that the subject is wonderful and that these are the advantages and perhaps disadvantages of whatever is to be studied or talked about. This is transaction (1) shown in Figure 18.

Students will generally respond from Adult, verbally agreeing that it sounds as if the subject may be wonderful, as in transaction (2). However, at the same time transactions (1) and (2) are going on, an ulterior set of transactions is being conducted, as shown in Figure 19.

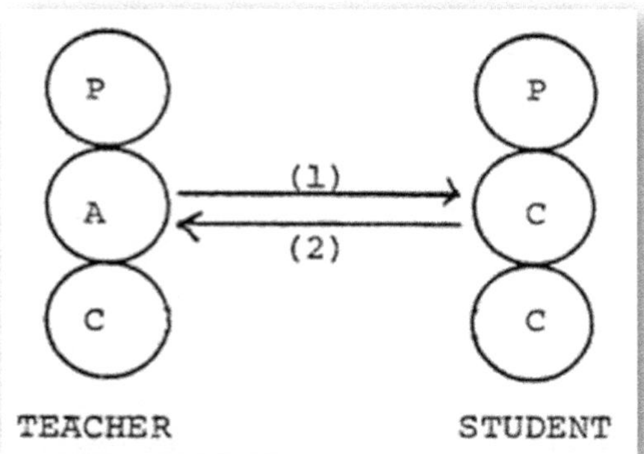

Figure 18. Opening Transactions of "Isn't education wonderful?"

On vector (3), the teacher is saying from the Child ego state (by body language, voice inflection, and in various covert ways) that he or she hopes the student will admire him or her and say good things about him or her, because his or her security or success depends on it. This ulterior transaction (3) is beamed at the Parent of the student.

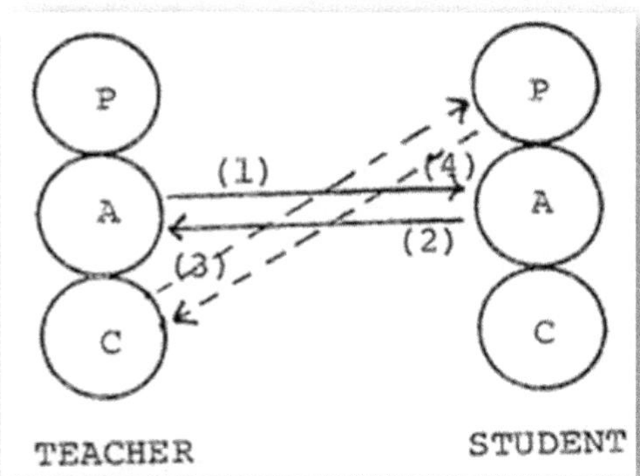

Figure 19. Intermediate Transactions of "Isn't Education Wonderful?"

The teacher initially sees himself or herself psychologically as the Victim of hapless, uneducated people not yet appreciating his or her knowledge.

Students will respond on vector (4) with a message that runs something to the effect of "well, let's see."

After several transactions, over minutes or days, a cross will eventually occur, as shown in Figure 20.

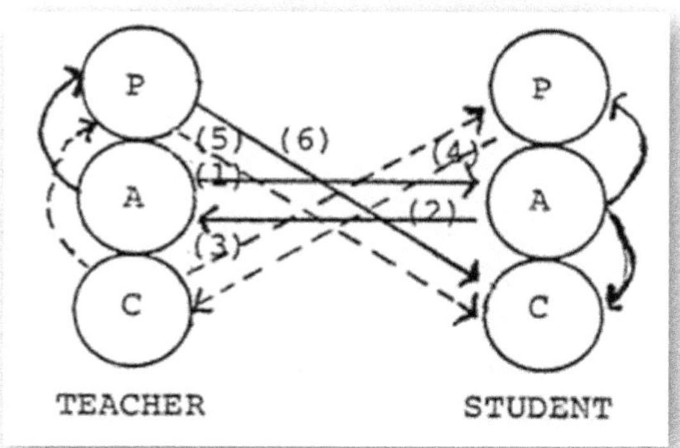

Figure 20. Crossed Transactions of "Isn't Education Wonderful?"

The teacher will move from psychological-level Victim to Persecutor by moving to Parent from Child and crossing the Parent-Child ulterior transactions of students. The effect will be to shift students into the Victim role from the Persecutor role at the psychological, covert, ulterior, unspoken level.

In response to this cross, students will shift at the social level from Adult to either Parent or Child. Some students will get heavily into Persecuting the teacher at the social level, and some will perhaps fall into contrition in Adapted Child, basically agreeing with the teacher, who is now coming from an I'm OK—you're not OK position.

The overall dynamics of the Game involve the teacher initially coming on as Rescuer at the social, overt level and Victim at the psychological, covert level. Students start as Victim at the social level and Persecutor at the psychological level. The teacher switches to Persecutor at the psychological level, and some students may retaliate by going to Persecutor from Victim at the social level. Once the Game has progressed this far, somebody may get sent to the principal's office for higher discipline.

The final switch comes when the teacher moves from Adult to Parent at the social level, beaming down laser-like Parent-Child transactions on vector (6), still espousing "isn't education wonderful?" as his or her defense or attack (Figure 21).

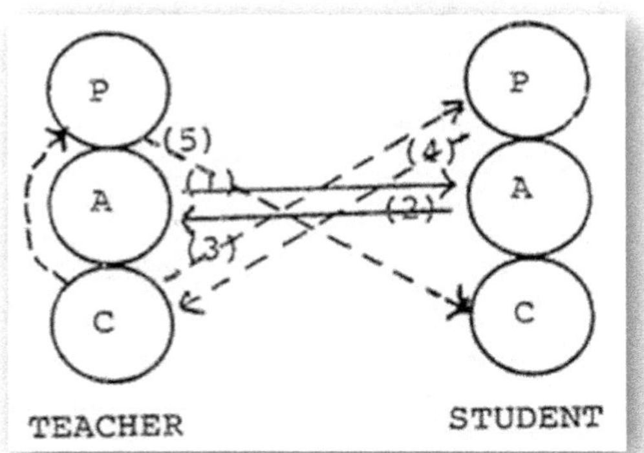

Figure 21. Payoff of "Isn't Education Wonderful.?"

The final payoff is confusion and hard feelings on the part of both teachers and students.

The whole thing might could have been prevented if only the teacher had been straight with the students and said: "I'm afraid what I have to teach isn't satisfactory to you, and you won't like me. However, despite that, I'd like to see what we can work out so that we can have an OK time together. I have a contract with the school to enable you to learn this material. I can use these measures to see whether you have learned the material. The school (or company) gives us some latitude in determining what we are to learn. Given this, what do you want to learn? Let's establish a workable contract so that we all can come out of this course in an OK position."

"So What?"

"So what?" (SW) is the student complement of "Isn't education wonderful?" (IEW) Whereas IEW involves grandiosity on the part of the teacher, SW involves discounting the teacher and the material by the student.

Whereas the teacher starting IEW attempts to make the material and himself or herself seem greater than it or he or she really is, SW involves an attempt on the part of the student to make the material or the teacher seem to be less significant than it or he or she really is.

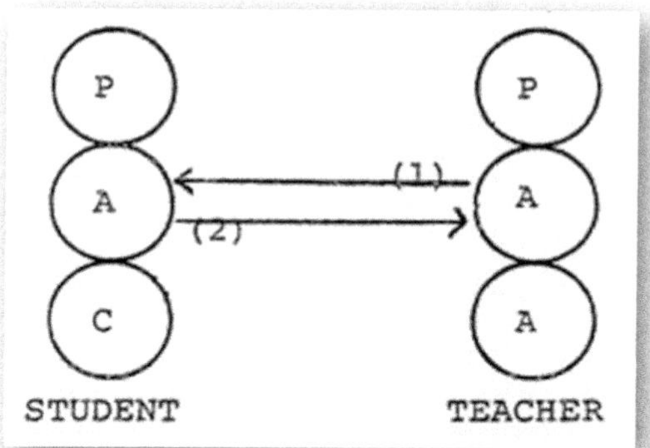

Figure 22. Opening Transactions of "So What?"

Transactions (1) and (2) are both Adult and pertain to the subject, its relevance, what is involved, and so on.

Shortly after the Adult preliminaries, the ulterior moves begin from the Parent of the student. The initial message on vector (3) is a variant of "this is not very good," "just what is the value of this?" or "I'm not getting as much out of this course as Mr., Mrs., Ms., or Dr. so-and-so's course." The teacher on vector (4), if hooked, will respond with a psychological variant of "well, let's wait and see; I'll show you how good I am."

The transactions up to this point are shown in Figure 23.

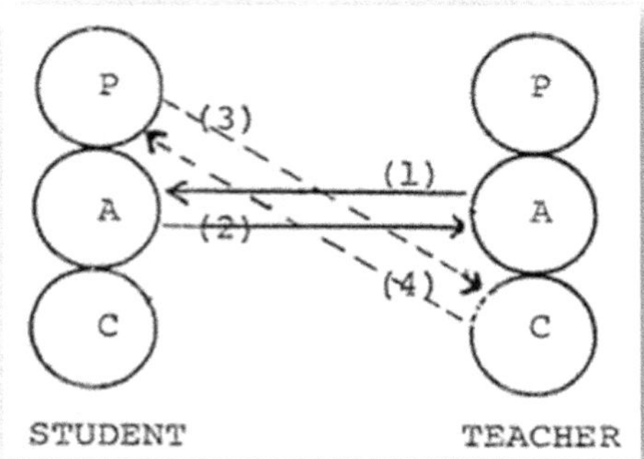

Figure 23. Intermediate Transactions of "So What?"

The Game reaches its payoff when the student moves from social-level Adult to Parent, issuing a variant of "so what?" "this is nothing new," and so on, as shown in Figure 24.

The dynamics of SW are similar to the dynamics of IEW. The teacher starts at the social level as a Rescuer, and the students start at the social level as Victims. At the psychological level, the students start as Persecutors, and the teacher, as Victim. "So what?" ends, however, with the student as Persecutor at both the social and psychological levels and the teacher as Victim at both levels. The feeling payoff for students is triumph.

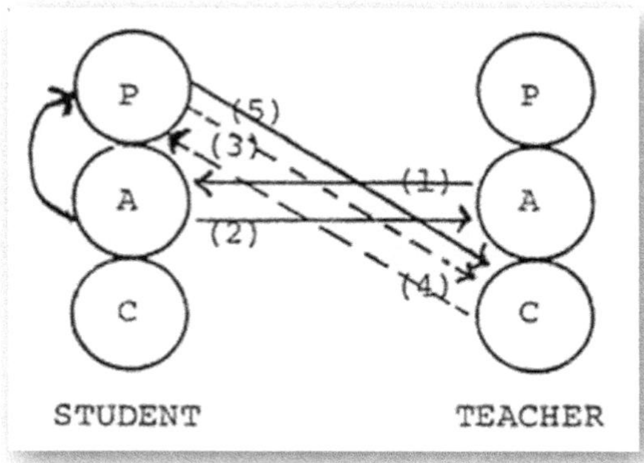

Figure 24. Payoff of "So What?"

Formula G Application

In my opinion, IEW and SW are the two most common classroom Games. Once one or two IEW or SW payoffs occur during a course, year, workshop, or semester, other Games will become more frequent.

Berne's Formula G for Games is as follows:

Con + Gimmick = Response → Cross → Switch → Payoff.

In the Game of IEW, the basic con, or unstraightness, on the part of the teacher is that he or she thinks the material is really so wonderful in the first place. The gimmick, or vulnerability, is a belief most students have that there really is something they might learn that will make them more secure in the world. The response on the part of the student is to pick up on the ulterior message and support the teacher in his or her ulterior moves by approving of the wonderfulness of the subject in order to feel secure. The crosses come when the teacher shifts his or her ulterior transaction from Child to Parent to Parent to Child and the social-level transaction from Adult to Adult to Parent to Child. The switches result in the teacher finally becoming a Persecutor at both social and psychological levels, with students being heavily invested in Victim or Persecutor. The Payoff is confusion and mistrust and perhaps triumph on the part of the teacher.

In the Game of SW, the basic con on the part of the starting student is that he or she really doesn't think the material or the teacher is any good. He or she probably just doesn't want to invest the energy required to learn, so he or she discounts the material or the teacher. The gimmick, or vulnerability, on the part of the teacher is a need for approval and perhaps love. The response is for the teacher to attempt to prove that he or she or the material is really good through ulterior transactions. The cross comes when the student moves from Adult at the social level into Parent and issues the final "so what?" The role switch on the part of the student is from Victim at the social level to Persecutor. The teacher becomes a Victim at both levels, and the student is triumphant.

Perspective

In IEW and SW, the main battle lines are between the Child of the teacher and the Parents of the students.

Since the Parents of the students involved in the Games are made up of videotapes of their actual parents' thinking, feeling, and doing, it follows that the teacher is doing battle with the teachings of the parents of his or her Game-playing students.

Assuming the teacher is aware of what is going on, the teacher could say things that would have an impact on the parents of the SW players in order to convince the students of their responsibilities to perform the Adult learning contract in the here and now.

It follows that students who have poor attitudes toward learning learned the poor attitudes as a result of what they were exposed to by their parent figures. It also follows that teachers who have poor teaching attitudes learned the poor attitudes as a result of what they were exposed to by parent figures, including teachers they had in the past.

Games such as IEW and SW are not played once or twice and then forgotten. Each Game payoff is the equivalent of a round in a boxing match. The next round may be a repeat of IEW or SW, or various other Game players may change their tactics and use different Games in their repertoires.

The only way to stop Games is for someone to see what is really going on and refuse to play.

As a practical matter, in many cases, the best thing a teacher can do is simply ignore the cons and "hooks" thrown out by his or her Game-playing students. In some cases, simply ignoring Game players will not work for long. In these cases, I think the best thing a teacher can do is talk with the student privately and say something like this: "I think you are trying to play Games with me, and I don't like it. When you do such and such in class, I think you are trying to set up a Game. I would appreciate it if you stop doing this."

In many cases, once the student sees that he or she has not fooled the teacher or manager, and his or her ulterior moves are exposed, he or she will stop. On the other hand, in some cases, the Games will continue, and the teacher or manager must continue using variations of the above approaches. What will definitely not work is to get on the Drama Triangle with students and employees and try to beat them at their own Games. You cannot beat a Game player by playing his or her Game. The only way you can win with a Game player is to communicate with the person in such a way as to place yourself in an I'm OK—you're OK position with the person.

An alternative is to diagnose the specific Games students and employees are playing and learn the standard social-level interventions that are listed on the Game matrix mentioned earlier. One way to neutralize the effects of "so what?" once the initial moves have been detected is to say something like this: "Why is it you don't think this material is any good?" This transaction should be directed from the Adult of the teacher to the Parent of the student.

Classroom Dramas

Both IEW and SW apply to theaters wherein the actors and actresses are similar in role to teachers, and the audience is similar in role to students.

In many cases, the more an actress or actor attempts to "break a leg" to please his or her audience, the more negative the response will be.

While there is probably no substitute for "knowing your stuff" and being confident in the classroom, teachers can sometimes be straight with their students about their weaknesses and fears as teachers. Fame and fortune are not in the cards for most teachers. Rarely are they applauded. Teaching is not dramatic, funny, or inherently entertaining. I suppose a certain amount of light comedy is OK in classrooms so long as the teacher does not go overboard with it and use his or her entertaining abilities to manipulate the students into giving him or her special favors.

What and how much students learn in classrooms is the relevant thing. How well the teacher entertains is a low-priority item.

Teachers, like everyone else, need strokes. They should get them in straight ways, however, rather than resorting to Games and theatrics in the classroom. And students can receive strokes without playing "so what?" or "isn't education wonderful?"

Both IEW and SW can be prevented if the teacher is aware that he or she does not have to be wonderful or teach wonderful material in order to satisfy his or her basic contract with the administration, the community, and the students.

I am sure it is somewhat "natural" for teachers to want to be considered "good teachers"—perhaps even great—but this desire, weakness, or vulnerability can get teachers hooked into Games if it is not controlled. Rather than doing his or her job, a teacher may become so invested in being wonderful that he or she gets into so many Games that he or she, in effect, becomes a poor teacher—that is, his or her learning contracts do not get fulfilled.

The daily existence of numerous Games in the classroom is prima facie evidence that the teacher is sometimes a nonwinner in an I'm OK—you're OK sense. The irony is that otherwise-OK teachers sometimes get themselves into not-OK positions by trying to be super-OK.

The way to stop IEW and SW is to do your job in a straightforward way and say, "I'm OK—you're OK," which does not mean "I'm great—you're OK."

It seems to me that one way or another, students and employees need to be taught that it's OK to know what you know right now. In other words, the student or employee isn't not OK because he or she doesn't already know what the teacher or manager knows. The student or employee need to be taught that learning is a basic process of life that produces satisfaction for the learner. Learning contracts are established to enable students and employees to acquire satisfaction and become what they are capable of becoming. The purpose is not to please the teacher or manager or become as smart, good, great, exalted, or OK as the teacher or manager.

Expecting students and employees to become as smart, good, great, exalted, or OK as the teacher or manager assures that a not-OK Game culture will exist in classrooms and businesses, since the underlying presumption is that students and employees are not OK—at least, not as OK as the teachers or managers.

I am sometimes amused or flattered that some students seem to think I am very knowledgeable. They seem to think I learned what I know about my subjects in the same time they spent doing their homework the night before. They don't seem to realize that after having repeated the courses I have taught over and over again over twenty-three years, I should remember much of the material. If you read and discuss what is in a book several times, it is difficult not to remember it. Some students and employees seem to think some teachers and managers have high IQs, for the same irrational reasons. While most teachers and managers probably have higher-than-average IQs, most are not gifted intellectually. Only a small percentage of teachers and managers are able to produce intellectual achievements outside the classroom or business that impact the larger environment.

While we're on the subject of IQs, as far as I am concerned, they are irrelevant in my classes. The relevant consideration is fulfilling the learning contract. Proving how smart you are or how high your IQ is falls into the same not-OK category of classroom environmental pollution as Games.

It seems to me that the relevant thing in life is getting the job done and achieving your mission. Being smart may help you achieve your goals and objectives, but attempting to prove you are smarter than others for sake of proving you are smarter than others seems a bit dumb, a waste of time and energy.

Being a winner with people is saying I'm OK—you're OK, which is not the same thing as saying I'm OK—you're OK, but my IQ is 140. Despite the fact it is impossible to precisely define and measure intelligence, it is obvious that some people are brighter than others—but this does not mean they are more OK than others.

As I see it, a person's IQ is basically a feature of the Adult ego state largely determined by physical brain structures and neural wiring determining how fast and well one can think, which is analogous to muscles, nerves, and other physical features determining how fast and well one can run. On the other hand, it's possible for a person to have a superior IQ but be so contaminated by his or her Parent or Child ego state that the Adult barely functions. Thus, it is possible for someone with an average Adult not having Parent or Child contamination to achieve more and lead a more satisfying life than a person with a better Adult.

What many parents, teachers, and managers often fail to realize is that human effectiveness and success is a function of all three ego states, not merely the Adult, which contains the subject content and thinking processes measured by IQ tests.

As I see it, the present trend in the United States of increasing the use of standardized tests will increase the level of not OKness we already have. It will set up a situation in which it will become increasingly difficult for teachers, students, administrators, parents, and anyone connected with education to maintain the I'm OK—you're OK position. I agree that standardized tests are useful in some cases, but I think their disadvantages outweigh their advantages.

Maintaining an I'm OK—you're OK attitude is not easy, given constant efforts by various apparatuses of society to recognize and create people who are more OK than others. Perhaps existential OKness is the best we can hope for.

A Hypothetical Classroom Case Example

The teacher comes into the classroom each day and mechanically performs classroom rituals. He or she nods and smiles to a few students. He or she says, "Good morning, Tommy," "Hi, Betty," and "How are you today, Sue?"

The students respond, "Good morning, Mr./Mrs./Miss/Dr./Ms. so-and-so."

This particular teacher takes the roll each day by calling each student's name aloud. Students respond, "Present." After the roll is taken, the teacher, almost every day, says, "As you know, our assignment for today is…I trust you have read the assignment.

"To begin with, I want to emphasize such and such about the material."

The teacher then emphasizes something about the material for ten or fifteen minutes. This emphasis plus the daily rituals have taken up about twenty-five minutes of a fifty-minute period.

Since there are twenty-five or so minutes left, and the students can't be turned out early, the teacher abruptly says, "Questions or comments?"

In most cases, the students have no questions or comments, so the teacher makes some up.

The questions are of the order of what was such and such, how do you do such and such, who was so-and-so, and who said what? The teacher says, "Mr./Miss so-and-so (or Tommy, Betty, and so on) what did so and so say," and so on. After about ten minutes of this questioning, with about fifteen minutes left in the period, sparks begin to fly. Various students begin to sleep, yawn, throw paper wads, look disinterested, and engage in other passive-aggressive behavior.

The teacher accelerates his or her questioning and insults some of the students in retaliation.

Most days, the remaining ten or fifteen minutes are devoted almost entirely to maintaining order and discipline.

Analysis of the Case

Several things in the above case could have been done differently. In the first place, is the roll taking necessary? Can't the teacher remember the names and faces of the students and visually scan the room to see if they are all there? Why say, "Good morning," every morning, whether it is good or not?

In the second place, does the teacher need to emphasize anything about the assigned material? Does he or she know something that is not in the book? If not, how does he or she know the students were not able to comprehend the material from reading it on their own?

Also, in the act of getting feedback from students, how does the teacher decide which student to call on? Does he or she call on particular students because he or she suspects the student does not understand or has not read the material, or does he or she think the student has read it and understands it? Or does he or she use some random process for calling on students?

Most of the time in the above case was spent on rituals, pastimes, and Games that had little to do with learning the assigned material.

The students (if they read the material) learned mainly from their reading. Very few of the students will be able to remember what the teacher emphasized ten minutes after the class is over.

The questions may or may not have engendered learning. The emphasizing and questions set up the moves of IEW and SW.

The Problem with Asking Questions to Students in Class

The problem with asking pointed questions to students in class is that the Drama Triangle is almost invariably brought into play. The teacher is usually seen as coming from the Persecutor or Rescuer position when he or she asks students specific questions. If he or she is coming from Persecutor, he or she will hope the student doesn't know the answer so that he or she can show the student up. If the teacher is coming from Rescuer, he or she will hope the student does know the answer so that the student will have a chance to shine.

This process of questioning places students in a Victim position. Some will dislike being placed in this position, and they will retaliate with their time-honored Games.

Rarely do teachers ask Adult questions in class (i.e., questions to get straight, needed information), because they are supposed to already know everything.

Two ways to cut down on Games in classrooms and businesses is for teachers and managers not to ask any questions or show their ignorance by asking questions to get real information. If the teacher doesn't ask any content-oriented questions, though, how will he or she get feedback regarding what the students are learning? Give them a test every day? Or written homework every day? This is generally not feasible from an Adult standpoint, because few teachers have enough time to conscientiously read and grade that much written work.

So how do you get feedback regarding homework and learning without asking pointed questions in class or giving a written test every day?

Eight

The Classroom De-Gamer

The Classroom De-Gamer is a "roulette" device I developed that enables teachers to get feedback from students regarding homework assignments without giving written tests every day and without setting up the Drama Triangle by calling on students to answer specific questions using a nonrandom selection process.

The Classroom De-Gamer is constructed of a three-quarter-inch-thick circular board that is twelve inches in diameter, with numbers affixed to allow for varying class sizes. I have published articles describing the device in *Research in Education* (1978), the *Transactional Analysis Journal* (1979), and *The Organizational Behavior Teaching Review* (1990).

To use the De-Gamer, I like to have students position their desks in an Orbit Layout. I place the De-Gamer in the center of the room.

I spin the arrow the first time myself. This is only time I will spin the arrow, barring absences of students.

The student the arrow lands on has the responsibility of talking about the assigned material. If specific questions are asked of De-Gamer-selected students, the questions are announced to the class as a whole before the spinning takes place.

The student initially pointed out spins the arrow next, and so it goes throughout the course. The last person pointed out spins the De-Gamer next.

If the room must be set up in the sometimes-unavoidable row-and-column layout, each student is assigned a number corresponding to numbers on the De-Gamer, and whoever's number the arrow lands on has the responsibility of saying what's what.

Advantages of the De-Gamer

The primary advantage of the De-Gamer is that it enables a teacher to get concrete feedback regarding material learned as part of the Adult learning contract without setting up the Drama Triangle.

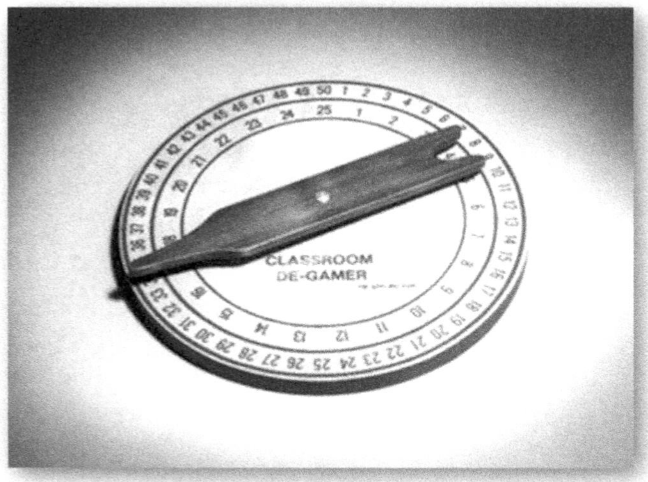

Figure 25. The Classroom De-Gamer.

In a classroom in which the De-Gamer is used properly, all ego states in students can see and feel that the teacher is not manipulating who gets called on for ulterior reasons. All ego states in students can see and feel that they are not being Persecuted or Rescued by a teacher playing a Game when they are called on to respond to classroom requirements and challenges.

Perhaps the major advantage of a De-Gamer is that it cathects Adult ego states, especially if group members are instructed to answer the following Adult Questions if randomly selected:

What is/are the problem/s?

What are the alternatives?

What do you recommend?

While no one should be taught to use the Adult ego state all the time, teaching business students to use the Adult ego state is especially appropriate, since, in the long run, being able to see current reality for what it is and assess and predict probabilities of recommended actions happening relatively accurately is a major determinant of satisfaction in competitive business environments.

Another advantage of the De-Gamer is that it brings about a more efficient utilization of class time. Less time is spent rehashing what the students know by emphasizing already-learned points.

Another advantage is that the De-Gamer focuses the attention of the class upon the Adult learning contract. Since less energy is now being spent playing Games, more energy is available for learning what is actually supposed to be learned.

I find that the De-Gamer also reduces the amount of time I spend on rituals and pastimes.

Disadvantages of the Classroom De-Gamer

The De-Gamer is at first threatening to many students. Ironically, while actual Persecuting or Rescuing has been banished from the classroom, some students psychologically view the probabilistic selection process facilitated by the De-Gamer as Persecuting or Rescuing. Some students are apparently so used to partiality of some sort (i.e. Games) being shown by teachers when they are called on in class that they are threatened when singled out by the obviously impartial De-Gamer.

I have participated with students as a student when the De-Gamer was used. When the De-Gamer landed on me, even though I was the teacher and should have known the material, I had an uneasy feeling. I felt as though some metaphysical force had caused the arrow to land on me.

Students tell me they feel some fear when the De-Gamer is spinning at the start of the class. When asked "what do you feel when the De-Gamer is being spun?" the almost-unanimous answer was "anxiety." Some of the students thought the anxiety (or "adrenalin," as one of them put it) helped them learn.

I teach college students. The reactions of high school, junior high, or grade school students may be different to some degree. I doubt the difference is extensive. Based on my experience, I believe the De-Gamer will work at any level.

Due to the adrenalin factor, perhaps the De-Gamer should be used less frequently at lower educational levels. There are a number of creative approaches that innovative teachers can use in conjunction with the De-Gamer at all educational levels.

Evidence the De-Gamer Works

I have acquired data indicating the effectiveness of the Classroom De-Gamer. At the end of the winter quarter 1978 and spring quarter 1978, I passed out the following questionnaire to my students.

1. I think the De-Gamer caused me to prepare more for this course than I would have had the De-Gamer not been used.
   Yes_____ No____
2. I think the De-Gamer caused me to learn more than would have been the case had the De-Gamer not been used.
   Yes____ No_____
3. I believe the De-Gamer made the learning process in this class more fair and just than would have been the case had the De-Gamer not been used.
   Yes_____ No______
4. I believe the De-Gamer reduced psychological Game playing in this class.
   Yes____ No_____

I taught Small Business Management and Production Management I in winter 1978 and Business Policy and Production Management II in spring 1978. There were 24 students in Small Business Management, 26 in Production Management I, 35 in Business Policy, and 19 in Production Management II.

Taking the 111 students as a group, regarding question 1, 94 percent said the De-Gamer caused them to prepare more for class than they would have had the De-Gamer not been used. Regarding question 2, 80 percent said the De-Gamer caused them to learn more than they would have had the De-Gamer not been used. Regarding question 3, 82 percent said they believed the De-Gamer caused the learning process to be more fair and just than would have been the case had the De-Gamer not been used. On question 4, 72 percent said they thought the De-Gamer reduced psychological Game playing.

The findings by course were as follows:

	Yes	Yes	Yes	Yes
Small Business Management	(1) 92%,	(2) 67%,	(3) 83%,	(4) 67%
Production Management II	(1) 96%,	(2) 92%,	(3) 81%,	(4) 76%
Business Policy	(1) 88%,	(2) 62%,	(3) 74%,	(4) 57%
Production Management II	(1) 100%,	(2) 95%,	(3) 84%,	(4) 84%

Analysis of the Findings

The questionnaires were anonymous and were placed in an envelope when I was not in the room. The students merely checked the appropriate blanks. There is no Adult reason that the students should not have been straight and Game-free in their transactions in filling out the questionnaire. There is some chance that bias entered into their responses, but it is minimal.

I think the findings from the above samples are valid and reliable. I believe the findings indicate that the De-Gamer does cause students to prepare more for homework assignments and learn more. I believe the findings indicate that the De-Gamer reduces Game playing in class and creates a more fair and just situation.

I think I can make two additional valid and reliable generalizations from an analysis of the findings by course. One is that the De-Gamer works better in "hard" courses than in "soft" courses. The other is that the smaller the class, the greater the De-Gamer's effects.

Small-business-management and business-policy courses are "softer" than Production courses. By *hard* and *soft*, I do not mean easier or less valuable. I see a soft course as one in which there is little that can be proved with hard data, where most of the generalizations or concepts are of the synthetic, inductive-opinion type. A hard course, on the other hand, is one in which many of the ideas, generalizations, and so on can be demonstrated by deductive logic and mathematics, based on the analysis of concrete facts and data.

Small business and business policy courses are, to a large extent, concerned with setting goals and objectives for businesses and determining basic purposes. This activity, a significant part of the business process, necessarily involves primarily intuitive abilities. It is easier for students to just make something up to say in class without reading the case beforehand in these courses than in the more mathematical courses. This is not to say that "just making something up" (i.e., creating something) is not a valuable part of a learning process, and some people are definitely better at doing it than others, which can be graded relatively.

This opens a Pandora's box of suboptimal OKness in schools. Much Game playing goes on regarding whose and which courses are hard, easy, interesting, boring, useful, and worthless. Some teachers deliberately attempt to make inherently soft courses into hard ones so they won't be considered easy Santa Clauses. There are hundreds of combinations of hard, soft, easy, hard-to-learn, useful, interesting, and worthless courses. Just because a course is hard, this doesn't mean it is valuable. I am sure a course in Egyptian hieroglyphics would be hard, but it would be next to worthless for most students.

The De-Gamer and Other Matters in My Human-Relations Course

The smaller the course, the higher the probability the arrow will land on a particular student on a given day, and, therefore, there is more pressure on students to do their homework in small classes than in large ones.

The main reason the De-Gamer works is that students know their fellow students know they had an Adult contract to read and study the assigned material and that they will lose points and face if caught unprepared. Even the most negative Parent and Child ego states in the room feel there is a positive reason to read and discuss homework under these conditions.

Regarding what students learn with the De-Gamer as measured by true-false/multiple-choice tests, I have some additional evidence that the De-Gamer works.

During the summer quarter 1978, using a standard textbook, I taught a human-relations course for junior-year business majors. There were about forty students in the course. The author placed some short cases in the book to embellish his text material, which consisted primarily of research findings. The cases were too short to facilitate any real analytical work, so we used essentially a Learning-the-Textbook Method.

As it turns out, practically nothing is always true in human behavior in the field of business. Most authors present the disjointed findings of behavior researchers from various areas that are qualified almost into nothingness. The author of the summer human-relations-course textbook, like all good textbook writers, also wrote an instructor's manual telling teachers how to teach out of his book. The instructor's manual, like all good instructor's manuals, also contained hundreds of true-false/multiple-choice/fill-in-the-blank/matching test questions, complete with answers for the teacher showing on which page of the textbook the answer was found. Since human-behavior research studies have not found any answers that apply in all cases, the "answers" to the test questions in the instructor's manual were of the order that so-and-so found that such and such was almost an answer and that so-and-so said such and such, regardless of whether what he or she said was true or relevant. Various numbers were found in the book from place to place, and lots of declarative sentences were used, which could be turned into test questions.

Since we had decided to use the Learning-the-Textbook Method in this course, with true-false and multiple-choice test questions prepared by the author for tests, the students would have to learn what was in the book. It took me some doing to get them to agree to abide by this learning contract from their Adult ego states, especially after the first test.

Most students in the course did poorly on the first test. They missed 40 or 50 percent of the textbook author's questions. Correcting the test in class, I had my instructor's manual and the textbook page numbers for answers in front of me so that I could look up the answers when students complained that they got points taken off that shouldn't have been taken off. Many points were taken off that shouldn't have been, because our management department's secretary left an answer off my answer key sheet. When I marked the Xs in the circles on the students' answer sheets, some of the Xs were for questions the students really got right. To say the least, this set loose a hornet's nest of Parent indignation and Child anguish in the students.

Some students were already disgusted with me in class, and the above incident added more fuel to the fire. I had said very little in class up to that point. I had come in every day and set the De-Gamer up in the center of the room. I used the Orbit Layout. I had made a few comments from time to time. On one or two days, I didn't say a single word. A student would spin the arrow at the beginning of the period, and the selected student would start a discussion of the assigned material; if I thought the students understood what was talked about in the chapter, I said nothing.

The first test was taken about three weeks into the quarter. By this time, many of the students were beginning to criticize the course in class. They didn't like the book. The author wasn't clear, they said. The test questions weren't fair. They wanted to use some other book or methods. I replied, "We've got an Adult learning contract to do it this way. It may not be any good or fair, but we all agreed to it, so let's keep it up."

Any student who disagreed with the learning contract could have dropped the course and gotten another teacher using other methods after the first day of class. We had alternative teachers and methods for the course. At the same time, any student taking severe umbrage to the course could drop it with no prejudice up until midquarter. I told them I thought they were doing pretty well, given the handicaps and unfairness they were exposed to in this course.

They did better on the second test. Two or three students made As on this test. They had learned how to answer 90 percent or more of the textbook author's questions right, according to the answer key taken from the instructor's manual.

During this interlude, after several invitations for me to lecture by various members of the class, I took a vote on whether I should lecture to them, and the almost-unanimous wish was that I would lecture. I then began to do some lecturing, which consisted of putting some transactional-analysis models on the chalkboard and adding my opinions on human behavior to those the textbook author gave.

I used true-false, multiple-choice questions taken from the instructor's manual for the third test. My TA and personal-opinion lectures on human behavior were freebies, I said. I told them I hoped they found my lectures interesting and useful. I was amazed at how well the students did on the third test. There were four or five As and no grades lower than C. I gave them several positive strokes for their achievement.

I told them that some of them did better on the test than I probably could or would have, and I was an expert on human behavior. I became a little concerned when I found out how much time some of the A students spent cramming for the test—I think it was something like eight hours. It was obvious that many of the students were doing their best to memorize the book for the test.

In the meantime, I had assigned the students the task of writing some cases of their own, taken from their work experience or current field research, which they distributed to each class member. They then discussed using the De-Gamer in the normal manner. After five or so weeks into the course, they began to discuss their cases along with the textbook.

At the first of the quarter, the students were covering a chapter a day in the book and had to have more material to fill out the quarter. They could discuss one of the textbook chapters in the Adult mode using the De-Gaming process in about fifteen minutes. The textbook, a normal-sized textbook of about five hundred pages, had only about twenty chapters, and we had fifty class sessions of fifty minutes each for the course. The remaining class time was devoted to their written cases and my occasional lectures. Rarely were they turned out early.

Final grades were determined 50 percent by their scores on the true-false/multiple-choice tests and 50 percent by their class participation. I always place a heavy weight on class participation—normally 80 percent of the final grade. Most (95 percent or so) of my courses entail the Case Method and no memorization for tests at all. I use case write-ups for tests. Students know—once you tell them what Games are—that playing Games will hurt their class-participation grades. This procedure alone precludes the playing out of many Games.

I use peer ratings on a scale of 0-4 (4 being equivalent to an A) to give students feedback regarding how the class as a whole saw each student. I think it is important that students know what students think about their performance. This teaches students how others perceive them in communication episodes similar to those of the class outside of class. This provides students with potent

Adult feedback that they can use to make significant decisions about how to communicate with others.

I have all of the students write down on a form a 0, 1, 2, 3, or 4 for each class member, corresponding to whether they think the student deserves an F, a D, a C, a B, or an A, respectively, for class participation. I sum these scores and divide by the number of evaluators. This provides a class average, which is usually valid, in my opinion. Some students are irresponsible, poor evaluators, but most are not. In my courses, it is obvious to the Adults of most students what grades most students deserve for class participation.

I consider it my responsibility to ultimately determine the class-participation grade. I use various criteria. The most important criteria are how well informed the student is; how accurate his or her observations, analyses, and recommendations are; and what sort of an impact the student has had on the class. Was the student a leader of the class? Did the student motivate the class to learn or have fun or play Games? Was the motivation positive or negative? Did the student listen well? Or did he or she frequently discount the class by sleeping, yawning, slouching down in his or her desk or chair, or whispering covertly to other students?

I tell students at the beginning of the quarter that they will be evaluated on the basis of their total participation in class, which includes not only what and how much they say but how well they motivate others by how well they listen. It comes as a surprise to most people that when someone teaches them, they can learn active, positive listening skills. Once they see what they are, active listening skills are not difficult to learn. A certain amount of effort is required to maintain an effective body posture and control ego states in such a way as to be congruent with what is going on. Since students are supposed to do some work in classes, it is not unreasonable to teach them to control their verbal and nonverbal transactions in order to contribute to the class.

Grading the active listening skills of students creates helping behavior in the classroom. Students are graded not only on the basis of what they selfishly learn for themselves to further their own success in life—they are also graded on the basis of how they help their fellow class members learn and grow and be successful, which is, after all, the best way to get successful and make it big in life anyway. This is what successful leaders and managers do in the business world.

Students, trainees, and employees have to be taught (sometimes with much repetition) that being smart and selfishly learning or memorizing material to further one's own ends is not necessarily excellent. I had some students in the above human-relations course who had A averages on the tests but C averages for class participation, and they thus received Bs in the course. There were some students who made Cs on the tests but who had As for class participation; they also received Bs.

Students in the human-relations course proved that students could memorize material for tests quite well when the Classroom De-Gamer is used and when the teacher does no emphasizing of the material in the text.

One of the most interesting things I learned in that course had to do with how students normally study for tests. The consensus of the class was that in most courses, they did not have to read the book word for word. They felt that most teachers who use the Lecture Method tell students, in one way or another, what will be on the tests. They do this by what they emphasize and spend extra time on and through the body language they use when lecturing about certain things. Thus, students don't have to pay much attention to the book. They mainly memorize their notes from the teacher's lectures, which, according to the students in the above class, did not require as much time or work as my classroom structure configuration.

All too often, students' attitude is "just tell me what's going to be on the test."

Another interesting thing about this human-relations class is that it was generally too Critical Parent and Adapted Child. There was not enough Natural Child and Nurturing Parent energy in the room. About midway through the course, it became apparent that most of the students had decided to do a good job of memorizing the material for the tests from Critical Parent and Adapted Child, but the class was boring and stiff.

One day, I told them I thought they were a dull group, which they were, relative to most of my classes. From quarter to quarter, semester-to-semester, or year-to-year, most classes will be populated with generally the same percentages of all ego states, but it will sometimes happen that some classes are overdeveloped or underdeveloped in various ego states, depending on the type of early conditioning the students in the class had. In this human-relations class, it appeared that 80 percent or so of the students must have been reared in families almost devoid of Natural Child fun and Nurturing Parent helping behavior. It seemed the only thing they cared about in class was their grade. There was little laughter or fun, and almost no one asked for or received any help or support.

A no-stroke economy had been set up, as they had apparently decided that the only thing that counted was memorizing the material for the tests. Another problem in this class was that the natural leaders were these Critical Parent/Adapted Child types. If there had been three or four leaders in the class who were better endowed with Nurturing Parent/Natural Child, the culture of the class would have been less dull.

When I told them they were dull, several of the Critical Parents were concerned. What Critical Parent wants their Adapted Child to be dull? I explained they needed to use more Natural Child and Nurturing Parent during class.

I also explained what Natural Child—Natural Child transactions were, and after I finished this, one shocked, indignant student from Critical Parent blurted out, "What do you want us to do, just sit here and bullshit"

I explained that I didn't think it would be a good idea for them to spend all their time bullshooting but that it would be a good idea to spend some time bullshooting.

"Not in the classroom!" the Critical Parent snapped back.

"Why not in the classroom?" I replied. I explained that in business school, we were training people to be business managers and salespeople and that out in the real world, if you don't know how to bullshoot, you won't get very far. I explained that bullshooting is a valuable skill for managers and salespeople.

Although some of the Critical Parents never bought this idea, most of the Adults got the point. The class began to spend more time in Natural Child pastiming. They started out spending maybe five minutes a day at it; by the end of the course, they spent fifteen or twenty minutes a day at it some days.

Telling the class they were a dull group caused them to be less dull. Near the end of the course, one student said from Adapted Child to my Critical Parent, "Dr. Stapleton, do you still think we're a dull group?"

"Not as dull as you were," I replied from my Adult to the student's Adult.

Some of the students, including the student who asked if I still thought they were a dull group, were pleased that I thought they had made some progress in becoming less dull.

The problem is that if you are trying to be not dull from Adapted Child to get your Critical Parent off your back, because a teacher thinks you are dull (when your Critical Parent wanted you to be dull in the first place), you are still operating from Adapted Child and are not spontaneously and joyfully saying and doing things from Natural Child. Therefore, a certain amount of dullness is still involved. While this class had become more lively than they were, they were still duller than most of my classes.

This lesson about being dull turned out to be very interesting to the students. It seemed to intensify their efforts to memorize the book. Apparently, they decided if they couldn't be not dull in their communicating in class, then they would at least be good scholars.

An exceptionally intense contest had somehow been set up among the students to see who could score highest on the tests, regardless of how unfair they thought the tests were. It seemed to me that even the least interested students in the class were drawn into this contest. It seems to me this indicates students will work to gain achievement strokes when they are denied Game strokes.

All in all, it was an interesting learning experience. I learned something from the course, and I think the students got something valuable from it. It wound up a generally OK class. Some of the students thought various students in the class and I were not OK, but most of us came out of the course in a winner position, i.e., I'm OK—you're OK. Some of the students told me they thought the course was one of the best they had had. One student had a 4.0 grade point average going into the course, having made a point to let me know about it during the course. She made a low A on the tests, but had a high C or low B in class participation, and, therefore, she got a B in the course. I haven't seen her since the course. I had some concerns about how she would react when she received the B and what effect this would have on her OKness, but my job is to enforce the Adult learning contract. I do not have a contract to see to it that 4.0 students keep a perfect average.

"OK, I'll Read It"

The students thought the De-Gamer was less effective for De-Gaming Games than it was for causing students to study and learn more, according to their survey responses.

I think the De-Gamer causes students to play one of the most pervasive student Games in the world (probably since the beginning of schools) less frequently. As far as I know, I am the first person to name this Game. I call it "OK, I'll read it."

"OK, I'll read it" (OKIRI) starts when teachers (usually from Adult) assign material for overnight reading or problem solving or analysis, transacting with the Adult of students. At the social level, the teacher is coming from Rescuer, and at the psychological level, from Persecutor. Students are Victims at both levels.

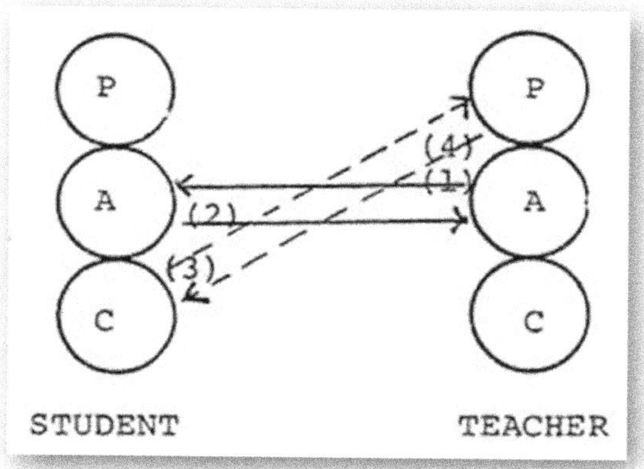

Figure 26. Opening Transactions of "OK, I'll Read It."

On transaction (1), the teacher says, "Here is your assignment for next time." Usually, there will be some requests for more information along transaction (2).

Usually, the teacher and students will slip off vectors (1) and (2) into a psychological set of transactions along vectors (3) and (4). On vector (3), the Child of the students attempts to reduce the work or complexity of the assignment from the Victim position, and the teacher, on vector (4), tells students why they should do what the teacher has already decided is good for them from the Persecutor drama position. In some cases, students will move from Adult at the social level to Parent and criticize the Child of the teacher for coming up with such an unreasonable assignment. The most significant switch, however, comes when the students move from the Adult level to Parent and from Victim to Persecutor, crossing transaction (6) with transaction (5).

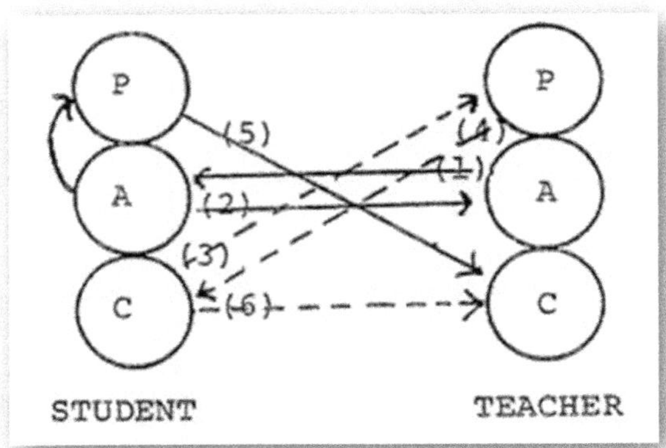

Figure 27. Payoff of "OK, I'll Read It."

On transaction (5), students communicate the message socially from Parent to the Child of the teacher: "OK, I'll read it." This message is a discount of the teacher and the material, a seeming noblesse oblige acquiescence, which is really a lie. Simultaneously, at the Child-Child level, an ulterior message is transmitted at transaction (6): "I have no intention of reading this crap. You are not smart enough to know what I should read."

These messages may be nonverbal. Students may nod their heads or change facial expressions or body posture to get their social and psychological messages, or discounts, across.

In many classrooms, teachers know students are playing Games with them about reading or doing homework, but they don't do much about it. And given many classroom configurations, it really doesn't make that much difference anyway. So the next day, when class starts, both the teacher and the students play the Game of pretending the students have read the material. This sets up the Drama Triangle and brings into play Persecutors, Rescuers, and Victims. The teacher again Rescues the students by not exposing the previous day's

OKIRI. The teacher winds up the Victim again at the psychological level, because he or she must accept the discount that he or she is not competent enough to know what should be done for homework. Students are Persecutors psychologically, because they get away with discounting the teacher and the material. One way to stop this Game, of course, is not to assign any homework. Is homework really necessary to learn? If it is, then students playing OKIRI will become the ultimate Victims.

Used every day, the Classroom De-Gamer significantly reduces the occurrence of the above Game. Since 94 percent of the students responding to my questionnaire said the De-Gamer caused them to prepare more for class than they otherwise would have, the De-Gamer is doing a better job of De-Gaming Games than most students think.

Emotional Reactions to the De-Gamer

At first, I felt some discomfort when I carried the De-Gamer around in the building. The students and faculty made derogatory comments about my "toy." My prototype model was painted in green, red, and yellow colors. The colors reminded students of Christmas, they said. I began to enjoy this when I realized the De-Gamer was setting up some Natural Child fun. There was some discounting around this, but it was a first-degree, almost-harmless Game. My newer models are made of hardwood, stained to match school desks and furniture. Onlookers rarely make comments anymore when I carry my De-Gamer to class.

There is always some tension in the room when the De-Gamer is spun at the beginning of the hour. It's like waiting for the kickoff of a football game. No one knows for sure who will have to carry the ball after the kickoff. Even though there may be forty or so students in the room, each student appears to feel that he or she may have to carry the ball. Seldom does the arrow point out a student who is not prepared. The arrow is never spun very often in a class, what with the excellent contributions many students volunteer after the kickoff is run back a ways.

I have contracts with students that if the arrow selects them to respond, and they are not prepared, if they have implied they were prepared by not telling me before the class started that they were not prepared, they will receive one letter grade lower as a final grade than would have otherwise been the case. While this might seem harsh, I contract that the grade-lowering provision will not apply if unprepared students tell me before class they are not prepared. This prevents the playing of OKIRI.

If particular students tell me they are not prepared frequently, then they are also playing a Game, and this Game must be dealt with.

I think it is important for the teacher to stay in the Adult ego state when the spinning process is going on. Not OKness can be set up in the classroom if the teacher allows his or her Critical Parent or Adapted Child to get hooked when students are being pointed out by the arrow. If the teacher excessively giggles or sneers when the arrow lands on someone, not OKness can be set up.

During some courses, the De-Gamer arrow seems to have a will of its own and stops in some parts of the room many more times than in other parts. Some students seem to get singled out every other day, while some students never get hit. In one class, a student spun the arrow before I could tell the class to get up and move to different positions. The arrow landed on a particular student. Before responding to the arrow, this student, along with thirty-seven other students in this class, moved randomly to a different desk in the room. The arrow was spun again…and it landed on him again! The spontaneous Natural Child energy that erupted in the room was powerful.

What is the probability of a student being hit twice in succession by a student-spun arrow in a room of thirty-eight students when the class members were randomly moved to different positions after the student was struck the first time?

This question ought to energize few Adult ego states.

To some extent, the De-Gaming process in the classroom simulates the occurrence of life events in the outside world. It sets up a situation in which students need to use their Adult ego states to be comfortable or successful. Most of the time, in most classrooms, there is little need for students to use the Adult ego state. The main requirement for success is to turn on the Adapted Child ego state and remember exactly what you are told. If you can do this, you will certainly receive an A.

What Kind of Teacher Am I?

I don't show up well on numerical-average faculty evaluations filled out by undergraduates. I am highly appreciated by some students and highly unappreciated by others.

I appeal to tough-minded, Adult-type students. Students who like to play Games don't like me. I am a competent teacher in the eyes of my colleagues, as evidenced by my promotion to full professor at age thirty-five. I develop good relationships with some students. Each year, I sent twenty or so graduates out into the world who majored in me. These are students who have taken courses with me for most or all of their free electives, from four to six courses. One of these students came by to see me four days before graduation. Since he was about to graduate, he decided to tell me how he saw the lay of the land at Georgia Southern. He was convinced I had the right approach to teaching. He wanted to know why more teachers don't use the case method. "That De-Gamer really works. In a lot of the courses you take, you don't learn anything," he said.

He had flunked some sort of exit exam and was in jeopardy of not graduating. He had retaken the exam but didn't know whether he had passed it the second time. I think this exam had to do with the constitution. At any rate, he thought it was ridiculous that he even had to take the exam. He was down on the test administrator and generally all college administrators. "Here I am, the customer," he said, "and they act like they're doing you a favor to let you out of here."

He was switching back and forth from Victim to Persecutor and was inviting me to Rescue him and join in the Persecution his Parent wanted to inflict on some administrators. This was a good student—a 2.8 or so grade-point type—and I personally liked him. He was a well-motivated, generally positive, go-getter type. I had observed him in class for five or six courses, and he generally stayed in an OK position, was well prepared, and had good things to say when he talked about the material. I decided to play some first-degree "ain't it awful" and "let's you and him fight" (Berne 1964) with him.

I pointed out he could go talk to the college president about the poor administrative performance he had seen, and that regarding the exit exam he had retaken, it might be a good idea to go talk to the "punk" administrator who would grade the thing and see if he passed it the second time.

"I just might do that," he said. "Just walk right in the president's office and talk to him like an Adult. You don't have to come on Child to these administrators, even the president, do you?"

"Not if you've graduated," I said.

"Yeah, well, I think I'll just go talk to the president."

I told him I thought that students had an Adult right to evaluate teachers and administrators, that no one was exempt from evaluation, that it goes on all the time everywhere.

"It sure is nice to have some teachers you can talk to," he said. "There aren't many teachers around here you can talk to."

This led him into wondering why I wasn't more popular with students. "You know," he said, "these freshmen and sophomores ask me, 'What's Stapleton like? Is he hard?' I tell them, 'No, he's not hard, but it's like having a test every day.'"

This student and I talked for thirty or so minutes in my office. We played some first-degree Games, did some pastiming and some Adult problem solving, exchanged positive strokes, and achieved a higher degree of intimacy than normally exists between students and teachers. We ended our encounter in an I'm OK—you're OK position.

The student was coming from a position of I'm OK—you're OK, but some of the administrators and other teachers are not OK. From an Adult standpoint, he was correct and accurately perceptive regarding some of the not OKness he had seen, but his Parent and Child had set up some Games around it. Before he talked to me, he had been more interested in enjoying the drama of the situation than taking some Adult action steps to correct the problem.

Despite his playing some Games, this was still a good student. I told him that I thought he was a good student and that I thought he would do well in his career. He told me about the job he already had lined up in first-level management at a good salary. Everything was rosy except the problem of graduating. Unless my guess is incorrect, this student will wind up more successful than most graduates. He will make it and be successful and powerful.

Many of my graduates report back that they have made it and are powerful and successful. Rightly or wrongly, they say my teaching helped them. I enjoy teaching and generally find it satisfying. I enjoy engaging in Adult-Adult discussions with students in a relatively Game-free atmosphere. This happens frequently in my classes. What is most satisfying about teaching to me is watching students figure things out and decide to become more capable.

Perspective

Games vary in degrees of seriousness. As pointed out in a previous chapter, there are first-degree, second-degree, and third-degree Games. First-degree Games are relatively innocuous, and third-degree Games are dangerous. I have encountered only one student whom I consider a potential third-degree Game player. In class, this student glared and glowered and absolutely refused to positively participate throughout the whole course. I gave him the D in the course he earned, giving him credit for his written work and the fact he was there in body. He then unleashed his full arsenal of Games, playing them not only with me but with my department head, the dean, and anyone else he thought could or would help Persecute me. He stopped me in the hall one day and escalated to the second degree. The white-hot anger showing in his face indicated he could have gone on to the third degree. The student did poorly not only in my course but also in several others. He flunked out of school and faded off into the sunset. I haven't seen the student for several years, but I have some scare whenever I think of him. I hope has he found a niche where he can be productive and has not been a menace to people around him.

Encountering one potential third-degree Game player is not bad. This indicates that the majority of college students are reasonably well-off in an OKness, Game-playing sense. I estimate that 80–90 percent of all college students play first-degree Games such as IEW, SW, and OKIRI in classrooms and offices with teachers. Most students "brownnose" to a certain extent. This reduces the efficiency and effectiveness of learning activities, but it does not result in serious harm. I estimate that 30–40 percent of all college students play some second-degree Games outside of the classroom with friends, family members, and so on, but this still will not put anyone in a hospital. I think college teachers and organizational trainers encounter fewer second- and third-degree Games among students and trainees than elementary, junior high, or high school teachers. Most of the heavy Game players drop out of the learning process before college and cannot function in most organizations that reward participants on the basis of outward, positive contributions and merit. On the other hand, based on my experience with public school learning situations, third-degree Games are rare in these situations. In general, teachers and trainers don't need to worry about third-degree Game players in ordinary learning situations. What teachers and trainers need to primarily do about Games is reduce first-degree Games so that more learning can take place.

Nine

How To Run Your Classes

How to run your classes is up to you. I have no idea what you teach, how you do what you do, or how effective or efficient you are. I have no idea how popular you are with your students or how fairly you have been appraised as a teacher by the people in your system who determine whether you are given poor, average, or good salary raises and promotions. What you are is a function of what you have decided to be.

You decided to be what you are because of the natural intelligence in your Little Professor (your A1) and your more grown-up Adult (your A2) and because of the parent figures and Parent data that existed in your earlier environments, which you have videotaped and stored in your electrode (your P1), your Parent before age seven, and your P2, the Parent you developed by copying others later in life after age seven.

You can probably identify specific teachers in the past whom you have copied in your teaching behavior and procedures. You probably use some of the same classroom layouts, teaching methods, testing procedures, ego states, Games, classroom rituals, pastimes, and activities that your favorite teachers used. It may be that you were lucky enough to have had good teachers from the first day of your life. If that is the case, and you have developed a teaching script based on that exposure (i.e., you videotaped your teachers' behaviors, feelings, thoughts, knowledge, mannerisms, and gestures and now replicate them), then it is likely you are appraised a "good teacher" in your system.

On the other hand, since there are no perfect teachers, if you have taken the path of least resistance by copying your teachers, it is likely you have some problems in your teaching in the here and now. You may be considered a "good teacher," but you will have some characteristics you could change for the better.

What to Change?

Eric Berne exhorted his students to "see what is really going on." Seeing what is really going on in your classroom, as everywhere else, entails seeing what the real feelings, desires, behaviors, and thoughts of people are. Berne (1970) said humans ought to be like Martians coming down to Earth for the first time to see what is really going on. Martians would not have already been taught how to see phenomena and events on Earth and would be less biased than Earthlings observing Earthlings.

To see what is really going on in your classroom, you need to think like a Martian and not allow your preconceived notions, which includes the teaching you introjected from others (i.e., your Parent tapes) to blind you. The probability of you doing things "just right" in your classroom is very low when you see how many alternatives you have for structuring the time, layouts, teaching methods, testing methods, rituals, pastimes, activities, Games, intimacy, ego states, and types of transactions in your classroom.

Considering only the alternative classroom layouts, teaching methods, and testing methods I have described in this book, you have 150 alternative classroom structure configurations you can choose among.

The alternatives for layouts are the Row-and-Column Layout, the Seminar Layout, the Horseshoe Layout, the Amphitheater Layout (assuming your school has amphitheater rooms you can use), the Circle Layout, and the Orbit Layout.

The alternatives for teaching methods are the Lecture Method, the Reading/Arithmetic/Discussion Method, the Case Method, the Learning-the-Textbook Method, and the What-Do-You-Want-to-Work-On Method.

The alternatives for testing are the Multiple-Choice/True-False/Matching/Fill-in-the-Blank/Short-Answer Test, the Solve-the-Problem Test, the Essay Test, the Case Write-Uup Test, and the No-Test Test.

The combinations of only these three classroom variables are 150 (6 alternative layouts × 5 alternative teaching methods × 5 alternative testing methods).

If you add a Classroom De-Gamer to the above three variables, you add 150 additional alternatives, for a total of 300 distinct alternative classroom configurations you can choose among.

When you add in alternatives for variables such as time-structuring patterns, ego states, and transactional patterns, the alternatives for classroom physical and social/psychological configurations explode into the thousands—over 90,000 (per the above discussion, 600 physical and procedure configurations × 6 time-structuring alternatives × 3 ego states × 9 transactional patterns). When you consider that many of these variables would be applied as percentages of the time in various configurations, the alternatives explode way beyond 90,000.

In light of this analysis, the notion of any classroom being set up "just right" seems absurd. How could you possibly prove your configuration was best, even if, by some quirk of fate, you had fallen upon the best configuration?

Alternatives for Classroom Management

Practically everything you do in the classroom involves alternatives and decisions. There are things you can say or do to keep yourself in an I'm OK—you're OK position. You can decide which ego state to communicate with when doing various things. You can decide to be more Adult and less Parent or more Child or whatever is appropriate. You can decide to see your students more for what they are in terms of ego states, transactions, Games, OK position, and scripts. You can decide to encourage your students to be what they are rather than try to have them conform to your preconceived expectations of what model students should be like. You can decide to encourage some students to change some aspects of their behavior or personalities.

You can decide to use whatever classroom layouts, teaching methods, and testing methods you think best from an Adult standpoint, given not only your Adult assessment of the situation but also the Parent requirements of your administrative system.

The two (so far as I know) original contributions I have made to classroom management are the Classroom De-Gamer and the Orbit Layout. Using the De-Gamer in an Orbit Layout with the rule that students must sit in different seats between different people each day maximizes the flexibility and adaptability requirements of classrooms.

Flexibility and adaptability lead to success in most social systems, regardless of how they are configured, including schools and businesses.

According to Eric Berne (1964), flexibility plus adaptability equals success. "Flexibility is the ability of a group member to modify or compromise the aims and objects of his individual proclivities in the process of adjustment, and adaptability is the ability to adapt social techniques to the confronting reality" (Berne 1964).

Flexibility entails an individual being able and willing to modify or alter aspects and aims of his or her personality or script, and adaptability entails an individual being able and willing to change his or her ideas about how things should be done—that is, his or her group imago. The group imago is the mental image a person carries around in his or her head regarding what a group should be like and how it should be run (Berne 1964).

For example, in order to be more successful, some students and employees need to change certain irritating personality characteristics. Some students and employees clown around too much. Some students and employees are too serious. Some should use more Parent, and some should use less Parent and more Child or whatever. Being able to change these aspects requires flexibility. Some students and employees have serious beliefs about how you should run things. For example, some students do not believe you should use Classroom De-Gamers. Some believe you should not grade students based on their participation in classroom discussions. Students in my classes who hold these beliefs and do not change them (or pretend to change them while they take my classes) generally get low grades. They are not adaptable enough to earn good grades, given the confronting reality my courses present. In a business, an employee might not like the rating system a supervisor uses for determining raises, or he or she might not like the tools or procedures the supervisor requires for getting the work done. Such employees, if hardheaded enough, are generally sluiced out of businesses over time. They are run off.

It is often useful to establish participatory groups in businesses including superiors and subordinates for the purpose of discussing and agreeing upon the methods of work and evaluation systems. Students can sometimes be included in the process of deciding upon the learning contract for the course. The ideal scenario is to include all parties as discussion participants when establishing work methods, evaluation systems, learning contracts, and the like for governing all parties or stakeholders in the system. Sometimes, this ideal scenario is not possible or practical.

Regardless of how the work methods, evaluation systems, and learning contracts are established, once they are established, all participants must flex and adapt to them if they want to be successful. Rarely do nonflexers and nonadapters possess sufficient power to change the established group culture or group imago to suit their personal tastes. Nonflexers and nonadapters to established group cultures and group imagoes, however established, are usually punished or run off. This seems to be a natural law of life since humans began to band together in groups for survival against other groups several millennia ago.

It seems that most people who are fired are not fired because of lacking the ability to do the job in a technical sense. They can memorize the procedures and possess the mental and physical dexterity to do what their jobs technically require at the required speed. They are fired because they will not or cannot flex and adapt to the organizational culture and imago.

Students must generally flex and adapt to the personalities and imagoes of teachers, not the other way around. Employees must generally flex and adapt to the personalities and imagoes of managers and owners, not the other way around. Even if a teacher wanted to, he or she could not flex and adapt to the personalities and imagoes of all of the students he or she is exposed to over the course of a year. Not only would trying to do so be stupid but trying to do so would create chaos. There would be nothing in the behavioral culture of the class any student could relate to as a given. There would be no order.

Managers, supervisors, and business owners dealing with employees can adapt more to the peculiar personalities and imagoes of employees without dysfunctional consequences, since they have fewer of them over time.

But the fact remains: subordinates of all sorts must generally flex and adapt to the established culture and imago of any organization.

The Orbit Layout, with the De-Gamer and the moving-about rule, creates a confronting reality in classrooms requiring much flexibility and adaptability, while, at the same time, it impartially enforces Adult (A2) knowledge- and skill-learning contracts. This would seem to be good teaching for students, given the importance of learning the significance of flexing and adapting for long-term survival.

Are you flexible and adaptable enough to experiment with it in your teaching, training, or meeting leading?

What You as a Teacher Can Manage

Your primary object of management is yourself. If you establish and enforce good Adult learning contracts with your students and employees and control yourself in such a way as not to get involved in Games, your students and employees will learn, and you will do a good job.

You can manage the following:

(1) Your contracts—Do your best to establish clear, clean, straight Adult contracts with students, employees, fellow supervisors, teachers, administrators, and owners. Don't enter into psychological contracts that entangle you in webs of Persecuting, Rescuing, and Victimizing that waste your energy and hurt your chances for real success and satisfaction. Be out-front with what you want to do, and get other parties to agree to it up-front. If you do what you set out to do in this manner, you did a good job.

(2) Your ego states—There is no reason for you to walk around all day in your Critical Parent or wear your Adapted Child to class or work. In most cases, in schools and businesses, it is probably best to stay generally Adult, with appropriate shifting to other ego states as circumstances merit.

(3) Your transactions—When communicating with your students or employees, fellow workers or teachers, and various superiors, beam most of your transactional vectors from your Adult to their Adults, with appropriate usage of other transactions as circumstances merit.

(4) Your rackets—If you have a mad, sad, glad, or scared feeling racket, do your best not to impose the racket on your students or employees or your peers and superiors. Just because you may have to feel sad all of the time, for example, in order to feel secure or comfortable, this does not mean those around you at work have to maintain a sad feeling. Even if you have to feel glad all the time, those around you still don't have to feel this feeling if they don't want to feel it.

(5) Your drivers—If you are possessed with a "hurry up," "please me," "be perfect," "be strong," or "try hard" driver, please don't impose the same on your students or employees or your peers or superiors.

(6) Your Games—Stay off the Drama Triangle, be straight, do what the Adult contact says to do, and watch out for ulterior transactions and ulterior contracts with students, employees, peers, and administrative superiors.

(7) Your permissions—In all the ways you can—from all three ego states if possible—tell your students it's OK for them to think, learn, be powerful, be successful, be themselves, make it, be the sex they are, feel what they feel, belong, be close, and be important.

(8) Your strokes—Give good strokes and lots of them. Don't give plastic, conditional strokes when others don't live up to the Adult learning contract. Positively stroke the existence of your students, employees, peers, and administrative superiors unconditionally. Maximize positive strokes; minimize negative strokes.

(9) Your time structuring—Spend an appropriate percentage of class and work time on rituals, pastimes, activities, and intimacy. Develop an appropriate balance. More time should be spent on activity than anything else.

(10) Your classroom layout—Use the appropriate layout, and don't let your or others' Critical Parent or Adapted Child make your layout decision for you.

(11) Your teaching methods—Use those methods that are most appropriate, given your Adult learning and work contract. Don't let your or others' Critical Parent or Adapted Child make this decision.

(12) Your testing and grading procedures—Again, use your Adult in deciding which procedure is most effective. Eliminate the Drama Triangle from your testing and grading as much as possible. Grade students and employees relative to how well they perform their Adult learning and work contracts and not according to how well they complement your script.

What Is an OK Teacher?

The major purpose of OK teaching is to cause relevant learning to occur. This forms the basis for the Adult contract that teachers and supervisors have with students, employees, and society. An OK teacher is a person who causes relevant learning to occur. I think any number of alternative classroom-structure configurations of layouts, teaching methods, and testing methods are OK, given the specific Adult learning contracts that are established.

An OK teacher is not necessarily a good speaker, a mathematical genius, a whiz kid in terms of memory, a creative genius, a good entertainer, or a good social worker.

An OK teacher is relatively racket- and Game-free in the classroom.

An OK teacher, in the majority of his or her transactions with students, employees, peers, superiors, and the public will feel, think, and act in such a way as to come out of those transactions I'm OK—you're OK.

An OK teacher does not always "try hard," "please me," "be perfect," "be strong," or "hurry up."

An OK teacher is not "locked" into a rigid set of ego states. He or she can decide to operate from various ego states when appropriate. Both Natural Child fun and Critical Parent "discipline" are appropriate at times. An OK teacher will be potent enough to offer some psychological Protection to students. An OK teacher will give students some psychological permission to think, learn, be successful, make it, feel what they feel, be who they are, be powerful, belong, be close, be the sex they are, grow up, and have fun. An OK teacher is not grandiose about himself or herself, the students, the subject matter, or learning. An OK teacher does not discount himself or herself, the students, the subject matter, or learning. An OK teacher sees what is really going on and calls the shots accordingly. An OK teacher respects truth and honesty.

It would probably be impossible for anyone to be an OK teacher all of the time, regardless of how many books on how to be a good teacher he or she has read. We are not OK some of the time. Writing and reading this book will not change that. But that's OK.

Ten

Inviting OKness

OK is being relatively free of physical illness, poverty, and despair. OK is enjoying life, oneself, other people, and activities. OK also has to do with a more subjective process of perception: OK is experiencing yourself, others, your group, the other group, and the world as OK. What is OK to one person may not be OK to another. OKness, like beauty, is to some extent in the eye of the beholder.

The general ethical view among transactional analysts is that all people are OK, despite the fact specific acts of feeling, thinking, and behaving may not be OK.

It is difficult to determine whether someone is operating from a somewhat chronically OK or not-OK position or a temporary OK or not-OK position. Where he or she is in the present is partially a function of past positions he or she was immersed in. Is present not OKness caused by something real in the present environment, or is past not OKness being reincarnated in the present through rackets, Games, or a script? A basic life position regarding OKness is decided at an early age and may be difficult to change.

It is difficult to move from basic not OKness to OKness. People are who and where they are because of the circumstances of their births and what they have decided in the past. Basic beliefs about the OKness of oneself and others are learned more or less accidentally by young children. A major source of information that children use to decide whether they and others are OK is the information transmitted nonverbally from the Child ego states of caregivers—more specifically, from the Parent in the Child, sometimes referred to as the Pig Parent or the electrode.

Even though parents and other parent figures may do the best they can to hide their true not-OK feelings and thoughts in their Parent of the Child, if they are there, the Little Professor in the Child of their children will probably detect them and may rightly decide that the parents are coming from a not-OK position. Unfortunately, the Little Professor may not decide this. The Little Professor may erroneously decide the parent is right and accept the negative messages the parent transmits to the child through the Parent in the Child of the parent, which were probably introjected from the Parent in the Child of the parent of the parent. If so, the child will introject and possibly permanently store the negative messages transmitted from the parent and may similarly transmit them to his or her offspring as an adult. Thus, basic Not OKness may be perpetuated from generation to generation down certain family lines.

If the parent is coming from a not-OK position a high percentage of the time, his or her children may decide that they are the cause of father's or mother's not OKness, and they may decide that they are not OK too, since they cannot make their mother or father OK.

By the same token, the Little Professors of students in classrooms and employees in businesses intuitively "know" when teachers and managers are coming from not-OK positions. Students and employees rarely use this data to take direct action. That is, they don't confront the teacher or manager about his or her not OKness, ask what's wrong, or tell administrators or parents about the specific not OKness they have seen, unless it's something extreme. In most cases, the astute students or employees picking up on the not OKness simply "don't like" the teacher or manager. They may not consciously know why they don't like the teacher or manager; they just know they don't. The answer lies in the Little Professor. The reasons why may not reach the Adult (A2) level.

Most people harbor some not-OK feeling, thinking, or behavior patterns of various kinds. People are not perfect. Most people, including students and employees, are willing to tolerate a relatively high degree of imperfection in others, including teachers and managers.

Not tolerating some imperfection in oneself and others is itself an imperfection. So, given the fact we are not perfect, and no one else is, most people (at some point or another) come to decide whether they should invest energy in changing some imperfection or leave it as it is and invest the same energy (and perhaps time and money) in having some fun or doing some work on the environment.

In general, in order to be happy, people must have goals, and they must achieve a reasonable percentage of them. The natural thing to do is just go out and get the job done, whatever it is. Do what it is that will solve the problem, make you happy, and so on.

If a reasonable percentage of goals are not achieved, the person is sabotaging himself or herself in some way for some reason. He or she sets unreasonable goals to start with, or he or she lacks psychological permission to achieve them. Or it may be that a person has permission and ability to achieve goals but does not have permission to enjoy the success.

Barring major calamities such as economic depressions and various forms of physical illness, people are responsible for their own objective OKness, even though it may be that their goal attainment and success (or lack of objective goal attainment and success) is caused by their basic life positions and subjective not OKness.

The OKness Continuum

On an OKness scale, from –1 (least OK) to +1 (most OK), most of us would probably be around 0. Various people would populate all points along the continuum. It is possible that people would be distributed along the continuum in the so-called normal curve. The normal curve is a bell-shaped curve with most frequencies occurring around the midpoint of a continuum. If the normal curve should apply to the above OKness scale, then 50 percent of the people would be relatively not OK, and 50 percent would be relatively OK. Two or 3 percent would be super-OK, and 2 or 3 percent would be super–not OK, and so on.

While it would probably be impossible to acquire data showing what percent of the population is at various points on the OKness continuum, the distribution of people along the OK continuum exists. In my opinion, most people in the lower end of the distribution are where they are because of scripts, not environmental circumstances. Regardless of the truth or falsity of this opinion, the fact that is that many people have some not-OK scripting. The relevant question, in my opinion, regarding this issue, is this: Are the benefits to be derived from making script changes equal to or greater than the costs of making the changes?

Medical doctors with psychotherapy certifications and various training in various psychotherapeutic disciplines behind them are at the top of the status heap of therapists and presumably are the most capable at helping people change their scripts. The going rate for MD-type psychotherapists in 1992 was in the neighborhood of $100 per hour.

Assuming you become convinced you are not as OK as you might be and have not had much success in increasing your basic OKness on your own, you might decide to consult a psychiatrist. What will the cost of making the change you desire be? How many hours will be required?

In many cases, where long-standing personality problems are involved, years of therapy will be required, usually one or two hours a week to start with, with less frequent visits later. The cost of correcting various imperfections and increasing OKness utilizing a psychiatrist can easily be thousands of dollars. How do you calculate the benefits of making personality changes to you, your children, your spouse, your friends, and so on? Simple relief from anxiety might be worth $1,000. Eliminating the ongoing misery of a bad script might be worth $100,000 or more.

In general, there is no precise, rational way to make the above decision. In the first place, therapists cannot diagnose personality problems with a sufficient degree of accuracy to precisely determine how long it will take to eliminate various personality problems (if indeed they can be eliminated) using various methods of therapy. Therefore, unlike other professionals and businessmen, they are unable to determine prices for various jobs. They can price only their time per hour, and, in many cases, the job continues until the patient/client decides to quit.

The psychotherapeutic industry is also somewhat uncertain as to whether people who come to practitioners for help should be called patients or clients. If the person asking for help is a patient, then he or she must be "sick." And if he or she is sick, he or she, if treated by a medical doctor, should get cured or well. But since the psychotherapeutic industry is also uncertain about whether they can actually cure these people seeking help, there is some doubt that getting well in in the cards. The most likely objective of treatment will be to make progress—that is, the patient/client will become more OK than he or she was before encountering and communicating with the psychiatrist.

I think the word *patient* should be eliminated from psychotherapy vocabulary unless a person is confined to a hospital. The vast majority of people who can use psychotherapy are not "sick" (in the normal sense of the word). They can function in most jobs and outwardly appear to get along OK. I think the word *client* is the better word. A person decides to increase his or her OKness to make life better, not to get well, and hires an expert to facilitate the process. Labeling people using psychotherapeutic services as *patients* may define them as not OK. They are presumed to be sick, crazy, or some other not-OK thing. In many cases, if friends or neighbors find out their friends have been using the services of a psychiatrist, the neighbors or friends may begin to think the person using psychotherapy is about 50 percent less OK than previously.

One of the costs of deciding to utilize psychotherapeutic services is dealing with the negative public relations it can create. In some cases, therapy can be obtained without anyone knowing about it. On the other hand, in some cases, it would not make any difference if people did find out about it. There is some not OKness around this whole issue, in any case. Assuming you should decide to consult a psychotherapist, what sort of therapist should you consult? An MD, a PhD psychologist, an MSW, a minister, a friend, the neighborhood "helpful Hanna," an Eastern guru, a Moonie, a biofeedback expert, a muscle-relaxing therapist? Of the scores of types of psychotherapy, which one should you pick?

One of the main objectives of many therapies (transactional analysis, in particular) is to enable people to become "autonomous" and self-reliant—that is, not needing to rely on others for help. To be autonomous means that people can use the Adult ego state in the here and now and make appropriate decisions given here-and-now data, facts, realities, and so on. The decisions of autonomous people are not automatic responses based on what they were taught and decided during the scripting process.

In order for people to become autonomous, in many cases, they must disobey their ancestors. They must ignore and violate their script injunctions. Many people are afraid to do this. The internal stress and strain and confusion that result from violating script injunctions are frequently too much to endure, so many people give up and let the script have its way, regardless of what it forbids and the happiness and success it precludes.

Consequently, one of the main reasons people may need psychotherapists is to obtain psychological permission to violate their script injunctions. If a therapist is to do any good, the client must see him or her as psychologically potent enough to psychologically protect the client from his or her own Parent, usually the P1 (the Pig Parent or electrode). Since the client expects to be punished because he or she violated the script injunctions, the therapist must stand ready to show the client that the script injunctions don't really count and protect the client from his or her fears.

Don't assume that just because someone has a shingle or certificate of some sort saying he or she is legally qualified to do psychotherapy that he or she will be a good therapist for you. Therapy is not like surgery or automobile repair. The therapist has a personality too, and his or her personality has something to do with how effectively he or she could do therapy with you. Some therapists are no doubt relatively ineffectual with all clients; some are relatively potent with all clients. There is probably as much or more variation in the quality of psychotherapists as there is in the quality of lawyers.

Assuming you decide to try some psychotherapy to seek psychological permission to violate some sabotaging, inhumane, or painful script injunctions you accepted and committed to in early childhood for your personal script, it might be a good idea to check around with other people who have had psychotherapy, if you can find any, and ask them whom they have had success with. Another idea is to shop around. Spend an hour or two with several therapists before you decide to stick with one of them. Another good idea is to attend workshops and conferences of various types put on by various psychotherapeutic associations, such as the International Transactional Analysis Association. There are many people at these workshops and conferences who have had therapy, and they are in a relatively good position to judge the effectiveness of various therapists.

Alternatives for Increasing OKness

For people who are relatively low on the OKness scale (from –1 to –0.5), some form of psychotherapy is probably needed. For people in the higher end of the OKness scale, psychotherapy becomes a luxury item, like Jaguar cars, horses, beach houses, mountain retreats, sailboats, and other items that are purchased for pure pleasure. You buy it because you want to have it, not because you have to have it. No one can tell you whether you should invest in psychotherapy if you are relatively OK. Your decision is related to how OK you want to get and how much money and time you have to spend.

There are alternatives for increasing OKness other than psychotherapy. The most obvious alternative that comes to mind is to read self-help books of various kinds (such as this one). Hundreds of books have been written on TA and Gestalt therapy in recent years. For example, Eric Berne wrote a book entitled *Layman's Guide to Psychotherapy and Psychoanalysis* (1957). For more information sources on TA contact the International Transactional Analysis Association, at http://itaaworld.org/.

Another method for increasing OKness at the upper end of the OKness scale is simply to think about where you are and where you want to go. Write down your goals and objectives and persist until you get what you want. The problem here is determining what it is you really want. On the other hand, be careful that you really want what you think you want. You might get it.

A good way of getting in touch with where you are in terms of your transactions is to develop what I refer to as a transactional profile. What this involves is seeing where you are in terms of your transactions so that you can decide whether to change using social control through your A2. At the higher end of the OKness scale, people can decide to become more OK by simply deciding to change some of their transactions. This is not psychotherapy, because there is no attempt to change what is in the Child ego state. The client decides with the Adult (A2) to present himself or herself differently to others and uses willpower to control his or her behavior. This will probably not help someone out of a chronic not-OK script position, but for relatively OK people who want to get more OK, it will probably help.

Developing Your Transactional Profile–Checking on Yourself

A transactional profile shows how you come across in public in terms of strokes, OK position, ego states, transactions, time structuring, time competency, and feelings.

What the profile amounts to is determining what percent of your waking hours you spend in various categories of the above variables. Stated another way, of all categories of a variable, what percent is each? Once you see where you are in terms of the variables, you can decide what, if anything, you want to do differently.

It is a good idea to get feedback from people who are close to you regarding how they see you in terms of the variables. Ask your family members how you come across to them in terms of these variables. This will tend to increase the objectivity of your profile.

Another technique is to talk to yourself in a mirror and record your conversation on a tape recorder. Better yet, have someone videotape you with audio. Looking at yourself in a mirror or seeing yourself on a screen, you can see yourself in your Parent, your Adult, and your Child. You can also hear yourself coming from Parent, Adult, and Child on the tape. You can judge from this what percent of the time, day in and day out, you operate from Parent, Adult, and Child.

It is probably easier to diagnose ego states listening to a tape recorder than it is talking to someone face to face. You can stop the tape and play it back to rehear nonverbal transactions, such as giggles, sighs, and the like, that you miss the first time through.

The following system can be used to develop a graph for each of the above variables. I first published a variation of this system in my book, *The Entrepreneur* (1985).

What it boils down to is that you have to check on yourself from time to time to see where you are. You must ask yourself these questions: What ego state have I just been using? What sort of transaction did I just have with that person or group? What ego state did I use, and what ego state did I hook in her, him, or them? How did the transaction end up? Did I end up OK, and they were also OK, or was I not OK, and they were OK or not OK—or what? What sort of strokes were involved? Did I give, receive, refuse to give, or refuse to accept positive strokes? Were the strokes conditional or unconditional? What am I feeling right now? Mad, glad, sad, or scared? How am I structuring my time? Am I withdrawing, pastiming, ritualizing, doing an activity, playing games, or being intimate? What sort of contracts do I need to deal with this?

Establish a time period for you to check on yourself. Decide whether you want to think about this sort of thing for a week, month, year, or whatever period of time. Say to yourself something like this: "I will check on myself once a day for a month to see where I am." You can also check on yourself twice a day, six times a day, once a week, or whatever seems right to you.

When you check on yourself, ask yourself these questions, and make a check beside the appropriate answer.

What ego state have I just been using?

Parent

Adult

Child

What was the transaction I just had?

Parent to Parent

Parent to Adult

Parent to Child

Adult to Parent

Adult to Adult

Adult to Child

Child to Parent

Child to Adult

Child to Child

How do I experience myself and the other after the transaction?

I'm OK—you're OK

I'm OK—you're not OK

I'm not OK—you're OK

I'm not OK—you're not OK

How were strokes handled in the transaction?

I gave positive conditional strokes.

I gave positive unconditional strokes.

I received positive conditional strokes.

I received positive unconditional strokes.

I gave negative conditional strokes.

I gave negative unconditional strokes.

I refused to give positive conditional strokes.

I refused to give positive unconditional strokes.

I refused to give negative conditional strokes.

I refused to give negative unconditional strokes.

I refused to accept positive conditional strokes.

I refused to accept positive unconditional strokes.

I refused to accept negative conditional strokes.

I refused to accept negative unconditional strokes.

What am I feeling right now?

Mad

Glad

Sad

Scared

What do I want right now?

Write something about this in a log of some sort, and give the date.

How am I structuring my time?

Withdrawing

Ritualizing

Pastiming

Doing an activity

Playing Games

Being intimate

A Not-OK Checklist

If I am feeling not OK, am I feeling not OK because of something that has recently happened, such as receiving negative strokes or failing at something, or am I feeling not OK for no apparent reason? If I feel not OK, what do I need to do to feel OK and be successful?

Write down what it is you need to do to feel OK or be successful.

Does your script give you permission to feel OK and be successful? If not, what sort of permissions do you need to get around script injunctions that are sabotaging you?

Write down what script permissions you need, if you need any.

How can you get the permissions you need if your script is holding you back?

Add It Up

When you decide you have spent as much time as you want to spend on this exercise checking on yourself and have made enough checkmarks, count them. How many total checks have you made for each question? Then count how many checks you have for each possible answer for each question. Then divide the number of checks for each possible answer by the total checks for the question. This will give you a percentage for each possible answer. These percentages will tell you approximately what percentage of the total time (your waking hours) you spend in various ego states, what percentage of your transactions are Adult to Adult (or whatever), what percentage of your strokes are positive or negative or conditional or unconditional, and so on.

Calculating these percentages will give you a profile that will enable you to better understand how you interact with others and how you come across in social situations. You can gain more certainty about the correctness of the percentages if you ask people who know you well if they agree with the percentages.

Analyzing the Data

Do you need to change something about your transactional profile? How can you know whether you need to change something about your profile? How much time, energy, and money would it take to change something about your transactional profile, if you should decide you should change something?

If you have been as happy and successful as you want to be, why consider changing your transactional profile? You already have what most people want. It seems to me that if you have been as happy and successful as you want to be, the only possible reason you might want to change your transactional profile would be that for some reason, you think the environment around you is changing in such a way that your previous successful transactional pattern will no longer yield happiness and success. Your company might be taken over, and you might get a new boss who wants different ego states and transactions with subordinates. Something like this might happen.

On the other hand, if you have not been as happy and successful as you would like, it is possible that changing your transactional profile might enable you to be happier and more successful. In this event, you need to think about the specific events that seem to be causing your unhappiness and lack of success. There are thousands of possible problems that cause people to be unhappy and unsuccessful. It is easy to focus on irrelevant problems. You should focus on those problems that are relevant to your specific case.

Many personality problems, thought problems, or emotional problems are not easy to solve. They may have evolved over a long period of time and are due to script messages and script decisions made over a long period of time. It is difficult to predict how very young children will respond to script messages, since they have not learned the rules of logic and lack sufficient experience to know whether any specific message is right or wrong. Regardless, once they incorporate certain programs and messages in their scripts, they develop behavior, feeling, and thinking patterns that tend to remain relatively stable, often throughout life. Such patterns are not easy to change. It may be that the logical choice is to simply accept yourself and others around you as best you can for what you and they are, regardless of what they decided caused them to be what they are.

One of the complexities of human affairs is that humans must not only discover and diagnose problems but they must also decide whether the problems are worth solving. Whether a problem is worth solving depends on the determination, willpower, intolerance, energy, intelligence, ambition, understanding, wisdom, physical health, age, marital status, and a host of other characteristics of the individual. Only you can decide whether many non-health-related problems are worth solving. When people get physically sick, they generally know they are sick. Most people are able to diagnose what is wrong with them. If you have a rash, you know it is a rash. If it does not go away, you consult a dermatologist and get some cream to control it. If you find yourself going to the bathroom much more than you should, you consult a doctor to see if you have diabetes, and so on. But personality-caused problems are different. If you find yourself always getting caught up in personality conflicts with your coworkers, there is probably something wrong with your personality. You probably play too many Games and cross too many transactions. Or you may be laying your feeling rackets on people around you. Or it could be any number of things. The point is that you can live a long time with many personality problems, even if they cause you to get fired over and over again. Whether you should change most of them is up to you.

You can change some personality problems simply by changing your transactional profile. You can establish contracts to use less Parent, or less Child, or more Parent or Adult, or whatever. There are things you can do or say or not do or say with certain people to get out of transactions with them in a more I'm OK—you're OK position.

You can contract with yourself to do the following:

- Use more or less Parent, Adult, or Child energy.
- Engage in more or less of the transactional combinations (Parent to Parent, Parent to Adult, Parent to Child, Adult to Parent, Adult to Adult, Adult to Child, and so on).
- Increase or decrease the number of your waking minutes you spend in withdrawing, ritualizing, pastiming, doing activities, playing Games, or engaging in intimacy.
- Do and say certain things with certain people at specific times that will enable you to maintain an I'm OK—you're OK attitude, and encourage them to have the same attitude toward you.

Check your feelings to see whether you are experiencing a natural mad, glad, sad, or scared feeling based on the circumstances or whether you are caught up on a feeling racket in which you are reincarnating feelings you felt in the past in similar circumstances, which may have been inappropriate at the time but which are certainly inappropriate in the present. You can contract to express appropriate feelings in appropriate ways.

You can contract with yourself to do whatever it is that will make you happy and successful so long as it is legal and does not cause harm to you or others. If you can't do it, you are setting unrealistic goals or sabotaging yourself in some way, possibly because of script injunctions that subconsciously tell you not to do what you consciously want to do.

Achievable goals are goals that you have Parent permission to achieve, have Adult ability to achieve, and have Child desire to achieve. In other words, if your Parent gives you permission to do it, if your Adult has the intelligence and ability to do it, and if your Child really wants to do it, chances are, you will do it. Conversely, if your Parent does not want you to do it, if your Adult does not know how to do it, and if your Child does not want you to do it, chances are, you won't do it.

Goals that are written down are probably more likely to be achieved than those that are not written down. Assuming you want to achieve you goals, it will help to write them down in a diary, log, notebook, or whatever.

Knowing Yourself

It seems to me that it is easier to know what you have Adult ability to do than it is to know what you have script permission to do and what you really want to do. I think most people have a pretty good idea about what they are good at and what they are not good at. Some people are good at math, and others are not. Some take to music, and others do not. Some are good readers and writers, and others are not. Some people can paint pretty pictures or write interesting stories, and others cannot. Some people can grow beautiful flowers, crops, and other plants, and some cannot. Some people can build square, defect-free houses, and some cannot. If you are not good at something, it may be that you just never tried to be good at it, didn't work at it, and so on. On the other hand, it may be you just don't have much natural ability for it.

I think success is a function of learning what you are good at and working hard and long at doing it. If you do what you are good at and work hard and long at doing it, you should be successful—if you do not have a script that psychologically prevents you from being successful or happy doing what seems natural. If you do have such a script, you can change it by doing an unnatural thing. You can enlist the help of a good psychotherapist to get permission to circumvent your psychological injunctions.

Use of the TA Profile

Once you get your TA profile developed, you can decide whether to change specific aspects. People cannot just up and decide to—presto—"get OK." Specific things must be worked on. This invites OKness. OKness is more or less a by-product of rational transacting in life. Rational transacting involves not only knowing where you are coming from and being aware of your profile; it also involves being aware of the other's transactional profile.

Assuming you have a perfectly OK TA profile, if you are not aware of where others are coming from, they can put you in not-OK positions. When someone cons you and cheats you out of money due to your ignorance of what that person was doing to you, you will experience some not OKness. By the same token, people can cheat you out of strokes and reduce your OKness. No matter how OK you are, you still have to defend yourself from the not OKness of others from time to time. The better you can "see what is really going on" with others in terms of their transactional patterns, the stronger your defenses will be, since you will be in a better position to take appropriate action to preserve your own OKness.

At the same time, a knowledge of your and others' transactional patterns will enable you, even when defending yourself, to help put your attacker in a more OK place than otherwise would have been the case. A good article to read on this is "Options" (1971), by Steve Karpman, MD. In this article, Karpman discusses his concept of "Verbate," which rhymes with *Karate*. "Verbate" is the "verbal art of self-defense."

Contracting for Change-Inviting OKness

A contract for change does not have to be elaborate or detailed. It is simply an agreement to do something. A person can contract with himself or herself to do something for himself or herself, or a person can contract to do something for someone else for something in return. In most cases, regarding transactional patterns of your own that invite not OKness in your classes, you will be contracting with yourself to make changes. Based on your transactional profile, you may now be aware of some not-OK transactional patterns you have been acting out. The following is a sample contract format that you can use to write down your contracts.

I, ________________, hereby contract to________________________________

____

by the ___________day of the month of _____________in the year___________.
If I do not fulfill this contract, since I have decided with my Child that I want to do it, decided with my Adult that I can do it, and decided with my Parent that I should do it, it will be because I have sabotaged myself by doing the following things in the following manner:

____

____

I and others will know I have executed the terms of this contract, because of the following tangible achievements in terms of creativity and production, impact on my environment, change in the way I relate to others, or change in the way I take care of my own needs:

____

____.

Signed this __________ day of __________in the year of __________.

Signed,

____

Some of the basic ideas for the above contract were taken from "Steps for Developing and Implementing Problem-Solving Contracts" (1974), by Graham Barnes.

Common classroom sabotages for teachers in classrooms include allowing themselves to get hooked into Games, operating from the Parent ego state too much, operating from the Adapted Child ego state too much, not setting clear learning contracts to start with, not being prepared, and so on.

I am not sure whether it is best to tell others about your contracts. If you do tell someone what you have contracted to do, pick out someone who will support you from all three of his or her ego states. Frequently, people will say from Adult that they think such and such is a good idea for you but will secretly hope from Parent or Child that you won't make it. Your Child may be aware that they don't really want you to do what you have contracted to do and may sabotage you to please the Child or Parent in himself or herself.

It is better not to tell anyone what you have contracted to do than to have the person you tell it to tell you not to make it. This phenomenon is more common than most people think. On the one hand, one would think that friends and family members would want their intimates to change for the better. On the other hand, however, since intimate relationships were established in the first place on the basis of interlocking scripts, there is a tendency for intimates to resist changes in each other in order to perpetuate the intimate relationship.

Contracting for change can be a lifetime process. Setting and achieving contracts is inherently satisfying. One of the best books I have read on the relations between goal-setting and attainment and satisfaction and happiness is *Psycho-Cybernetics: A New Way to Get More Living out Of Life* (1960), by Maxwell Maltz, MD.

You can invite OKness in your classroom by changing yourself through the contracting process. You can also invite OKness in your classroom by inviting your students to set contracts.

Getting Students to Set Contracts

It is, of course, much easier for you to set your own contracts to increase your OKness than it is to get students to set contracts to increase their OKness.

A teacher is not a therapist and should not attempt to "do therapy." But in practice, a teacher does perform functions that are therapeutic. Teachers sometimes do change the behavior of their students, if only for the time students are in their classes. Getting out the paddle changes behavior. Threatening to flunk students if they don't stop doing things, such as cutting class or sleeping in class, changes behavior. On the other hand, when students are really sad or scared because of real problems, such as deaths in families, divorces, or economic calamities, it behooves teachers to nurture such students from Nurturing Parent, providing what protection they can.

There is no way a teacher cannot do at times what therapists sometimes do and still be a genuine, loving human being. Basic good humanness requires a certain amount of supporting, nurturing, and so on in the teaching function.

On the other end of the spectrum, I do not think it is a good idea for teachers to always be "analyzing" their students and thinking up ways for students to make major personality changes, in effect playing the Game of psychiatry (Berne 1964).

Assuming you were to memorize this book and become totally convinced it is "the way," you might go to school and start applying the various TA labels to everyone you see—your fellow teachers, your students, and your administrators. Some of this is OK and inevitable. On the other hand, if you go around telling people, "You're playing Games," "You sure do like to come on Parent," "You're playing 'stupid,'" "You're a NIGYSOB player," or "Why do you always operate out of your Adapted Child?" for example, you will almost inevitably set up the Game of psychiatry.

Since others most likely will not know the TA words you have memorized, if you throw them around, you, in effect, will come across as a Persecutor. The people you apply them to will probably see themselves, perhaps correctly, as Victims of whatever you have in mind, which they, of course, will not be able to understand. You will be coming from an I'm OK—you're not OK position. In the Game of psychiatry, people come across Adult socially, appearing to be concerned with correcting imperfections, but at the Parent-Child ulterior, psychological level, they are creating some drama strokes for themselves and enjoying the inherent Persecuting or Rescuing.

The way not to play psychiatry is, first of all, to be sure when you decide to correct some ill or imperfection that you are doing it for technical, Adult reasons. In the classroom, the technical, Adult reason to correct imperfections and ills is to make sure the Adult learning contract is fulfilled. Where I am, as a teacher, you have the right and responsibility to confront students about their feeling, thinking, and behavior problems that are undermining their and your learning contract. On the other hand, you do not have a right to intervene in their natural evolution, which does not affect the learning contract. Assuming they fulfill the contact, students have a perfect right to grow up to be whatever they want to be, assuming they stay within the bounds of the law.

Should you teach your students some TA words? As far as I am concerned, this is OK. If your students know basic terms such as *Parent*, *Adult*, *Child*, *Game*, *Script*, and so forth, when you do talk with students regarding not-OK behavior that is detrimental to the learning contract, you can use some TA words and get your meaning across more clearly and efficiently. One term you will want to teach for sure, if you do define or teach any TA words, is *unconditional positive strokes*.

I think it is best not to use some TA words frequently. The optimum strategy is to think with them but beam your transactional vectors across with ordinary conversational synonyms. Use your TA looking glass to see what is really going on, but use common words to tell others what you have seen. Use words and examples—the more concrete, the better—that will appeal to all ego states in whomever you are communicating with. Even when doing this, you need to watch setting up the Drama Triangle.

Assuming it is obvious a student is a heavy Game player of some sort, should you tell the student in private that he or she is a such-and-such Game player? In general, I don't think you should, especially with younger students. It might be OK at times to tell such students that they are "playing Games" and that you want them to stop, but I still don't think it is a good idea to label the specific Games, such as "kick me," "stupid," "do me something," "so what?" "gee, you're wonderful, Professor," or whatever it is the student is playing. It might be OK to label "OK, I'll read it," since this Game is so especially relevant to the learning contract.

I think it is wise for teachers to use more Adult than Parent or Child in one-on-one conferences with students regarding problems. I think the teacher should be straight regarding the feedback he or she gives. In appropriate words, the teacher can tell the student how he or she really sees what is going on. Words like "I don't like what you are doing," "This is what I see you doing," "I want you to stop," and so on are OK.

One of the most important things to remember in dealing with problem students is to separate the behavior from the person. It is OK to see and define specific feelings, thoughts, and behaviors as not OK. It is not OK, however, to define the student as a not-OK human specimen.

Inviting the problem student to do something or stop doing something to further the learning contact is OK. Asking, "Will you establish a contract to start or stop doing such and such?" will work. In many cases, once the student sees that his or her ulterior moves have been detected in a one-on-one conference, he or she will agree to accept your contract from all three ego states. Sometimes, however, they will accept, but only from one or two ego states. The unaccepting ego states may sabotage the contract. In any case, using the contract procedure is better than saying, "If you don't stop or start doing such and such, I'm going to send you to the principal's office."

Most of the contracts you invite your students to establish will be unwritten. You will give the invitation in a matter of seconds, perhaps at recess or casually as students come or go from the room. At times, you will want to call them into a private office. The acceptance will usually be given quickly. "Yes, I will."

It's no big deal. In general, this is all there is to it. On the other hand, you can invite your students to write down their contracts according to some format, as I have invited you to do. But what happens if your OKness invitations are not accepted? What happens if you should have a -3 not-OK monster in your class, a chronically I'm OK—you're not OK/the school's not OK/the world's not OK type who ignores all of your positive efforts and constantly attempts to make a fool out of you and undermine your effectiveness?

In general, I think students such as the above should be separated from normal classrooms and placed with people who are trained and skilled to treat problem students. Otherwise, the learning contract for all students will be threatened to some degree. Parents should be informed of the not-OK behavior.

If the problem student simply refuses to learn or participate but does not interfere with the learning of other students, and if all OKness invitations have been ignored, then the teacher has little or no alternative left but to flunk the student. The student should be held back, flunked out of school, or whatever is done to this type of student in various systems. Socially passing students when they don't learn the material is a social ill. This discounts the material, the teacher, the student, and the value of learning itself. Therefore, the way to invite OKness with students who obstinately refuse to learn is to grade them according to what they have learned and call the shots as they are.

I think it is important to bear in mind that Games, while they are unstraight and devious, and while they do cause some disruption and inefficiency in learning situations, are serious attempts on the part of human beings to get basic needs met, which is a positive act.

If learning situations were totally De-Gamed, some students and trainees would be deprived of strokes they could have gotten through Games. In such case, some students will need to be taught how to get strokes and needs met in other ways. School and training systems might consider providing structures outside of regular classrooms that have as a basic purpose providing unconditional positive strokes. On the other hand, in regular classrooms, the learning contract is the main objective.

The Learning Contract

Class, Grade, etc.________________

Period: from ______________20____to______________20______________.

Subject material to be taught/learned________________________________
____
____
____

Teaching methods to be used.______________________________________
____
____
____

Testing methods to be used.______________________________________
____
____
____

Policies:

Tardiness____
____
____
____

Absences______________________________

Talking in Class______________________________

Gum chewing______________________________

Smoking______________________________

Other______________________________

Students' responsibilities for homework assignments________________

Teacher's responsibilities in class (lecturing, facilitating discussions, etc.)

Students' responsibilities in class (note taking, orally participating, nonverbally participating, etc.)__________________________________

Basic time-structuring pattern (percent of time generally to be spent on withdrawal, rituals, pastimes, Games, activities, and intimacy)________________

Means of seeing whether the contract is being fulfilled (observation, tests, De-Gamer, etc.)____

Rewards/penalties for contract performance/nonperformance______________

Things that might sabotage the contract (Games, using too much Parent, Adapted Child, etc.)____

Personal contracts (both teacher's and students' contracts for dealing with the things that might sabotage the learning contract)________________________

Inviting The System to Increase OKness

OKness in the learning environment is a function of students, teachers—and the system. Systems, like people, populate an OKness continuum. Some systems are –1 (very not OK), and some systems are +1 (very OK). Most systems fall somewhere in between.

What kind of a system am I talking about? I am talking about a system of people in an administrative hierarchy. In any administrative hierarchy, some people have more authority than others, as well as more responsibility. A chain of command exists wherein individuals must report to and be evaluated by certain superiors.

People in positions of higher authority usually have more impact on the OKness of a system than people in lower positions. All top leaders are not equally influential. Some leaders impose their will on almost everyone in one way or another in their systems; other leaders (perhaps effective ones) are rarely seen or felt. The effectiveness of a leader is a function of both what he or she does and what he or she does not do. If the right things are thought, felt, and done (or not felt, thought, or done) by higher leaders, the system will be more OK than otherwise.

I published an article in the July 1979 issue of the *Transactional Analysis Journal* titled "The Chain of Ego States" in which I pointed out some interesting aspects of human systems. I have reprinted a diagram I termed the Chain of Ego States in Figure 28.

The Chain of Ego States points out that, since all superiors and subordinates have three ego states, messages are transmitted from all three ego states. These messages flow up and down and across the organizational chains of command, which, I point out in the article, are three in number: the Parent chain of command, the Adult chain of command, and the Child chain of command.

Most of the Parent and Child messages of the Chain of ego states are derived from the personal life scripts of leaders. Therefore, it follows that the living or dead ancestors of a leader may actually have more influence in a system than anyone now involved.

Whether a system is OK or not depends upon whether the system does what the sign on the door says. The sign on the doors of schools and training facilities says Education and Training. If the energy of the system is primarily forcing students, trainees, teachers, trainers, and administrators to conform to Parent or Child organizational script messages, then the system is less OK than it might be.

The way to change not-OK systems into OK systems is to focus the attention of the system's leaders and members upon doing what the sign on the door says and encourage more communication on the Adult chain of command. Some Parent script messages or commands in organizations are OK if they are means to the end. It is OK to work hard, for example, if working hard does not get in the way of learning in learning environments. The important thing is to learn, not do busy work. In other words, doing what you have an Adult contract to do is more important than doing anything, or being anything, which I have listed as Parent messages in Figure 28. As you can see, many of the Child messages in Figure 28 are limiting and handicapping. Parent messages can also be limiting and handicapping, especially those based on biases and prejudices regarding physical characteristics and personality factors.

In not not-OK systems, people are sometimes hired and fired or given good grades or poor grades depending upon whether they conform to the Parent and Child messages of the Chain of Ego States. Over time, as people in NOT not-OK systems are sluiced, only certain scripty types remain, and the organizational script gets solidified. These organizations are the most difficult of all to change.

Since most leaders and members of most organizations have not read my "Chain of Ego States" article and have not learned TA, quite naturally, they are unaware of the Chain of Ego States. One way to increase the OKness of systems is to invite leaders and members of the system to create their own Chain of Ego States diagrams, with messages peculiar to their systems. Most people, once they become aware of these phenomena, can see they exist in their systems. Once leaders and members get in Adult touch with the Parent and Child commands of their systems, they can be invited to think about where the messages came from.

Creating awareness of these messages may help cause the originators and perpetuators of NOT not-OK Parent and Child commands to stop placing them on the organizational chains of command.

I do not have space in this book to discuss in any detail organizational analysis and development. I would like to say, however, that there are many people in this country, (yours truly included) who consult in this area. If you or some leader or member of your system would like to learn more about organizational analysis and development, you can write me at the address printed on the cover copyright page of the book.

Unfortunately, in some systems, teachers and trainers are forbidden to establish good, Adult learning contracts because of irrational Parent and Child commands flowing on the organization's Chain of Ego States. That being the case, before learning in such systems can be greatly improved, the originators or perpetuators of the not-OK script messages must change or be changed.

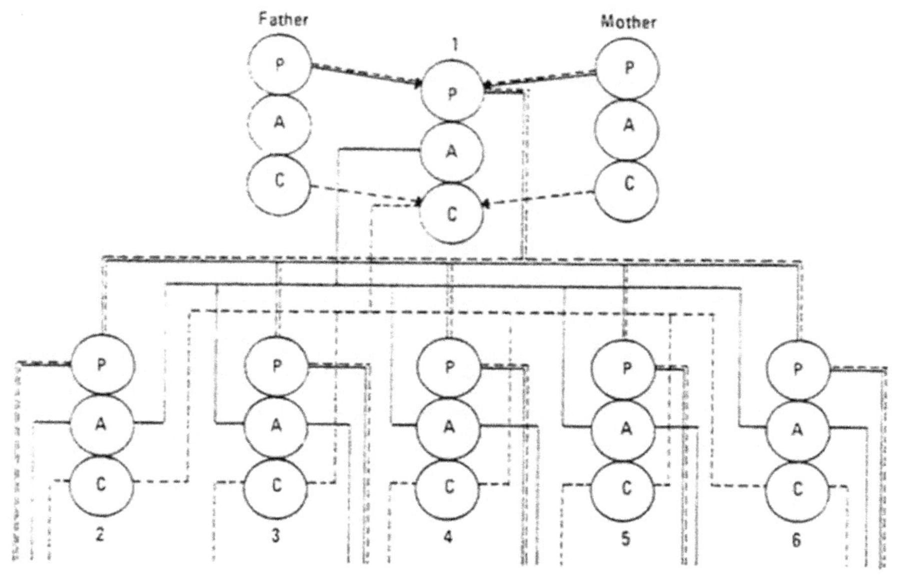

Figure 28.
THE CHAIN OF EGO STATES—A P--A--C Chain of Command Organizational Script Matrix.

PARENT CHAIN OF COMMAND MESSAGES: Be productive. Work hard. Make money. Be strong. Hurry up. Be firm. Be slow. Be pompous. Be polite. Be serious and reverent. Be silly and irreverent. Walk fast. Use emphatic hand gestures. Make small talk. Don't violate the chain of command. Go through channels. Be attractive. Be unattractive. Be short. Be tall. Look harried. Please me. Be perfect. Make the organization look good. Use innocuous, euphemistic words. Take your glasses off, and point with them. Wear a pinstriped suit. Dress nicely. Drive a Buick Electra. Play golf. Drink scotch. Cross your legs nonchalantly. Stroll coolly. Have another beer. Have some wine. Don't wear a tie or dress nicely. Go bowling with the guys/gals. Ride a bicycle. Get a Toyota. Be a nice gal/guy. Act/be old/young.

ADULT CHAIN OF COMMAND MESSAGES: Hiring costs are $100; firing costs are $97. We need 1,000one thousand more units a month to keep up with the present sales rate. Enrollment increased/decreased X percent. X percent of our students /trainees report back that our teaching/training was beneficial to them. X percent of our students think they learn valuable, relevant learning in our classes/courses/programs.

CHILD CHAIN OF COMMAND MESSAGES: Don't think. Don't feel. Don't be powerful. Don't feel what you feel, feel what I want you to feel. Don't be close. Don't be you, be what I attribute you to be. Don't belong. Don't be well or sane. Don't be sexual. Don't be intelligent. Don't be imaginative. Don't make it. Don't feel glad. Don't learn. Don't achieve. Don't grow up. Don't be energetic and confident. Don't be spontaneous.

Organizational change can come about by the script message originators and perpetuators simply deciding to clean up their acts. On the other hand, in some cases, therapy may be desirable. In some cases, unfortunately, the script originators or perpetuators must be replaced. In most systems, teachers and trainers must generally accept what is communicated on the Chain of Ego States. Sometimes, it is best to move to another, more OK, system.

Like it or not, reality has it that in most organizations, that subordinates must be adaptable and flexible to succeed and get ahead. This entails being able and willing to adapt one's group imago (i.e., his or her basic conception of how to run an organization) to suit the group imago of her or his boss up the chain of command—and being able and willing to flex his or her personality to suit the personality of the boss. In general, it's the boss's way or the highway in most organizations, especially in corporations, where cronyism is generally rampant in the upper echelons.

A Winner's Perspective

Classical TA game and script theory indicates that people are destined for certain outcomes in life by what happens to them and what they decide in their early years. Berne (1972) developed a life script formula:

> Early parental influence → Programming → Commitment → Important behavior → Payoff.

Early parental influence and programming include rackets, Games, script messages, feelings, teachings, and specific rules and procedures taught and learned in the family of origin and in the larger environment, including the families of friends, neighbors, and relatives. People may not decide to accept all of the early parental influence and programming, but they will accept some of it, which becomes a commitment, determining good and bad behavior and payoffs.

Where negative script payoffs are involved, TA can become a gloomy, heavy, depressing discipline, partially deserving, perhaps, of the sometimes-applied phrase "that TA crap." In some respects, TA provides crap models—models that clearly illuminate the dark, sinister, pessimistic side of life. TA did not create the crap, but TA can be used to shine a spotlight on the crap, making it seem that more crap exists than good stuff.

Are some people doomed by their family scripting, their early decisions, or their subconscious minds? Are some people doomed to live lives of misery, anger, guilt, fear, or depression? The unsatisfactory answer is that yes, this is more or less true of some people if left in a state of nature. By a state of nature, I mean they are left largely uninfluenced by various educational sources that have the power to bring about a change in the process. But the process itself is not completely hard, either, even given the state of nature assumption.

No doubt, some people do make more or less spontaneous changes in their personalities. Given today's knowledge, there is no reason for anyone to be doomed by poor scripting and early decisions. Therapy and support are available to help prevent loser script outcomes. There is no technical reason why anyone should not be a winner in life.

One of the problems many people have is holding on to old hurts, anger, guilt, and fear that they have experienced with parents. Some people blame their parents for their poor lives. This helps ensure that their quality of life will remain poor, since they then feel justified in not doing anything to make their lives better. Such people sulk and pout their way through their whole lives, almost continually feeling angry, fearful, or guilty about what they did or didn't get from their parents.

It is true that many people have not had and do not have adequate parents and that some people had and have parents who are basically loving, caring, competent and brave. But this is a fact of life. No amount of ranting or railing or sulking or pouting will change the fact. Life is still not fair for all people.

Harry Boyd (1976) makes a clear distinction between "responsibility" and "blame." I think this is a good distinction for all of us to make. While it may be true that some parents are responsible for the poor life script payoffs of their offspring, they are not to blame. Parents were also once children, and whatever scripts they passed on to their children were probably passed on to them by their parents and so on, back into history. Several generations may be responsible but not to blame.

As Harry Truman was fond of emphasizing, the buck has to stop somewhere. In order for things to get better, a winner must "own" responsibility for his or her own life, regardless of the early parental influence and programming. The winner decides to "let go" of the not-OK early parental influence and programming and stops using this material to run his or her life. The Adapted Child is put on the back burner, so to speak.

Harry Boyd (1978) has developed a useful diagram that combines both structural and functional aspects of ego states and illuminates this.

According to Boyd, there is no such thing as a truly "natural" Child ego state. From the moment birth, people are subjected to civilizing pressures from parents. Thus, Boyd asserts, even the C_1 is part of the Adapted Child ego state. The A_1 and the P_1 are also part of the Adapted Child—that is, the part of the Child that adapted to parental pressure. On the other hand, Boyd asserts there is a "Free Child" element in the C_2, as shown in Figure 29.

The Free Child is a part of the C_2, which can be spontaneous and Game-free in the here and now, irrespective of the early parental influence, programming, and commitment. Thus, there is the possibility an individual can become successful and happy, despite a depressing script.

What winners who have poor scripts do is shut down or ignore the Adapted Child, which contains Game behavior, and learn to operate from Free Child and the A_2 and P_2. This is not easy and may require therapy or outside intervention, but it can be done. It is a relatively simple matter to reprogram the A_2 and P_2 with rational data, knowledge, skills, and so on through ordinary teaching and training facilities. As Muriel James and Dorothy Jongeward (1973) point out in the title to a popular TA/Gestalt book, people are born to win. Various techniques are available to reparent the Parent ego state.

De-Gaming learning processes and motivating learners are not trouble-free procedures. Some pressure and tension are created by deciding not to play Games. But these negative effects are less than the negative effects of allowing Games to dominate the learning process. Students and employees don't learn the subject material and skills they are supposed to learn when Games are being played.

Allowing Games to go on in learning situations tacitly reinforces non-winner behavior. De-Gaming learning situations deprives some students and employees of the opportunity to get some basic hope- and fear-type Adapted Child needs met. By refusing to play Games, the teacher or manager cannot be the perfect Parent the Game players want, and some disappointment is inevitable. But not playing Games also encourages learners to be real winners.

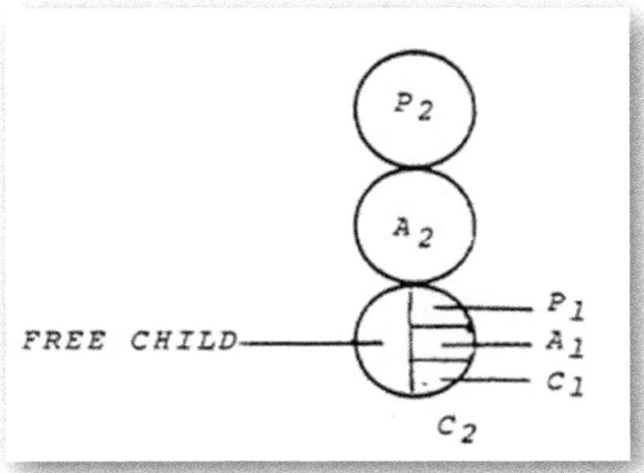

Figure 29. The Free Child.

A degree of toughness is required. Students who have been involved in Games in class occasionally come by my office to talk things over. They know that things are not going well for them in class and that their Games have been detected. In most cases, the long-standing frustration, grief, sadness, helplessness or whatever behind the Games comes out. In some cases, the students shed real tears. Part of the emotion behind the tears is relief that the Game has been detected by another human being and will not bring on the usual payoff.

I do not do therapy with students. I stay in Adult. Out of the one hundred or so cases of students who wanted to talk about their Games in my office, not one has regressed or become irrational. Most of these talks ended I'm OK—you're OK. In almost all cases, the student did better in his or her classwork after the talk in my office about the Game.

Transactional analysis and other scientific approaches to human understanding teach that feeling, thinking, and behavior forms, problems, and outcomes have identifiable causes. Time, money, and energy are normally required to ferret out the causes and to ta and take corrective action. While we humans still have more questions than answers about our existence, we are still learning, and the sum total of our knowledge is increasing.

It is possible in the future that all people may be able to think and feel for themselves, express their thoughts truthfully, set their own goals, determine their own legal and ethical behavior patterns, and be winners.

I take the view that human life is an ongoing experiment. A reading of history shows that humans have not been able to discover, develop, and implement a set, permanent configuration of thoughts, behavior, policies, rules, strategies, institutions, and technology for living life.

Feelings in human affairs, however, probably have not changed. The basic feelings—mad, sad, glad, and scared—remain the same from one decade, century, or millennium to another. They are therefore precious, a way of relating to all mankind in all time.

On my pilgrim's journey in life, given the trials and experiments I have been exposed to and have conducted, I have come to think that what I have written in this book is relevant. It is altogether possible that some years down the road, I will come to decide that what I wrote in this book in 1979 and 2015 was wrong and perhaps should not have been written at all.

We continually take action without being fully informed with facts or educated enough with decision models. We continually run the risk—if we decide or do anything—of being wrong. We may win, we may lose, or we may neither win nor lose but gain experience. Given this, we always need qualities such as unconditional courage, faith, hope, and love.

Eleven

Summary And Conclusions

I was thirty-eight years old when I wrote most of the first ten chapters of this book. I made a few revisions here and there recently and a professional editor, Maria, at Create Space, performed a line edit for all chapters, except this one, making hundreds of technical changes; but the content and wording of the writing in the first ten chapters is pretty much like it was in 1979 when it was first published in *De-Gaming Teaching and Learning.* I also appreciate Maria's advice and suggestions regarding the overall flow, tone, and content of *Born to Learn,* helping me decide to cut out three new chapters I had written and use this one instead.

I am now seventy-five years old, having been retired from university teaching ten years. My health has held up fairly well, although my memory is not as good as it used to be. I am not as idealistic as I used to be, but I have not given up on the human race. This chapter will give you a sample of how I am functioning now as a thinker and writer, relative to how I functioned at age thirty-eight in the first ten chapters.

ITAA Conferences and Workshops

Through the years I participated in TA conferences conducted by the International Transactional Analysis Association in places around Earth like

Chapel Hill, North Carolina, USA; San Francisco, California, USA; Stamford, Connecticut, USA; Chicago, Illinois, USA; Calgary, Alberta, Canada; Halifax, Nova Scotia, Canada; Zurich, Switzerland; Utrecht, Holland; and Edinburgh, Scotland.

Probably the most memorable ITAA conference was the last one I attended, in 2005, in Edinburgh, in the continuing education facilities of Heriot-Watt University, the year I retired from university teaching. I participated there in a workshop conducted by Gianpiero Petrigleiri, MD, a former president of the ITAA, from Italy, now a professor of organizational behavior at INSEAD in France, one of the best business schools around Earth, ranked 10th in the world by the *Economist* magazine in a recent issue, using his case he had written involving a student of his when he was a visiting professor at the University of Copenhagen, using a case method discussion process similar to mine.

I participated in a workshop for TA writers conducted by Anne de Graaf, an organizational consultant in the Netherlands, and a member of the Board of Trustees of the ITAA, who had recently published a new TA book titled *Einstein and the Art of Sailing: A New Perspective on the Role of Leadership.* Participating in these workshops were several long-term TA organizational experts, including Abe Wagner, of Denver, Colorado, USA, the author of a best-selling TA book titled *Say it Straight or You'll Say it Crooked.* Abe has been delivering speeches to large groups of corporate employees around Earth using ideas in this book for over 30 years.

Gianpiero Petriglieri and his colleague Jack Wood in their *Transactional Analysis Journal* article "Transcending Polarization: Beyond Binary Thinking" (2005), integrating transactional analysis, Jungian psychology, Hegelian dialectics, some of the philosophy of Betrand Russell, and some recent findings and ideas of LeDoux (1994, 1996), have provided new insight into organizational processes and problems. They point out humans are neurologically wired in their brains to process new stimuli either by thinking or feeling as electrical impulses flow through the brain as a result of seeing, hearing, or feeling something outside their heads, and people may react to new objects, information and ideas rationally and/or emotionally in appropriate and beneficial ways or in destructive and unproductive ways. Conflicts and differences naturally develop. The ideal approach is to work them out through dialectical discussion. One person has an idea, another disagrees. Assuming people say what they think and believe not playing Games these disagreements can be resolved through dialectics. One person's thesis is contested by another person's antithesis so as to develop a synthesis everyone can live with. Unfortunately the dialectical process often does not work because people become polarized in their theses and antitheses. Such polarizations get set in concrete as dogmas, doctrines, and the like resulting in either/or, one or zero (1 or 0), binary thinking. One may become identified as a conservative or a progressive, a rationalist or a dogmatist, or whatever the dualist labeling combination, and the dialectic may stop, resulting in problems. The challenge is to keep the dialectical process flowing so as to continually create new emergent ideas and processes.

Anne de Graaf in his workshop, after informing us he was not a boy named Sue, Anne being a male name in Holland, pronounced *ah-nn*, said he invited readers of his book to consider themselves Einsteins sailing their small sailboats on Lake Zurich, controlling and using ego states, transactions, scripts, and time structuring patterns to deftly navigate satisfying career courses in organizations and groups.

Graham Barnes, PhD, the founder of the Southeast Institute at Chapel Hill, North Carolina, USA, attended the conference. Born a US citizen he had become also a citizen of Sweden where he lived at the time. He is a long-term clinical certified transactional analyst, a Harvard graduate, whom I first encountered at the Southeast Institute in 1975, becoming my first sponsor for my TA certification program. He attended Abilene Christian College, ACC, a Church of Christ school, at Abilene, Texas in the 1950s, unbeknownst to me, whilst I was attending Hardin-Simmons University, H-SU, also in Abilene, a Baptist college on the other side of town, on a basketball scholarship, having been reared a Methodist. Graham was awarded the Eric

Berne Memorial Award, the highest award you can get in the ITAA, at the Edinburgh conference.

Graham and I happened to coincide in Utrecht, the Netherlands in July 2002 at a world ITTA conference. He had recently finished his PhD, I assume at a Swedish university, and he wanted me to read his dissertation, which I have yet to read. I have however read his book *Justice, Love and Wisdom: Linking Psychotherapy to Second-Order Cybernetics* (1994) that among various presentations and analyses documents his experiences and achievements working with leaders in Croatia to help rebuild that country after the cultural and military explosion in Yugoslavia in the early 1990s. Graham's reading and research significantly exceed the norm achieved by most scholars. His learning forays in World 1, World 2, and World 3, have been assiduous, long and productive.

World 1, World 2, and World 3–The Content of Learning

What is it possible to know? Karl R. Popper, a philosopher, and John C. Eccles, a brain scientist, in their book *The Self and Its Brain* (1977) assert there are three worlds that one might know something about—what they call World 1, World 2, and World 3. According to Popper and Eccles (1977, p 16), "World 1 includes hydrogen and helium, the heavier elements, liquids and crystals, and living organisms; World 2 includes consciousness of self and of death, and sentience or animal consciousness; and World 3 includes works of art and science and technology, human language, and theories of self and of death."

Eric Berne, MD was caused to invent the I'm OK—You're OK conceptualization with the four life positions, I+You+, I+You-, I-You-, and I-You+, and Martin Groder, MD was caused to invent the OK diagram with five dimensions, I+-, You +-, We +-, They +-, and It+-. Both diagrams reflect the subjective OKness of individuals, organizations, and groups, that is, OKness as they perceive it, based on cause-effect chains determining their positions.

Subjective OKness as perceived by individuals exists for individuals, organizations and groups around Earth in various relationships in various degrees. The same is not true for TA variables such as ego states, transactions, strokes, scripts, Games, and time structuring patterns. Some of us think they objectively exist. Some critics argue TA variables cannot be observed, much less measured by an objective observer. Probably the most common criticism of TA through the years was it's too simplistic and is too reductionistic. Perhaps the most damning criticism of TA is that it reifies metaphors into concrete phenomena, creating distortions of reality. At the same time, most people who know anything about TA will concede a major strength of TA is it makes complex psychological processes more understandable for laypeople. I overheard a middle aged female member from India at the Edinburgh conference tell another female member in the hall between sessions, "All TA is doing is helping people be happier frogs."

One can build the case OKness with respect to TA and the ITAA is inherently subjective, being dependent on the eye, feelings and opinions of the beholder. I am convinced I can observe subjective OKness, ego states, transactions, Games, scripts and time structuring patterns in people and I can gauge subjective OKness in others with some ordinal accuracy in a quasi-objective way, as I pointed out earlier in this book, giving me more ability than most to "see where people are really coming from." On the other hand, it's a fact TA and ITAA as brands have not fared well in terms of subjective OKness with consumers, especially in the US, since sales and customers significantly declined after 1980, implying most psychotherapy consumers consider TA and the ITAA either not-OK or not very OK.

The OKness of TA

Ted Novey published an article titled "Measuring the Effectiveness of Transactional Analysis: An International Study," (2002) in the *Transactional Analysis Journal* presenting research data and evidence showing people who had consulted psychotherapists who used TA were more satisfied with the results of their therapy than were people who had consulted psychotherapists using other psychotherapeutic disciplines, which is not necessarily a high rating for TA if most other psychotherapies are not rated highly. It seems to me most humans have received messages causing them to harbor low opinions of all forms of psychotherapeutic organizations, disciplines and techniques, caused by dogma and doctrine people were caused to learn in organizations and groups such as families, political parties, and religions.

The ITAA has always been a supporter of human rights for all humans around Earth, including lesbian, gay, bisexual, and transgender people, who are objectively caused to be what they are just like everybody else. LGBTQ people are as OK as anyone, including cisgender heterosexuals.

Based on this line of reasoning it follows all humans are equal morally, ethically and existentially, not to blame or praise for being what they are in terms of sex, age, gender, sexual orientation, intelligence, family history, education, talent, achievement, physical beauty, color, religion, profession, occupation, nationality, ethnicity, or whatever the identifying characteristic, condition, or feature might be, thanks to having been caused to be what they are by accidental or inevitable cause-effect chains.

A recurring error through the ages in my opinion is that humans blame other humans, gods and themselves for willfully causing their problems and suffering, and praise other humans, gods and themselves for willfully causing their good deeds and fortunes, when both the bad and good were accidentally or inevitably caused in natural cause-effect chains.

Something causing this error to be corrected might finally cause peace to exist on Earth.

Humans not analyzing the nature of human action and learning and being forced to conform to dogma and doctrine to survive in organizational cultures cause this error in my opinion. Learning happens when humans are caused to encounter new phenomena and experience their effects, which inevitably occurs in natural cause-effect chains. These phenomena include in my opinion feelings, thoughts and decisions that occur inside human brains and new information encountered externally in observations, conversations and written material as humans age. Natural cause-effect chains it seems to me are infinite in length or duration or they somehow accidentally started with the Big Bang.

Not to Blame or Praise

Most people are hero worshippers, foolishly admiring, idolizing, envying and fawning over beautiful, intelligent, talented, highly accomplished human beings; narcissistic rich people, movie stars, and beauty queens; and famous musicians, athletes, writers, scientists and politicians, never stopping to think they were caused to be how they are by accidental/inevitable cause-effect chains.

One can build the case all individuals, organizations and groups are existentially OK since all were caused to be what they are by accidental/inevitable cause-effect chains coursing through infinity in which they accidentally or inevitably happened to be linked. Since there are myriad infinite cause-effect chains there is no such thing as normal or natural OK conditions, features, or characteristics existing for all individuals, organizations and groups in all cause-effect chains. On the other hand, all individuals, organizations and groups are normal and natural with respect to their particular chain, since nothing other than what is was possible on that chain. What is natural for specific individuals, organizations and groups is what a particular differentiated accidental/inevitable cause-effect chain produced, and therefore one differentiated condition is as natural, and existentially OK, as another when looked at from the perspective of a theoretical objective observer observing all chains.

Unfortunately, regardless of particular conditions, characteristics or features being normal or natural as caused by cause-effect chains, individuals oftentimes find themselves in environments, organizations and groups in not-OK positions because of their natural features or conditions, forcing them to create or fake new features or conditions to get along. LGBTQ humans, for example, even today, are at risk of harm from not-OK people in certain environments, being considered not only not-OK but diabolically not-OK, as if they caused themselves to be what they are and had committed heinous crimes being what they are. The net result is their cause-effect chains require them to either take serious risks being themselves or hide their feature or identity, however unfair this might be. Unfortunatrely subjective not-OKness is, for all practical purposes, what reality is according to cause-effect chains in some places around Earth, since humans in many cause-effect chains have been caused to be relatively ignorant, mean, cruel, and vicious by doctrines, dogma, and practices they inevitably and accidentally encountered in organizations and groups.

I have discussed the question of free will at some length in my book *Business Voyages: Mental Maps, Scripts, Schemata and Tools for Discovering and Co-Constructing Your Own Business Worlds* (2011) and I have concluded free will probably does not exist, given that all events, even feelings, thoughts, wants, and decisions in humans are *caused.* Admittedly the jury is still out on this issue. If you ask Google on your computer, "Does free will exist?," you will find thousands of results, with about as many asserting it does not exist as existing. I began to think at about age twenty that free will does not exist; and I was caused to take a harder stance on the issue by the writing of A. L. Goldman, a philosopher, who pointed out in his book *A Theory of Human Action* (1970) that if all effects have causes, then feelings, thoughts, wants, decisions and the like, being effects, were caused. It seems to me if such things are caused then free will does not exist. Many people assert free will exists because humans are free to choose among alternatives, which they are, but it seems to me they are caused to choose whatever they choose by decision criteria previously caused to be stored in their memories. There is now a fair amount of neurological and brain research indicating all decisions are made subconsciously in the absence of free will.

Ludwig Wittgenstein in his book of propositions *Prototractatus* (1921) postulated, "All that happens happens by accident." He also postulated in *Prototractus,* "The case is all there is."

Can something be accidental and inevitable at the same time? Yes, depending on perspectives. What appears to be accidental can in reality be caused, resulting in what philosophers call an antinomy, a condition, feature, or phenomenon that is both A and non-A at the same time. One can build the case responsibility is such a condition. Martin Buber asserted in his book *I and Thou* (1958) that people are simultaneously responsible and non-responsible for the consequences of their decisions and actions.

The Nature of Organizational Life

Eric Berne in his book *The Structure and Dynamics of Organizations and Groups* (1963), defined success in organizations and groups as, Success = Adaptability + Flexibility, where adaptability is being willing and able to adapt one's subjective beliefs and opinions regarding how an organization or group should be run to those of the leader in control of the organization or group, however insane she or he might be, and flexibility is being willing and able to flex one's personality, that is, one's ego states, transactions, and other transactional analysis variables, to suit the leader in control of the organization or group, meaning most humans have to do a lot of faking and dissembling to survive or get ahead or get along in most organizations and groups, as caused by cause-effect chains. Hopefully this faking/dissembling phenomenon and process sooner or later will be extinguished by cause-effect chains, but organizational behavior has required faking and dissembling for millennia, causing all manner of agitations, migrations, conquests, and violence.

The alternatives to adapting and flexing to organizational leaders include arguing and reasoning with them attempting to convert them to your way of looking at things and transacting, attempting to overthrow them from within, or leaving. In most organizations it's my way or the highway (from the perspective of the leader), and most people mostly operating from Free or Rebel Child ego states are run off or sluiced out of most organizations over time, if they do not leave of what one might consider their own free will before it happens. Probably the major reason I became a university professor is that professors have to do relatively little adapting and flexing, especially after they get tenure, thanks to academic freedom in good universities. For some reason I always did like to think for myself and do my own thing.

Some successful people had to do relatively little adapting and flexing because of having been among the lucky few who accidentally and inevitably were born in cause-effect chains in which their natural ego states and scripts were useful, valued, and rewarded. If you grew up in one town and bought into the culture and stayed there, becoming what Martin Groder called a "normal" person, assuming the town culture and economy stayed intact long enough, you might not have to do much adapting and flexing to get along or be successful.

Eric Berne also asserted in his *Structure and Dynamics of Organizations and Groups* that the main task of organizational consultants was to locate agitations and cohesions among leaders and members of organizations, at the external boundaries of the organization with other organizations, and at internal boundaries between the top leader and leaders of the subsets of the organization, and between leaders and members of any subset.

Why Tenure is Necessary in Colleges and Universities

I am convinced tenure is necessary in colleges and universities to preserve and encourage intellectual honesty. Even after getting tenure many professors and administrators adapt and flex to administrators and students to get high salary raises and promotions. In the absence of tenure only a small fraction of professors in my opinion would speak truth to those in power not wanting to hear it, jeopardizing their jobs, salary raises, and promotions.

Unfortunately the main way to receive more monetary compensation than others in most universities is to get ordained as an administrator, after having been a teacher and researcher, exempted from the competitive rigors of teaching, research, and publishing, because of playing Games producing personality and political satisfactions with cronies. Once ordained as a member of the administrator caste and defined as being more OK than teachers and researchers, administrators receive larger salaries than teachers that become relatively larger year after year thanks to percentage-based raises applied to everyone. Adapted Child and Critical Parent ego states generally generate higher salaries than Adult, Free Child, and Nurturing Parent ego states in universities in the long run. Most administrators had little desire to be teachers and researchers in the first place or they were mediocre or below teachers and researchers. Administrative work is not inherently more valuable than teaching and research, nor does it require more talent, skill, and energy. Administrator salaries are higher than teacher and researcher salaries simply because administrators are granted more power in the organization by the political process, and they cause the salary checks to be written as they are. The work load per administrator has decreased in recent years as evidenced by the higher percentage of administrators relative to professors in most colleges and universities.

On the other hand, I am convinced universities are in general among the most OK organizations on Earth. Or at least they used to be.

Money has become an increasing contaminant in the last ten years. Students have been punished with tuition increases and high-priced textbooks, professors have had slim to no cost of living increases, fewer professors can get tenure, and administrator salaries have significantly increased. Football coaches and college presidents have done very well for themselves in recent years, with more and more of them receiving over one million dollars per year in salary, over ten times more than most full professors, because of adapting and flexing to rich donors and winning ball games, creating salary inequities and agitations among fellow members of their universities, assuming football coaches and presidents are actually members of their universities. Unfortunately this phenomenon shows what politicians and rich donors value most in universities, certainly not learning.

Intellectual Honesty in Public Life

To make a living in Mainstream Media (MSM) and in public life, including politics and university administration, with the exception of a few comedians who use Critical Parent and Adult ego state energy in funny, entertaining, and ironic ways, most humans have to discount real life and write, speak, and communicate in happy, entertaining ways. Indeed, one can build the case that most successful people in MSM and politics are professional players of the Game known in TA as "Greenhouse", focusing on happy, cheerful events and issues, making few truly Adult or Critical Parent ego state comments about what is really going on in reality, creating a false entertaining reality of pleasantness and happiness. They have to be experts participating in a "happiness racket", wherein people are not supposed to feel what they feel but feel happy. The script message is Don't feel what you feel, feel what I want you to feel, that is, happy, so I can earn my pay as an entertainer.

Some people say modern humans have been entertained to death, an intellectual death, caused by successful professionals engaged in a massive global happiness racket distracting people from reality itself, causing victims to focus on superficial, pleasant, and happy facts and considerations instead of understanding reality and taking action to correct problems.

Just today (January 3, 2016) I heard a couple of female professional commentators on National Public Radio discussing the fact the TV program *American Idol*, after fifteen years was shutting down. Having never seen a single episode of the program I am by no means an expert on how well the show did its job. According to the two loquacious, Barbie Doll talking commentators, it is shutting down because it was not entertaining enough. The problem, they said, was that the show format allowed contestants to get on stage who just were not "good" enough. Some of the contestants were "troubled" they said, and some were just not pleasant to watch. In other words they were dismal failures as happiness racketeers. They allowed their true feelings and attitudes to show.

What I call a Barbie Doll talking female is a generally young female who has done everything she can to make herself sound sexy and interesting with a fake accent not developed in the course of her natural development. I think this is generally called culture-free speech, or something of that nature. Loquacious males do the same thing in some cases, Ken Doll talking males, using fake accents to make themselves sound sexy and interesting, especially talking about sports as commentators on TV, apparently a coveted career-path nowadays.

I always did enjoy hearing natural accents from different parts of Spaceship Earth, such as English, Scottish, and Irish accents on BBC. After seventy-five years I still have my natural Texas accent. Most people can identify it anywhere; some sometimes confuse it with an Alabama accent. There are advantages to everyone trying to sound happy, sexy, and upbeat like everyone else, perhaps equalizing and entertaining people more, taking their minds off their troubles, but it's still fake, a low level form of Game-playing and racketeering, performed for ulterior motives using the Adapted Child ego state, designed to please Critical Parent ego states in others, casting a script message everywhere that it's not only OK to discount Adult reality and its true causes and implications, but you had better do it if you want to make it in the Adapted Child—Critical Parent make-believe Walt Disney world of MSM.

Sanders or Trump, or Barbie-like Hillary or Ken-like Marco?

It's refreshing to me to hear Bernie Sanders and Donald Trump (despite his bigotry and fascism) using their authentic accents running for US president, however not-OK Mainstream Media apparently think it is.

We shall soon see what the US culture at large thinks about the matter. Mainstream Media have been wishing and predicting all along that the Barbie-like Hillary and the Ken-like Marco will wind up the two choices on the presidential ballot this fall, after winning this year's American Idol-like presidential unreality show, having best satisfied the fantasy, entertainment, and ego needs of Adapted Child—Critical Parent, non-Adult US voters.

Maslow's Hierarchy of Needs

Regardless of the causes, one can see significant differences in OKness among individuals, organizations and groups around Earth. Some are better off than others in terms of food, clothing, shelter and medicine, and in terms of other needs, such as those postulated by Abraham Maslow in his hierarchy of needs—safety, belonging, love, esteem, and self-actualization (Maslow, 1943). For more detail regarding Abraham Maslow and his hierarchy of needs see https://en.wikipedia.org/wiki/Abraham_Maslow.

Buckminster Fuller in his book *Operating Manual for Spaceship Earth* (1969) asserted humans were continuing to learn and were evolving new systems for managing organizations and groups through what he called *synergistic* learning, which he defined as learning in a whole system not predicted by observing its sub-systems. He predicted this learning would eventually cause humans to learn how to manage their whole system, Spaceship Earth, in such a way as to humanely enable all humans to get their needs met. He thought the computer was the best hope for humanity.

Jack Dusay, MD, of San Francisco, California, a protégé of Eric Berne, a long-term certified clinical transactional analyst told me in a personal conversation in the late 1970s his research had shown if you can change the functioning and structures of organizations and groups, including families, you can change the neural wiring in the brains of people subjected to them, which can enable people to function more rationally, cohesively and productively, which is a tall order, considering you would have intervene in such a way as to add another accidental new link of causation for individuals in their natural cause-effect chains. Jack Dusay is the innovator of the Ego-Gram, a widely used process for estimating the ego state usage of individuals, described in his *TAJ* article, "Egograms and the Constancy Hypothesis," (1971).

Unfortunately there has never been any serious management of the total system of organizations and groups around Earth, including 200 or so so-called sovereign nations playing blind man's bluff attempting to improve the human affairs of their rulers, subjects and citizens at the expense of other nations in a system generally referred to as capitalism. In this regard the US has been a relative winner, having gained control of about twenty-five percent of Earth's resources through imperialistic operations around Earth through time, which it allocates, however unfairly, among about six percent of Earth's human population within the physical boundaries of the US. This dog-eat-dog management system has not only been sub-optimum but in many cases catastrophic, proving what is good for sub-systems may be disastrous for the whole. Among the many obvious defects and deficiencies of this dog-eat-dog system is its causing and allowing of obscenely unfair income and wealth inequalities among humans around Earth, with the richest ten percent of humans now controlling about eighty percent of Earth's resources and wealth, with their share increasing geometrically year after year with no end in sight. This dog-eat-dog process scripts humans to believe individuals, organizations and groups increasing their wealth without limit at the expense of others is actually moral behavior, which causes humans to become callous, cynical, apathetic and uncaring regarding the suffering of others, as it causes the whole system to become increasingly irrational, agitated and dysfunctional through time, constantly inching forward toward another all-out war.

I have covered these issues in greater detail in my book *Business Voyages,* plus I have become somewhat of an armchair political quarterback in recent years reading and writing articles in Internet journals such as the *Intrepid Report, MWC News, Counterpunch, and Consortium News*, and on my webpage at www.effectivelearning.net and my Facebook page at https://www.facebook.com/richard.stapleton.397.

The more I learn about the foreign and domestic policies of the US government the more depressed I become. We US citizens in many ways have indeed created one of the best nations in the history of mankind, a melting pot of outcasts, rejects, visionaries, rebels and entrepreneurs of older nations that led all nations in human development and progress; but we also have a tarnished and blemished record, replete with exterminating natives to steal their land; capturing, importing, and exploiting Africans as slaves on Southern cotton farms; and invading, destabilizing, and destroying other countries and governments through time to gain easy and cheap access to their natural resources. We have been as immoral in this regard as most other imperialistic, agitated, flag-waving, chauvinistic, hubristic and demented political, religious, and ethnic organizations and groups throughout human history. Whether any US president, no matter how intelligent or ethical, can do much to change the imperialistic fascist drives, instincts and vested interests of the current US military-industrial-corporate-banking-intelligence complex, or the inertia and morass of the US Congress, Supreme Court, and administrative bureaucracies remains to be seen. Most US politicians have poor comprehension of the causes of relevant management issues and problems around Earth, or could care less about them, spending most of their time and energy telling their poorly-informed credulous voters back home ideological fairy tales pandering for more campaign money and votes to get reelected.

Business and Organizational Scripts

Up to now in this book *Born to Learn* I have focused on the basic reductionistic *life* script model of TA formulated by Eric Berne, Bob and Mary Goulding, Claude Steiner and others. I discussed earlier in this book the nature of the De-gaming case method process I used in my business courses, but I have not said much about the nature of the cases I used in my courses and the nature of the scripts they contained. *Business* and *organizational* scripts are algorithmic-like sequences replete with words and phrases members have to learn to do their jobs created in the act of doing business through time by the leaders and members of organizations and groups. Scripts are the way things are done in particular differentiated organizations and departments, and employees rise and fall depending on how well they can learn, adapt to, and flex with them.

Scripts do to humans in organizations what Do and If statements do to AI computer programs and real robots, telling them what to do and say when exposed to certain types of stimuli. The employee cannot be her or himself much of the time during working hours. S/he has to follow and act out the script or scripts the organization requires. Some organizations are scriptier than others. The scriptiest business organization I ever studied was Disney World. Employees were called characters and were almost completely scripted when they were *on stage* paid to pretend they were Walt Disney characters such as Mickey Mouse wearing costumes, walking in a certain way, talking in a certain way, and saying prescribed lines during working hours. Most organizations do not script their employees to this degree, but they script them nevertheless.

High on the list of scripted organizational members and leaders are the nuns and priests of the Catholic Church. All military organizations are highly scripted. Organizational scripts are a form of artificial intelligence. Unfortunately in many cases businesses are now scripting customers. If you don't believe it just telephone a large insurance company sometime and try to do business with the AI robot on the other end of the line with a mechanical voice. You have to become a robot yourself to supply the specific numbers and information the programmed voice requires in a precise algorithmic sequence to tend to your business. Insurance companies are also outsourcing their jobs to customers, forcing customers to spend time on the Internet doing work employees used to do. Restaurants are inherently scripty businesses for employees and customers. Most require about the same words, phrases, and algorithmic physical movements for getting seated, served, eating, and paying the check.

There are hundreds of different scripts leaders and members use to do their jobs and tend to routine mundane chores of daily life in millions of differentiated organizations and groups around Earth. Most people only learn a few organizational and business scripts, depending on the types of organizations they work for during their lives. You don't have to learn that many scripts to do the same job for one business in one town all your life. The more businesses you work for in various functions at various levels in more places the more scripts you have to learn. Some scripts are better than others for certain types of businesses, organizations and business functions. I do not have space in this book to cover in any detail how business and organizational scripts relate to financial planning and control. If interested in more detail regarding this issue read my book *Business Voyages,* about 745 pages, about three dollars as an eBook at Amazon.com.

One of the best academic books I have read explaining the nature of and the necessity for business and organizational scripts is *Scripts, Plans, Goals, and Understanding*, by Schank and Abelson (1977):

> By subscribing to a script-based theory of understanding, we are making some strong claims about the nature of the understanding process. In order to understand the actions that are going on in a given situation, a person must have been in that situation before. That is, understanding is knowledge-based. The actions of others make sense only insofar as they are part of a stored pattern of actions that have been previously experienced. Deviations from the standard pattern are handled with some difficulty.
>
> . . . . Understanding, then, is a process by which people match what they see and hear to pre-stored groupings of actions that they have already experienced. New information is understood in terms of old information . . . . We will meet other bases for understanding, but we view human understanding as heavily script-based. A human understander (sic) comes equipped with thousands of scripts. He uses these scripts almost without thinking (Shank & Abelson, 1977, pp. 67-68).
>
> . . . . Understanding, then, is sometimes all plan-based, sometimes all script-based, and sometimes a mix. The main point is that in order to understand you must predict and in order to predict there must be knowledge of how events connect (Shank & Abelson, 1977, p. 78.)

What Schank and Abelson call "plan-based" understanding is determined by external data and research in the here and now using the neo-psyche, the Adult ego state. Script-based understanding is largely based on scripts stored in human brains largely involving the Parent and Child ego states. To get the right scripts in one's head it is sometimes necessary to knock the wrong scripts out. The case method is good for this, since it causes students to seriously argue against one another about which script to instantiate in which situation using the Adult, Free Child, and Nurtuiring Parent ego states.

Schank and Abelson also discussed similarities between the human scripting process and AI (artificial intelligence) programming of scripts in computers. In order to create artifical intelligence in computers humans have to first program something in a computer that the AI algorithm can compare new data it reads in against.

The best bit about the case method is that it causes students to argue back and forth among themselves in class using their Nurturing Parent, Adult, and Free Child ego states about which scripts to instantiate in which situations, which not only causes them to learn new scripts espoused by other students but to modify the scripts they came to class with. The process is dialectic. One thesis is challenged by a different thesis leading to a new synthesis that becomes a new thesis, and new learning, to be challenged later by an even better thesis, and on and on it goes in the best of human worlds, that continue to improve, not getting bogged down with dogma and doctrine to be memorized using Adapted Child and Critical Parent ego states.

During the course of my 38-year career teaching business policy and entrepreneurship in business schools I read thousands of cases containing hundreds of business and organizational scripts, not that I could do what most of them required, but I at least knew they existed because of reading the cases. I now have two light oak-stained birch plywood boxes 3' x 3' x 4' with tops on them in my Stapleton Learning Company office almost completely filled with over a thousand graded business cases and plans averaging about ten double-spaced typewritten pages written by my students through the years, each containing at least one business script the student casewriter had learned working in business before taking the course. I have also saved on my bookshelf some of the casebooks I used in my courses researched and written by business professors at Harvard, Stanford and the University of Alabama, most containing about 30 cases containing several business and organization scripts in each case. I also saved three casebooks of my own containing cases I wrote. "The devil is in the details," and there are a lot of devils in those cases piled in those plywood boxes.

My students were required to read these cases before class, even those they wrote, which were copied for discussion by all class members, and accept the draconian possibilities posed by the Classroom De-Gamer. I am convinced this process caused them to learn about business organizations and groups and the many differentiated scripts they contain and require, enabling them to know more about the business world in general than people not educated by such a process. Such a process is at first threatening and a bit scary, as students begin to learn there is a lot more out there than they had heretofore imagined; but after a semester or two discussing a case a day most students became more confident they could learn what they would need to learn to function with satisfaction in the real business world outside their home towns.

In general the most successful entrepreneurs are people who know more scripts than others and know better than others which scripts to instantiate, i.e. implement, in different situations and markets at various times.

See my article, "Academic Entrepreneurship: Using the Case Method to Simulate Competitive Business Markets," published by the Organizational Behavior Teaching Society in the *Organizational Behavior Teaching Review* (Stapleton, 1990) for more detail regarding how the De-gaming case method process worked in class.

I reprinted in *Business Voyages* several research articles published in professional journals, including the immediately above one, showing the de-Gaming case method process worked better than alternative teaching methods for teaching business policy and entrepreneurship. I am the *only* teacher I know of who has *any* quantitative longitudinal data showing his teaching methods worked better in the real world for his students than alternative teaching methods used by other teachers in the same courses, published in *Business Voyages* and in refereed professional journals and proceedings.

Unfortunately even if people today are successful in their careers or small businesses, many may have little to show for their efforts in the end if the US economy continues to unravel and deteriorate, if more and more good jobs are eliminated and shipped overseas, if jobs continue to pay less and less, if the rich continue to get richer while the poor get poorer, if aggregate demand continues to decline, if the returns on invested retirement money continue to decline, if home prices continue to fall, if Social Security is abolished or severely curtailed, if violence in socieity continues to escalate, and if other adverse trends continue.

Toward the Creation of Spaceship Earth, Incorporated

As I pointed out in my article, "Toward the Creation of Spaceship Earth, Incorporated," first published in *MWC News* (Media with Conscience) at http://mwcnews.net/focus/analysis/31023-spaceship-earth-incorporated.html, discussed earlier in this book, it seems to me there is no way to create a rational, cohesive management system for Earth as a whole so long as you have grinding poverty and chronic premature deaths in various countries around Earth. So, you have to have a system that guarantees a livable income for all Earthians. Once you do this you can begin to create systems to make life satisfying for everyone, including aggressive competitive people who must do battle against others in athletics, business, politics or whatever for satisfaction. Killing people in actual wars, however, should be outlawed and banished from Earth. My big idea in the article is that computers would basically plan, produce and distribute the basic necessities of life—food, clothing, shelter and medicine—around Earth using linear programming models. Beyond that you could have all manner of decentralized small business entrepreneurial ventures everywhere, as well as all sorts of social and therapeutic discussion groups to make life satisfying and meaningful for all, perhaps even preserving differentiated languages, religions, cultures and the like around Earth. While this idea is little more than business science fiction at present, if humans survive aboard Spaceship Earth for several more centuries, I think most likely something similar to it shall evolve.

> The upshot of this linear programming discussion is that if computers and computer programs become powerful enough, they might eventually store data in matrices for food, clothing, shelter, energy, transportation, and medicine requirements for every single human living on Planet Earth. These requirements could be summed to develop the

> total requirement for food, clothing, shelter, energy, etc. for Earth as a whole, per week, month, year, or whatever. An X_j matrix stored in a magnum computer system might contain all the various products required by humans, a B_i matrix in the linear programming formulation might contain all the types of resources available to produce the required goods, which will constrain production below some limit, an A_{ij} matrix in the LP model might contain the amount of various resources required to produce one unit of each necessity of life, or X_j, and a C_j matrix in the linear programming formulation might contain the relative utility of each alternative good, or X_j. The magnum computer system could then scientifically compute the optimum number of units of all the alternative products to produce for all humans then living on Earth. Once the goods are produced the magnum computer system could then scientifically distribute them among all humans living on Earth using another quantitative management science technique known as the transportation model to minimize transportation costs. Such a process would insure that all Earth's resources necessary to sustain human life were used in an optimum manner and were consumed fairly (Stapleton, 2011, p 635).

Linear programming based on linear algebra makes it possible to simulaneously solve a system containing any number of equations with any number of variables, assuming your computer is large and powerful enough.

The general form of the linear programming model in this case is Max C_jX_j, s.t. (subject to) $A_{ij}X_j$ <, =, or > b_i, where

C = the relative utility or value of an alternative good necessary for a healthy dignified human life,

X = the number of units of a good to be produced,

A = a matrix containing sufficient rows and columns to store the specific number of a good to be produced as constrained by a specific form of raw material required to produce the required good,

b = the total quantity of a specific raw material available for allocating among the alternative goods,

$_{j}$ = the number of possible goods to be produced and the number of columns in the A matrix,

$_{i}$ = the quantities of the different forms of raw material to be allocated to the optimum number of specific goods to be produced, and the number of rows in the A matrix.

You may remember simultaneously solving two equations with two variables in basic algebra, which is analogous to solving a matrix system with two rows and two columns. It's a bit more complicated solving a matrix system of simultaneous equations containing any number of rows and columns or equations and variables, but a computer can do it. The algorithm for the process has long been programmed. While formatting LP formulations for the production and distribution system of Spaceship Earth would be a formidable problem, having never been done before, requiring the establishment of data bases necessary to aggregate the numbers necessary to plug into the above mathematical formulation and similar formulations, it seems to me it could be done by an international scientific organization such as NASA, the US space agency. Unfortunately solving the technical problems would be easy compared to solving the political problems necessary to implement the system, caused by plain ole fear, irrationality, ignorance, greed, selfishness, unfairness, obtuseness, and callousness.

How much would such a system cost to install, maintain, and operate? I have no earthly idea, but I bet it would be much less than two hundred countries aboard Spaceship Earth now spend on their so-called military defense systems, probably over two trillion dollars per year, some six hundred billion dollars per year now being spent by the US alone on its military operating expenses.

If you want to learn more about linear programming just punch "linear programming" into Google on your computer.

The Functioning of Political Organizations

As I understand it Eric Berne, MD was convinced the ITAA should be a scientific professional organization with no political responsibilities or aspirations, leaving such considerations to citizens and politicians, limiting the scope of

ITAA activities to fostering good psychotherapy treatment and services for individuals, organizations and groups, and providing services for professionals in related fields, like a good medical doctor adhering to a Hippocratic oath with patients. His basic idea as I understand it was certified transactional analysis professionals should more or less consider irrelevant problems caused by the Four Horsemen of the Apocalypse, since they are caused by the *force majeur,* and focus on their practical professional actions that might cause people to be more rational, functional and satisfied in the here and now. If so, I am not sure this is possible for conscientious citizens of supposed democracies such as the US who happen to have become certified transactional analysts. In my case I am also an economist and a management scientist, and I cannot ignore obvious political and economic wolves at the door. I will do whatever I can to cause humans to function economically and politically more rationally and sustainably, even using Critical Parent ego state energy if it seems appropriate. See my Facebook page at https://www.facebook.com/richard.stapleton.397 for some of my articles and postings using Critical Parent energy.

It seems to me voters should use more than Adapted Child and Critical Parent energy participating in the political process. They should use their Adult ego states as much as possible to really understand the facts of problems and issues of current human affairs around Earth; and they should use their Nurturing Parent energy to decide whether policies and actions are moral, ethical, fair and just; and they should use their positive Critical Parent energy to criticize politicians and citizens who advocate and support obviously stupid, deleterious, harmful, unfair and unjust policies and actions—to hopefully cause learning aboard Spaceship Earth that might cause rational, harmonious, cohesive and satisfying human life indefinitely around Earth.

Alan "Jake" Jacobs, a certified transactional analyst out of Chicago whom I encountered at the Southeast Institute in Chapel Hill in the 1970s, a track star who tied the American collegiate 70 yard dash record (7.0 seconds) in1956, who won two NCAA silver medals in the 100 and 220 yard dashes, with best times in the 100 yard dash (9.4 seconds) and in the 220 (20.6 seconds), of Jewish descent, who had relatives gassed by the Germans at Auschwitz-Birkenau, an amateur photographer who traveled there trying to get a better feel and understanding for what went on there, taking numerous photos of the place he showed us at Chapel Hill, who was dealing with a good bit of psychological unfinished business about Auschwitz at the time, wrote a seminal article, "Aspects of Survival: Triumph Over Death and Onliness," published in the *Transactional Analysis Journal* (Jacobs, 1991), caused by his family holocaust history, research, therapy and travel. He concluded in this article what is necessary to cause human atrocities such as genocides and holocausts, in addition to causes such as a not-OK group having desires to steal the land and goods of another group having different ethnic, cultural and religious beliefs and practices, which the perpetrator group has been caused to hate over time caused by living in or near the same geographic territory causing their sense of superiority and security to be threatened, is the causation of a charismatic leader, a kind of master, or monster, who enjoys a sense of aloneness brought about by causing the deaths of many others, who attracts numerous followers and true-believers who also enjoy these feelings, facilitated by passive by-standers not necessarily enjoying these feelings, who sit back and watch it happen.

Jake pointed out in "Aspects of Survival" some 200 million humans were killed in the 20th century in genocides and democides, deaths of people caused by their own governments, most instigated and implemented by monstrously not-OK leaders such as Hitler, Stalin, Mao, Pot Pol and others, and their true-believers.

(The best time I ever had in high school in the 100 yard dash was 11.4 seconds. I did not run track in college).

We have organizations and groups in the US today advocating insane, barbaric and inhumane ideas similar to those believed and implemented by the Nazi's in Germany during World War II almost as bizarre as, and of the same order as, the abominable practices of the ISIS terrorist group of Iraq and Syria. Such groups propagate their nonsensical hate-mongering drivel on websites on the Internet and elsewhere. I am a supporter of the Southern Poverty Law Center, of Montgomery, Alabama, that takes legal action in US courts against not-OK organizations, groups and individuals when they commit hate crimes against people in the US they consider not-OK, such as African Americans, Hispanics, Jews and LGBTQ people, in schools and elsewhere. You can read articles about cases the Southern Poverty Law Center has litigated against white supremacy hate groups and others in their publications on their website at https://www.splcenter.org/. White supremacy and neo-Nazi hate groups also exist today in most countries of Europe.

Can horrors such as World War II happen again? Based on the historical frequencies of wars throughout human history, it's likely. We can only hope enough humans and their governments have learned the consequences of total all-out war are now too horrible to contemplate happening, and therefore such wars won't happen again. While some of these terrorist groups in the Middle East such as ISIS waging so-called war now might like to escalate to a total war it's probably impossible for them to develop the capability to massively bomb cities and civilians like Germany, England and the US did during World War II. But apparently they can kill, torture and raise hell for a long time, capturing and controlling small parcels of territory, running off the original inhabitants, parading around like heroes, blowing themselves and others up in suicide bombings, believing this will cause them to be rewarded in heaven beyond their wildest dreams. How long they will keep this insanity up remains to be seen.

Perhaps the biggest threat for all Earthians caused by terrorist groups such as ISIS is that one of them might somehow disable a nuclear power reactor somewhere causing a manmade Fukushima. According to Harvey Wasserman in his article in the *Intrepid Report* December 2, 2015, "Nuclear Reactors Make ISIS an Apocalyptic Threat," at http://www.intrepidreport.com/archives/16930, transmission power lines supplying power to atomic reactors in Ukraine were blown up by terrorists on or about November 30, 2015, dangerously cutting power to the reactors, which, if completely cut off for a sufficient period of time would cause coolant to be shut off for radioactive cores and spent fuel pools, causing melt-downs, causing an environmental catastrophe.

Wasserman is convinced all nuclear reactors for electric power plants around Earth should be decommissioned as soon as possible for the above reasons, to be replaced as soon as possible by solar panels, which are rapidly improving in efficiency with production costs declining rapidly, thanks to significant learning going on in this industry.

Meanwhile real nations such as Turkey, the US, Russia, Iran and others mill around the Middle East doing one thing or another, killing a few people here and there, but killing nothing like the numbers of people Germany, Russia, England, Japan, and the US killed in all-out real war in World War I and II. The US, Russia, Turkey, Saudi Arabia and Iran are now dilly-dallying around Syria vying for minor imperialistic advantages and gains, doing what their leaders feel appropriate given the fantasies, needs and desires of members of their organizations and groups back home.

The whole situation in the Middle East is disastrous, a dystopian nightmare come true. Basic causes stem from agitations among organizations and groups going back centuries caused by disparate religious beliefs and struggles for resources, exacerbated by the competitive capitalistic economic system and the advent of the infernal combustion engine around 1900 requiring oil for fuel and lubrication in cars, trucks, airplanes and ships. The Middle East happened to sit atop huge quantities of oil which developed countries needed for their cars, trucks, airplanes and ships, which led to political and military actions in the region to secure oil supplies, especially during World War I and II, Great Britain being the primary imperialist until World War II, having pretty much political control of the region up to then, establishing alliances with rulers, sheiks and the like, even redrawing the boundaries of countries, even establishing the nation of Israel in 1948 in the area.

The US pretty much took over after World War II as the chief imperialist in the Mid-East and has pretty much controlled the region since through alliances and military invasions, and by training troops and pilots for various monarchs, while selling them airplanes, tanks and other military hardware and munitions. Some say the US is the primary cause of the madness in the region today, caused by invading Iraq in 2003, destroying a Sunni dictator and government, setting up a proxy Shiite government, causing constant agitations among Sunnis and Shiites not only in Iraq but throughout the region. Apparently the US has actually funded some terrorist groups in the region to destabilize this that or the other country attempting to manipulate things in favor of the US economy and US corporations.

ISIS, which stands for the Islamic State of Iraq and Syria, includes Sunni leaders and members whom the US displaced with their invasion and conquering of Iraq in 2003. The entire Mideast region and parts of Africa are now agitated with competing and warring religious organizations and groups fighting among themselves, who are funded by rich monarchs, sheiks and others in various Islamic countries believing in various forms of Islam to fight against other brands of Islamism, and Christianity, playing a third-degree Game of, "Let's you and them fight", somewhat like rich oligarchs fund professional sports teams to fight against other sports teams playing various games in Western nations.

The US now has military personnel stationed around Spaceship Earth doing one thing or another. The US spends more per year on its military teams than the next seven largest military-spending nations combined. How wonderful it is the US can always sell some more treasury bonds to get more "money" when real tax money runs out every fiscal year to pay its troops, pilots, and sailors and other military bills. The total discretionary cost of the US military is now about $600 billion per year, about 54 percent of the discretionary spending in the federal budget, a major cause of the yearly US budget deficit and total debt, which by November 4, 2015 had cumulated to $18,775,249,838,371, according to the US Debt Clock at http://www.usdebtclock.org//. Some say the US now has 800 military bases in over 100 countries scattered around Earth.

Evolution of the Current Economic Predicament

Thanks to ideas Republican voters and politicians had been caused to believe by 1980 the US has been caused to go deeper and deeper in debt after cutting taxes for large corporations and the elite rich while increasing military expenses, which Reaganite Republicans in 1980 said would increase aggregate demand in the domestic economy causing the creation of good civilian jobs. Unfortunately, largely due to large US corporations outsourcing jobs to low wage countries and using more and more computers and automated systems good civilian jobs in the US have decreased since 1980.

The US Federal Reserve System has tried, especially since 2007, to remedy the situation with monetary policy by flooding the US economic casino with trillions of digital dollars created out of thin air by simply punching digits into their accounts, which were "spent" buying back US Treasury Bonds and other debt assets of dubious quality owned by US banks, giving banks more "money" to lend out, which should have spurred economic activity in the civilian sector creating good jobs. Unfortunately this did not happen. Jobs were created but they were not good jobs, and millions of unemployed workers quit looking for new jobs, lowering the unemployment rate, since they were no longer counted as unemployed. While the US economy now supposedly has low unemployment there is little economic growth and insufficient aggregate demand.

Most of the new digital money created since 2007, over three trillion dollars worth, was not loaned to entreprneurs and small business owners who would use it to create more business activity and good civilian jobs. Instead, the money largely wound up in the hands of large corporations and the elite rich who used it to buy stock in the stock market, inflating their paper wealth even more, increasing inequality even more. Consequently the US now in December 2015 has an inflated stock market which could start falling at any time, and another recession is imminent. Debt is high all around, not only the government debt. Consumers have borrowed money to go to college and buy new cars. House prices have increased since 2007 but demand for houses is low and prices will probably crash again when marked to the actual market. How much longer the US Federal Reserve can continue creating new digital money to keep the economy going with monetary policy remains to be seen.

If only Democrat Lyndon Johnson had not escalated the Vietnam War after John F. Kennedy was caused to be assasinated in 1963; if only the US government had raised the taxes of large corporations and the elite rich and had used the new tax money to create good infrastructure jobs in the US, instead of taxes for large corporations and the elite rich being lowered by fifty percent or more after the Reagan Republican revolution in 1980; if only the US Congress had curtailed the outsourcing of good US jobs since 1980, protecting their lower and middle class constituents; if only the Glass-Steagall Act had not been repealed by neocons in 1999, to enrich bankers in too big to fail banks; if only Republican Bush II had not invaded Afghanistan and Iraq, to enrich the military-industrial-intelligence complex—the US would not be in the not-OK position it is in now, economically, politically, morally, and ethically.

And, alas, if only a frog had wings. . . .

The Assassination of John F. Kennedy

The asassination of John F. Kennedy is by far the most famous, riveting, and foreboding unresolved murder in US history. The official government story has been that he was shot by a lone mentally deranged gunman, but there is considerable evidence, proof many say, he was caused to be assassinated by agents within the US government, caused by his threatening the interests of the US military-industrial-intelligence complex by the way he responded to the Cuban Communist revolution, by his planning to quickly get the US military out of Vietnam, and by his planning to raise the taxes of the US oil industry, among other causes.

To see compelling evidence or proof JFK was killed by a conspiracy see this video at http://www.soldiersforpeaceinternational.org/2013/03/speaking-unspeakable.html forwarded to me in March 2015 by Rick Staggenborg, MD, of Coos Bay, Oregon, a psychiatrist specializing in PTSD and other trauma-related conditions, founder of Take Back America for the People and Soldiers for Peace International, and a candidate for the US Senate from Oregon in 2010, who may make another run for the US Senate in 2016.

As you will see in the video a secret service agent had been running on the street holding on to the right rear side of the topless car JFK was riding in to protect him, to use his own body if necessary to shield JFK from assassin bullets; but shortly before JFK was shot, as you can see in the film, the secret service agent received a message instructing him to move away from the car. He turned around and waved his arms and hands up and down in dismay, looking back at someone in the car immediately following the car JFK was in, as if to say, "What the f… is going on?" Seconds later JFK was shot, most likely by two shooters from two different locations.

If this video does not prove a conspiracy was behind the assassination, it proves how utterly stupid and incompetent the US secret service agency can be.

I had recently published articles on the Internet about the JFK assassination taking the position it was probably impossible to prove JFK was killed by a conspiracy; but after I saw the video Staggenborg sent me as an email attachment I became convinced beyond a reasonable doubt a conspiracy of some sort caused JFK to be assassinated. I had seen the Zapruder film, available on the Internet, showing the actual shooting of JFK, but I had not seen this film showing the secret service agent being caused to move away from the JFK car before the shooting occurred.

The JFK assassination is another example proving how difficult it is to convict humans in large organizations such as governments of a crime. The problem now is that if the real shooters of JFK were still alive and something caused them to want to confess how could they prove they actually did it? How could any of the conspirators prove they were involved if something were to cause them to want to set the record straight? Hundreds if not thousands of books and articles have been published and several movies have been made since 1963 attempting to prove JFK was or was not killed by a conspiracy. In the end the government truth definers will probably win. If no can prove a conspiracy did it to a majority of humans, then it must be the lone deranged gunman caused himself to do it, using his own free will, as improbable as this seems, just like the US government said in the first place; and if this happens so it shall be read in history books so long as humans shall live aboard Spaceship Earth.

While the leaders of countries fighting wars would like their members to believe they are victims and innocent good guys, heroically rescuing innocent victims from persecutors, on a Drama Triangle, there is no such thing as a totally innocent country in a war. All countries fighting a war allowed the unjust and unfair conditions that caused the war in the first place. Countries enjoying advantages caused by unfair conditions caused for others act as if they think they are naturally entitled to enjoy better conditions than other countries because of their superiority before war breaks out. While terrorist groups in the Middle East have inflicted unfair and barbarous suffering on innocent victims, they were caused to do what they are doing by unjust and unfair causes others, including the US, England, France, Russia, Iran, Saudi Arabia, and many others caused, took advantage of and allowed. Some say the US is now funding ISIS indirectly though its allies in the region who funnel US funny money to various terrorist groups in the region.

The US in my opinion should not have invaded and destroyed Iraq, a nation not posing a military threat to the US, and it should not have done the killing it did in Vietnam, Cambodia and other places in Southeast Asia, attacking and destroying governments not posing a military threat to the US; nor should it have destroyed innocent people and the infrastructure and environments of those places, leaving live bombs lying about the countryside to cripple and maim innocent people to this day. Why did the US do this? It did it because its political and military leaders were caused to do it by psychological causes and impulses, needs for political power and glory, desires to control more resources, career vested interests, and because a majority of its citizens were caused to go along to get along with the leaders, with many harboring atavistic patriotic desires to fight for god, glory and the American flag to become heroes, and to alleviate the boredom, tedium and frustrations of their banal daily lives in the organizations and groups they accidentally and inevitably encountered at home caused by their natural cause-effect life chains.

The Need for Artificial Intelligence

War is hell but it also satisfies basic human hungers for stimulus, recognition and structure, especially if the warrior can stay alive and in one piece and come back home a hero, with veterans benefits and lifetime retirement income, after the war is over.

War is the most destructive third-degree tissue-tearing psychological Game on Earth, a dangerous sport indeed.

Figuring out how to produce an optimum OKness level for all species aboard Spaceship Earth using the human Adult ego state is not a simple problem. Some humans are now worrying about computers and artificial intelligence being a serious threat, fearing they might eventually take over Earth and decide to render humans extinct, since computers with AI programming will eventually become capable of processing digitized Adult neo-psyche ego state data and information thousands if not millions of times faster than individual humans, in quantities of digits humans can only imagine.

On the other hand, it seems to me computers and artificial intelligence taking over so as to fairly plan, produce and distribute the necessities of life for all humans may be the only hope for Earthians in the long run, considering humans have naturally been caused up to now to co-construct countries, religions, economic systems, cultures, and military organizations and groups causing constant war and existential threats such as over-fecundity, resource depletions, global warming and climate change.

This assumes the last human programmer that writes the last line of computer code that finally enables the magnum AI program to get smart enough to automatrically control the Earthian production and distribution system leaves the AI program with permanently locked-in digitized Parent and Child ego state programming and data that insures all Earthian species can survive for satisfying natural lifespans indefinitely, until a *force majeur* event such as a gigantic asteroid accidentally/inevitably crashing into Earth, or the sun burning out in a billion years, ends it all.

I explained how a magnum AI computer program written by humans using linear programming and the Fortran IV computer language might optimize the production of the necessities of life for all humans in my book, *Business Voyages: Mental Maps, Scripts, Schemata and Tools for Discovering and Co-Constructing Your Own Business Worlds,* after constructing a scientific organization similar to the US space program, NASA.

This idea first happened in my brain in 1969 after taking courses in computer simulations and linear programming in the Texas Tech business doctoral program taught by Dr. Richard Barton, who had recently earned a PhD from the University of California at Berkeley in management science, who caused more new learning to happen in me than any other professor in any course in the doctoral program. I included a model of my magnum linear programming application in the appendix of my doctoral dissertation, *An Analysis of Rural Manpower Migration Patterns in the South Plains Region of*

Texas (Stapleton, 1970), which was supported by a grant from the Office of Manpower Evaluation and Research, US Department of Labor, which was published in 1970 in the National Technical Information Service (PB188048).

Humans keep on learning and thinking while asleep at night. Some of my better ideas have been caused to occur in my brain when I was asleep, certainly not of my own free will. While dreams often appear crazy and bizarre if you can remember them and think about them after you wake up quite often you can see they were not quite as crazy or as shameful or as scary or as wonderful and satisfying as you thought they were when they were going on in your brain when you were asleep, and you can see they were caused by stimuli you had recently been exposed to when you were awake, perhaps even stimuli you were exposed to in academic classes or when doing academic homework.

Considering what happened in the Great Depression and in World War I and II, and in Korea and Vietnam in the 20th Century on Earth; and in Afghanistan, Iraq, Egypt, Tunisia, Libya and Syria in the 21st Century; and in the "wars" in Serbia, Kosovo, Bosnia and Croatia; and in China, Cambodia, Rwanda and Somalia, and elsewhere, in the 20th Century; humans can only hope Earthian history does not keep repeating itself, however OK they might think they are because of learning and using TA, or because of learning, believing, or pretending to believe, family, religious, political and economic dogma, doctrine and scripts naturally pushed up and out on the outer branches of family trees from parents to children generation after generation for millennia around Earth.

The Role of TA in the Overall Scheme of Things

If it's any consolation, certified clinical transactional analysts doing one on one psychotherapy can cause some humans to become more rational, functional, OK and satisfied in their Earthly lives than otherwise would have been the case, regardless of how subjectively and objectively OK, or not-OK, the countries, families, religions, cultures, organizations and groups they are linked with are around Earth.

It seems to me it's less certain certified organizational transactional analysts can cause most organizations and groups to become more OK and satisfied than they otherwise would have been, since it is difficult for an organizational consultant to establish a level of trust with leaders and members of an organization conducive to bringing about such a result. I did it with one manufacturing organization with 300 or so members back in the late 1970s and early 1980s, lecturing and presenting TA models to all members in groups of 50 or so, using the row and column classroom layout, at the outset of the program in a college continuing education facility during the plant work hours, then conducting group meetings spasmodically during work hours as needed over five years at the plant with 10 groups with 20 or so members in each group in hourly meetings, using the circle classroom layout, using the Classroom De-Gamer to randomly select the leader of the day for the group to start the discussion by answering the Three Adult Questions, what's the problem, what are the alternatives, and what do you recommend, designed to cathect I'm OK—You're OK, Adult—Adult transactions. Each group included members from the production, scheduling, production control, finance, and computer departments, including members from all ranks and job descriptions in the department chain of command.

Among other things the experience caused them to improve their OKness and cohesion, invent a new scheduling and control system for the plant, replace their old computer with a new bigger and faster one, and install the new system throughout the plant, which improved the efficiency and profitability of the organization.

Everything was OK until the parent company owning the plant sold it, and the new corporate parent company outsourced most of the jobs of their newly acquired plant to a facility in a low wage country, thereby annihilating the OKness of the organization.

See my eBook, *Recommendations for Waking Up From the American Nightmare*, published in 2012 at Amazon.com at http://www.amazon.com/Richard-John-Stapleton/e/B001KHS3P6, for the full story of this case.

Most leaders of most organizations and groups would not trust a certified organizational transactional analyst doing organizational development as much as most individual clients would trust a certified clinical transactional analyst doing psychotherapy, especially if the clinical CTA had a MD degree. Trust is a rare commodity in organizations and groups, especially when it comes to discussing money and secrets, and most top leaders of large organizations would know a certified transactional analyst organizational consultant could not know much about the specific cause-effect chains determining the financial OKness of the organization for all stakeholders, especially the top leaders and stockholders. Therefore most so-called organizational consulting is not consulting about how to make the organization more OK as a whole based on analyzing and discussing relevant facts, data and information to develop better feelings, behaviors and systems; rather in most cases it entails the so-called consultant dispensing generic canned dog and pony show observations, ideology and encouragement, with no group participation, for the purpose of making members temporarily feel better than they otherwise would have, which is perhaps worth something in some cases. Some people used to do this using TA concepts and diagrams. I tried it myself but I had little talent for or interest in the art. Most teachers do it using standard textbooks in all school systems, from first grade through college, with the script being less prevalent in doctoral programs and in elite business schools.

I think this generalization applies to most organizations, including the largest organizations on Earth, such as nations and religions, led by leaders who are generally charismatic people considered attractive by members of their organizations and groups who wear expensive suits, robes and other types of uniforms and costumes who generally dispense generic canned observations, ideology, and encouragement, aka fairy tales, in their public appearances, talks, sermons, speeches, lessons, and the like to make their organizational members and stakeholders feel better than they otherwise would have about their business, political and spiritual affairs, to hopefully keep their jobs and to keep their organizational cash flow flowing.

Unfortunately, in many ways the Earthian capitalistic dog-eat-dog economic system discourages and retards serious human learning, primarily by enabling large often too big to fail corporations to divide, conquer and dumb down their dispensable employees in various departments, divisions, sub-systems and the like, forcing them to keep their noses to the grindstone day in an day out, if they are lucky enough to keep their jobs, focusing on little but doing their detailed algorithmic mundane jobs when at work, causing them to learn little of value after work because of fatigue, causing them to crash at home with reality shows, sports, soap operas and evangelical preachers on TV; digital movies; sports pages; detective novels; romance novels; and, perish the thought, video games; and in many cases over-sedate themselves with beer, wine and whiskey, or marijuana, or pain pills, or whatever the pain reliever might be, which enables the elite rich lucky enough to have been caused to own and control large corporations to better exploit them at work and as consumers, widening ever more the gulf between rich and poor humans around Earth.

Probably most personnel managers are caused to harbor and radiate attitudes similar to those of the personnel manager of a manufacturing plant with 700 members I tried to sell some TA organizational consulting to in the mid-1980s, who told me, "We don't want our employees to know nothin', about that, except what *we* teach em'."

That plant completely shut down a few years later. The large cavernous facility once housing its equipment, managers, and workers has now sat empty twenty-five years decaying amongst trespassing weeds and brush.

You will find about 1,450,000 results if you ask Google on your computer, "Why is it most humans do not learn very much?"

Learn very much compared to what?

It follows that no one is an A student when it comes to knowing everything possible to learn in Worlds 1, 2, and 3, as defined by Popper and Eccles (1977) listed above. No one could get ninety percent or more of it right on any sort of objective test. Some people know more of it than others, but nobody could make an *absolute* D, that is, get sixty percent of it right, on an objective test. All humans are dummies relative to the total learning content possible to know aboard Spaceship Earth. The best you could hope for on a real life report card would be to know more about Worlds 1, 2, and 3 than most people know around Earth, maybe as much as the top ten percent know, giving you a *relative* A, which cannot be proved with standardized tests.

The Three Adult Questions—What is the problem? What are the alternatives? What do you recommend?

A relevant question is, "Why do most people not learn as much as they might?"

Heeding my advice in this book answering this question, here is my subjective answer, answering the Three Adult Questions. The problem of most humans not learning as much as they might is caused by subjectively not-OK parents, teachers, neighborhoods, communities, schools, religions, businesses, corporations, governments and cultures that script people to be less OK, functional, knowledgeable and rational than they would have been had they been taught and influenced in OK ways. What are the alternatives? The fundamental alternatives are business as usual or change. What do you recommend? I recommend all humans, especially parents, attempting to teach, train or educate humans, especially children, be required to use a classroom de-Gamer and a circle classroom layout at least some of the time in their educational activities and discussions—to cathect all ego states and encourage I'm OK—You're OK, Adult—Adult transactions—while answering and discussing the Three Adult Questions: What is the problem? What are the alternatives? What do you recommend?

I also recommend that de-Gamers be used to randomly select as many politicians and as many congressional committee members as possible to bust up vested interests in one of the most dysfunctional, Game-infested groups on Earth, the US Congress. This is not a novel idea. The ancient Greeks had this idea and used it as early as 600 bce. The process is known as *sortition.*

All humans have Adult ego states that can be cathected, even children at young ages. A soft drink bottle as in playing the childhood game *Spin the Bottle* works well as a classroom de-Gamer to randomly select the leader from the group to attempt to answer the Three Adult Questions in a circle classroom layout to start the discussion among all members. Read my book *Business Voyages* for more detail for rules and procedures I used to govern the discussion process after the randomly selected leader broke the ice. One essential rule is no one can interrupt anyone once someone has the floor. Another one is there can be no side communicating of any sort in the room for the whole session. Members cannot transact overtly or covertly with members around them in the circle, using body language, eye contact, smirks, frowns, and the like, discounting the speaker. Everybody has to pay Adult attention to what the current speaker is saying whether they like it or not. Anyone can respond to any speaker once the speaker has finished, disagreeing or agreeing with what was said, and may bring up another problem if appropriate in the context of the discussion, at least according to my rules. You might be able to figure out better rules than those I used.

What does *cathect* mean? In the case of this book cathect means to turn on or energize an ego state—a state of being, energy, cognition and emotion in the human psyche—for achieving goals and interacting with fellow humans in appropriate ways to produce satisfaction for everyone.

How long should a discussion last? Long enough for the group members to comprehend the system under consideration, the system being the interrelations between relevant focal point entities of the system, that is, the relevant points necessary to comprehend the problem, alternatives and recommendations. According to R. Buckminster Fuller in his *Operating Manual for Spaceship Earth* (1969) comprehension entails separating the relevant from the irrelevant in the system under consideration. It takes time to do this. According to Fuller, Comprehension = $(N^2\text{-}N/2)$ where N = the number of relevant focal points in the system. The greater the number of relevant points the greater the interrelations among them and the greater the comprehension required and produced.

When most members of the discussion group comprehend the system it's time to stop. Most paper cases in my classes of about 30 students took about one hour. Real cases and systems in your organizations and groups may take more or less time, perhaps several hourly sessions for one system. Stick with the discussion until it seems most members have comprehended the relevant problems, alternatives and recommendations of the system under consideration.

Read my course syllabus for BA 450, Busines Policy and Strategy, the capstone course for the undergraduate business program at Georgia Southern University, in *Business Voyages,* which I used 35 years, for more detail regarding how to conduct a de-Gamed discussion process.

It seems to me in order to have better governments you have to have better voters who will elect better politicians; and to have better voters you have to have better educational systems; and the place to start in my opinion is creating continuing education groups and forums for all adults everywhere, creating spaces where adults can discuss relevant adult issues in Game-free ways.

The Need for More and Better Adult Learning

The Open Forum at the Rathskeller Pub in Franklin, North Carolina, started and directed by Heidi and George, is an excellent model. My wife and I have a log cabin near Franklin in the Western North Carolina mountains and when there we attend and participate in the Open Forum, usually consisting of about 20 members, ranging in age from early twenties to late eighties, from all walks of life, from college students to medical doctors, sitting in a circle classroom layout with a glass of wine, a beer, or a latte in hand.

Heidi and George do not use a classroom de-Gamer to elicit answers for the Three Adult Questions: What is the problem, what are the alternatives, and what do you recommend? Instead they preannounce a topic, such as, Does free will exist?, or Does capitalism dumb people down?, or Are all Republicans bigoted?, and the first person to hold up a hand gets to talk first, with everyone holding up hands getting to talk in the order in which he or she raised their hand, with no deviation from this rule. The process is Game-free. Any participant can say whatever she or he wants to say so long as it is not obscene or vicious. And the process works. The group members enjoy the process and they learn. The people there might be wrong about what they say, but if so they are honestly wrong. They are not playing Games. They do not say what they say to curry favor with group members or to get ahead. They are saying in general what they truly feel, think, and believe. More relevant general truth gets discussed in this group than in any group I now relate to. Anyone can attend simply by showing up. The experience is free, except for the price of a glass of wine, a beer, or a latte, if you so choose.

I have been influenced in recent years by my long-time friend William John Cox, of Long Beach, California, with whom I reconnected on the Internet about six years ago, who told me about the *Intrepid Report* and other Internet journals as publishing outlets. Wm and I were friends in the 1940s at Wolfforth, Texas, sitting in the same Methodist Sunday School class in 1945, playing on the same high school football team in 1954. He became a police officer, attorney, public prosecutor, author and social activist, living in Long Beach, California, who wrote the police manual for the Los Angeles Police Department (LAPD) and several books on fair practices in law and politics, including a book about the Holocaust. He has created a website for the United States Voters Rights Amendment at http://usvra.us/, which he conceived and founded, promoting an amendment needed to correct defects and loopholes in the US Constitution that have allowed voter suppression and anti-social actions by Republican politicians and judges in Congress and on the US Supreme Court that have sabotaged democracy in the US. Wm recommends making a voting day for the US presidency and Congress a paid national holiday, providing time for political discussions in a Game-free way among voters at the grass roots level around the country, making write-in votes possible, and making the vote a paper vote to insure against voter fraud. Wm is the author of *You're Not Stupid! Get the Truth: A Brief on the Bush Presidency* (2004). I am now on the board of directors of the USVRA organization. I recommend you support this effort, or a similar one, to amend the US Constitution to make the above changes.

Who do I recommend as US president in 2016? Bernie Sanders without a doubt. Not only is Sanders the only viable candidate not beholden to the elite rich; he has far and away been caused to learn and create the best ideas for leading the US aboard Spaceship Earth for the next four years.

No one can be fully OK in her or his perceived world unless most people, organizations, and groups in that world are perceived to be at least somewhat OK. It seems to me all humans philosophically realizing all humans are caused to be what they are by accidental/inevitable cause-effect chains, and therefore are not to blame or praise, would facilitate everyone being subjectively OK all the time, and would, in the long run, facilitate all humans being objectively OK based on rational data, analysis, and criteria.

Despite humans being caused to be and do and therefore not being to blame or praise, OK leaders and members must cause subjectively not-OK members to obey rules and laws applying to everyone in their organizations and groups. Otherwise chaos ensues. Figuring out appropriate, fair, and just rules, laws, and systems for everyone in organizations and groups using all ego states is not a simple task, especially in the largest organizations on Earth such as nations.

What Spaceship Earth needs is a large computerized international corporation, having no board of directors or ceo to corrupt its operations for personal gain, in which all humans are unconditionally and automatically issued one share of ownership stock at birth, that will automatically, optimally, and fairly produce and distribute to stockholders as dividends the necessities of life as needed throughout their lifetimes, with the stock share terminating at the death of the shareholder. This system might finally untie the Gordian Knot of irrationality, fear, ignorance, selfishness, greed, unfairness, obtuseness, and hatred that has caused not-OKness for all individuals, organizations, and groups aboard Spaceship Earth, in various ways and in various degrees of severity, since time immemorial, before it's too late.

Bibliography

Adzema, Michael (2013). *Experience Is Divinity.* Amazon.com, 2013.

Allen, J. R. and B. A. Allen. "Scripts and Permissions: Some Unexamined Assumptions and Connotations." *Transactional Analysis Journal* 18 (1988): 283–293.

Allen, J. R. and B. A. Allen. "Towards a Constructivist TA." In *The Stamford Papers: Selections from the 29th Annual ITAA Conference*, edited by B. R. Loria, 1–22. Madison, WI: Omnipress, 1991.

Allen, J. R. "Concepts, Competencies, and Interpretative Communities." *Transactional Analysis Journal* 33, no. 2 (2003): 126–147.

Allen, Jon and Dorothy Webb. "Stroking, Existential Position and Mood in College Students," *Transactional Analysis Journal* 5, no. 3 (1975).

Amundson, Norman. "TA with Elementary School Children: A Pilot Study." *Transactional Analysis Journal* 5, no. 3 (1975).

Anderson, R. C. (1977). "The Notion of Schemata and the Educational Enterprise: General Discussion of the Conference." In *Schooling and the Acquisition of Knowledge*, edited by R. C. Anderson, W. E. Spiro, and W. E. Montague. Hillsdale, NJ: Lawrence Erlbaum Associates, Publishers.

Arnold, Tim and Richard Simpson. "The Effects of TA on Emotionally Disturbed School-Age Boys." *Transactional Analysis Journal* 5, no. 3 (1975).

Barnes, Graham. *Steps for Developing and Implementing Problem-Solving Contracts.* Chapel Hill, NC: Southeast Institute, 1974.

Barnes, Graham. "What Is a School of Transactional Analysis?" In *Transactional Analysis after Eric Berne: Teachings and Practices of Three TA Schools*, edited by Graham Barnes. New York: Harper's College Press, 1977.

Barnes, Graham. *Justice, Love, and Wisdom: Linking Psychotherapy to Second-Order Cybernetics.* Zabreb, Croatia: Medicinska Naklada, 1994.

Bateson, Gregory. *Steps to an Ecology of Mind: The New Information Sciences Can Lead to a New Understanding of Man.* New York: Ballantine Books, 1972.

Berne, Eric. *A Layman's Guide to Psychiatry and Psychoanalysis.* New York: Simon and Schuster, 1957.

Berne, Eric. "Classification of Positions." *Transactional Analysis Bulletin* 1, no. 3 (1962).

Berne, Eric. "Ego States in Psychotherapy." *American Journal of Psychotherapy* 11, no. 2 (1957).

Berne, Eric. *The Structure and Dynamics of Organizations and Groups.* New York: Grove Press, 1963.

Berne, Eric. "Trading Stamps." *Transactional Analysis Bulletin* 3, no. 10 (1964).

Berne, Eric. *Games People Play: The Psychology of Human Relationships.* New York: Grove Press, 1970.

Berne, Eric. *What Do You Say After You Say Hello? The Psychology of Human Destiny.* New York: Grove Press, 1970.

Boyd, Harry. "Second-Order Structure in the Child." *Transactional Analysis Journal* 8, no. 1 (1978).

Boyd, Harry. "Scripts and Scenarios." *Transactional Analysis Journal* 6, no. 3 (1976).

Boyd, Harry. "The Structure and Sequence of Psychotherapy." *Transactional Analysis Journal* 6, no. 2 (1976).

Buber, Martin. *I and Thou.* Translated by Ronald Gregor Smith. New York: Charles Scribner's Sons. (1985).

Childs-Gowell, E. *Bodyscript Blockbusting.* Seattle, Washington: Self-published, 1979.

Childs-Gowell, E. *Good Grief Rituals.* Station Hill Press, 1992.

Childs-Gowell, E. *Regression and Protection: How to Provide Safety When Working with Deeply Wounded Clients.* Seattle, Washington: Self-published, 2001.

Christensen, C. R. and A. J. Hanson. *Teaching and the Case Method.* New York: McGraw-Hill, 1986.

Christensen, C. R. *Education for Judgment: The Artistry of Discussion Leadership.* New York: McGraw-Hill, 1992.

Cox, William John. *You're not Stupid! Get the Truth: A Brief on the Bush Presidency.* Joshua Tree, CA: Progressive Press, 2004.

Dewey, John. *Democracy in Education: An Introduction to the Philosophy of Education.* New York: The Macmillan Company, 1935.

Dooley, A. R., and W. Skinner. "Casing Case Method Methods." *Academy of Management Review* 2, no. 2 (April 1977).

Dressel, P. L. *Evaluation in Higher Education.* Boston: Houghton Mifflin Company, 1961.

Dusay, John. "Egograms and the Constancy Hypothesis." *Transactional Analysis Journal* 2, no. 3 (1972).

Edwards, Paul and Sally Edwards. *Game Matrix (a Chart).* Kansas City, Missouri: PAA Publications, 1975.

English, Fanita. "The Substitution Factor: Rackets and Real Feelings, Part I." *Transactional Analysis Journal* 1, no. 4 (1971).

English, Fanita. "Rackets and Real Feelings, Part II." *Transactional Analysis Journal* 2, no. 1 (1972).

English, Fanita. "Whither Scripts?" *Transactional Analysis Journal* 18 (1988): 292–303.

Epictetus (80), From the *Discourses of Epictetus.* Translated by T. W. Rolleston. New York: The Mershon Company, undated. Taken from *The Administrator: Cases on Human Aspects of Management*, by Glover, John; Hower, Ralph; and Tagiuri, Renato, eds. Homewood, Illinois: Richard D. Irwin Inc., 1979.

Ernst, Franklin. "The OK Corral: The Grid for Get on With." *Transactional Analysis Journal* 1, no. 4 (1971).

Ernst, Jennie Lou. Using Transactional Analysis in a High School Learning Disability Grouping, *Transactional Analysis Journal* 1, no. 4 (1971).

Ernst, Kenneth. *Games Students Play, and What to Do About Them.* Millbrae, CA: Celestial Arts Publishing, 1972.

Erskine, Richard and Jerry Maisenbacher. "The Effects of a TA Class on Socially Maladjusted High School Students." *Transactional Analysis Journal* 5, no. 3 (1975).

"Ethical Principles of the ITAA." *The Script* 3, no. 3 (1978).

Fischer, Judith D. "The Use and Effects of Student Ratings in Legal Writing Courses: A Plea for Holistic Evaluation of Teaching." *Legal Writing: The Journal of the Legal Writing Institute* 10 (2004).

Frazier, Thomas. The Application of Transactional Analysis Principles in the Classroom of a Correctional School." *Transactional Analysis Journal* 1, no. 4.

Freire, Paulo. *Pedagogy of the Oppressed.* New York: Herder and Herder, 1970.

Fuller, R. Buckminster. *Operating Manual for Spaceship Earth.* New York: Simon and Schuster, 1969.

Gagne, R. M. *The Conditions of Learning* (third. ed.). Holt, Rinehart & Winston, 1977.

Giroux, Henry. *Border Crossings: Cultural Workers and the Politics of Education.* New York: Routledge, 1992.

Goldman, A. L. *A Theory of Human Action.* New Jersey: Princeton University Press, 1970.

Goulding, Robert and Mary Goulding. "Injunctions, Decisions, and Redecisions." *Transactional Analysis Journal* 6, no. 1 (1976).

Greenwald, A. G., and G. M. Gillmore. "Grading Leniency Is a Removable Contaminant of Student Ratings." *American Psychologist* 52, no. 11 (1997): 1209–1216.

Greenwald, A. G. and G. M. Gillmore. "No Pain, No Gain? The Importance of Measuring Course Workload in Student Ratings of Instruction." *Journal of Educational Psychology* 89, no. 4 (1997): 743–751.

Groder, Martin. "Groder's 5 OK Diagrams." In *Transactional Analysis after Eric Berne: Teachings and Practices of Three TA Schools*, edited by Graham Barnes. New York: Harper's College Press, 1977.

Groder, Martin. *Organizational Development Workshop.* Chapel Hill, NC: Southeast Institute, 1975.

Hough, Pat. "Teachers and Stroking." *Transactional Analysis Journal* 1, no. 3 (1971).

Hesterly, Otho. "How to Use TA in the Public Schools." Little Rock, AR: Self-published pamphlet, 1971. Available from Transactional Publications, 1772 Vallejo Street, San Francisco, CA.

Jacobs, Alan. "Aspects of Survival: Triumph over Death and Onliness." *Transactional Analysis Journal.* 21, no. 1(1991): 4–11.

James, John. "The Game Plan," *Transactional Analysis Journal* 3, no. 3 (1973).

James, John. Positive Payoffs, *Transactional Analysis Journal* 6, no. 3 (1976).

James, Muriel and Dorothy Jongeward. *Born to Win: Transactional Analysis with Gestalt Experiments.* Reading, MA: Addison-Wesley Publishing Co., 1973.

James, Muriel and Dorothy Jongeward. *The People Book: TA for Students.* Reading, Mass.: Addison-Wesley Publishing Co., 1972.

James, Muriel. "Self-Reparenting: Application to Script Analysis." *Transactional Analysis Journal* 4, no. 3 (1974).

Johnson, Lois. "Imprinting: A Variable in Script Analysis." *Transactional Analysis Journal* 8, no. 2 (1978).

Kahler, Taibi and Hedges Capers. "The Miniscript." *Transactional Analysis Journal* 4, no. 1 (1974).

Karpman, Stephen. "The Bias Box for Competing Psychotherapies." *Transactional Analysis Journal* 5, no. 2 (1975).

Karpman, Stephen. "Eric Berne Memorial Scientific Award Lecture." *Transactional Analysis Journal* 3, no. 1 (1973).

Karpman, Stephen. "Fairy Tales and Script Drama Analysis." *Transactional Analysis Bulletin* 7, no. 26 (1958).

Karpman, Stephen. "Options." *Transactional Analysis Journal* 1, no. 1 (1971).

LeDoux. J. *The Emotional Brain: The Mysterious Underpinnings of Emotional Life. New York:* Touchstone Books (1966).

LeDoux, J. *Synaptic Self: How our Brains Become Who We Are.* New York: Penguin Putnam (2002).

Loria, B. R. "Integrative Family Therapy: A Constructivist Perspective." In *The Stamford Papers: Selections from the 29th Annual ITAA Conference*, edited by B. R. Loria, 34-41. Madison, WI: Omnipress, 1991.

Loria, B. R., ed. *The Stamford Papers: Selections from the 29th Annual ITAA Conference*, 1–22. Madison, WI: Omnipress, 1991.

Maltz, Maxwell. *Psycho-Cybernetics: A New Way to Get More Living out of Life.* New York: Prentice-Hall, 1960.

Maslow, Abriham. "A Theory of Human Motivation," *Psychological Review*, 1943, Vol. 50, No 4, pp 370-396 (1943).

Maturana, H. R. and F. J. Varela. *Autopoiesis and Cognition: The Realization of Living*. Dordrecht, Holland: D. Reidel Publishing Company, 1980.

Maturana, H. R. and F. J. Varela. *The Tree of Knowledge*. Boston: New Science Library, 1987.

Maury, D. H. *Recollections of a Virginian in the Mexican, Indian and Civil Wars*. New York: Charles Scribner's Sons, 1894.

Maury, M.F. *Physical geography of the seas*. New York: Harper & Brothers. Now available from .com as *The Physical Geography of the Seas and Its Meteorology*. Dover Publications, 2003.

McKenna, Jim. "Stroking Profile: Applications to Script Analysis." *Transactional Analysis Journal* 4, no. 4 (1971).

Maisenbacher, Jerry and Richard Erskine. "Time Structuring for 'Problem' Students." *Transactional Analysis Journal* 6, no. 2 (1976).

Menninger, Joan. "Reteachering." *Transactional Analysis Journal* 7, no. 1 (1977).

Novey, Theodore. "Measuring the Effectiveness of Transactional Analysis: An International Study", *Transactional Analysis Journal* 32, no. 1 (2002): 8–25.

Osnes, Russell. "Spot Reparenting." *Transactional Analysis Journal* 4, no. 3 (1974).

Pascal, Blaise, *The Pensees (thoughts): A Defense of the Christian Religion*. Wikipedia, The Free Encyclopedia. En.wikipedia. org/wiki/Pensees, 1669.

Perls, Fritz. *The Gestalt Approach: Eye Witness to Therapy.* Palo Alto, CA: Science and Behavior Books, 1973.

Perls, Fritz. *Gestalt Therapy Verbatim*. Moab, UT: Real People Press, 1959.

Popper, K. R. and J. C. Eccles. *The Self and Its Brain.* Berlin: Springer International, 1977.

Schiff, Aaron Lee and Jacqui Lee Schiff. "Passivity." *Transactional Analysis Journal* 1, no. 1 (1971).

Schiff, Jacqui Lee. *All My Children*. New York: Pyramid Books, 1972.

Schank, R.C. and Abelson, R.P., *Scripts, Plans, Goals, and Understanding.* Hillsdale, New Jersey: Lawrence Erlbaum Associates, Publishers, 1977.

Simon, H.A, *Administrative Behavior: A study of Decision- Making Processes in Administrative Organizational (4th ed.).* New York: The Free Press, (1997).

Stapleton, R. J. *An Analysis of Rural Manpower Migration Patterns in the South Plains Region of Texas.* (Doctoral dissertation). Washington, DC: Department of Labor, Office of Manpower Evaluation and Research, National Technical Information Service (PB188048), 1970.

Stapleton, Richard. *Managing Creatively: Action Learning in Action.* Washington, DC: University Press of America, 1976.

Stapleton, Richard. "Classroom De-Gamer", *Research in Education*, Materials Clearinghouse, School of Education, University of Michigan, Ann Arbor, Michigan (1978).

Stapleton, Richard. "The Chain of Ego States", *Transactional Analysis Journal* 8, no. 3 (1978).

Stapleton, R. J. "The Classroom De-Gamer." *Transactional Analysis Journal* 9, no. 2 (April 1979): 145–146.

Stapleton, R. J. *De-Gaming Teaching and Learning: How to Motivate Learners and Invite OKness.* Statesboro, GA: Effective Learning Publications, 1979.

Stapleton, R. J. *The Entrepreneur: Concepts and Cases on Creativity in Business.* Lanham, Maryland: University Press of America, 1985.

Stapleton, R. J. "Academic Entrepreneurship: Using the Case Method to Simulate Competitive Business Markets." *Organizational Behavior Teaching Review* 14, no. 4 (1989–1990): 88–104.

Stapleton, R. J., G. Murkison, and D. C. Stapleton. "Feedback Regarding a Game-Free Case Method Process Used to Educate General Management and Entrepreneurship Students." *Proceedings of the 1993 Annual Meeting of the Southeast CHAPTER of the Institute for Management Science* (October, 1993).

Stapleton, R. J., G. Murkison, and D. C. Stapleton. "Realistically Estimating the Magnitude and Significance of Business Learning: Longitudinal Feedback Regarding a Management Learning Process." *Manuscript.* Georgia Southern University, 1994.

Stapleton, R. J. and D. C. Stapleton. "Teaching Business Using the Case Method and Transactional Analysis: A Constructivist Approach." *Transactional Analysis Journal,* 28, no. 2 (1998): 157–167.

Stapleton, R. J. and G. Murkison. "Optimizing the Fairness of Student Evaluations: A Study of Correlations between Instructor Excellence, Study Production, Learning Production, and Expected Grades." *The Journal of Management Education* 25, no. 3 (2001): 269–292.

Stapleton, R. J. *Business Voyages: Mental Maps, Scripts, Schemata and Tools for Discovering and Co-Constructing Your Own Business Worlds.* Statesboro, Georgia: Effective Learning Publications, 2012.

Stapleton, R. J. *Recommendations for Waking Up From the American Nightmare.* Amazon.com, 2013.

Stapleton, R. J. "Toward the Creation of Spaceship Earth Incorporated." *MWC News.* Monday, September 9, 2013. http://mwcnews.net/focus/analysis/31023-spaceship-earth-incorporated.html.

Stapleton, R. J. "Waiting on a Hurricane in the Summer of 2015." *MWC News.* August 15, 2015. http://mwcnews.net/focus/politics/53583-waiting-on-a-hurricane.html.

Steiner, Claude. *Games Alcoholics Play: The Analysis of Life Scripts.* New York, Grove Press, 1971.

Steiner, Claude. *Scripts People Live: Transactional Analysis of Life Scripts.* New York: Grove Press, 1974.

Steiner, Claude. "The Stroke Economy." *Transactional Analysis Journal* 1, no. 3 (1971).

Thweatt, William. "My High School Counselor Said I Should Be a Forest Ranger." *Transactional Analysis Journal* 5, no. 3 (1969).

Towl, A. R. *To Study Administration by Cases.* Boston: Harvard University Press, 1969.

Von Foerster, Heinz. "On Constructing a Reality." In *The Invented Reality: How Do We Know What We Believe We Know*. Edited by Paul Watzlawick. New York: W. W. Norton and Company, 1984.

Von Glaserfeld, E. *The Construction of Knowledge: Contribution to Conceptual Semantics.* Salinas, CA: Intersystems Publications, 1988.

Wasserman, Harvey. "Nuclear Reactors Make ISIS an Apocalyptic Threat," *Intrepid Report.* (December 2, 2015). http://.intrepidreport.com/archives/16930.

Wittgenstein, Ludwig, *Philosophical Investigations.* Translated by G.E.M. Anscombe. Oxford: Basil Blackwell, 1968. First published in 1953.

Wittgenstein, Ludwig, *Prototractatus* (an early version of *Tractatus Logico-Philosophicus*). Edited by B. F. McGuinness, T. Nyberg, and G. H. von Wright. Translated by D. F. Pears and B. F. McGuinness. Includes a historical introduction by G. H. von Wright and a facsimile of the author's manuscript. Ithaca, New York: Cornell University Press, 1971. First published in 1921.

Wood, J. D. and Gianpiero Petriglieri. "Transcending Polarization: Beyond Binary Thinking," *Transactional Analysis Journal,* Vol. 33, No. 1, (2005), pp. 31-39.

Appendix 1

You can find here a full PDF copy of "Optimizing the Fairness of Student Evaluations: A Study of Correlations between Instructor Excellence, Study Production, Learning Production, and Expected Grades," by Richard John Stapleton and Gene Murkison of Georgia Southern University, published in the *Journal of Management Education,* the official journal of the Organizational Behavior Teaching Society, as the lead article of their issue of June 2001.

"Optimizing the Fairness of Student Evaluations" has by now in January 2016 been cited as a reference in sixty professional, refereed journal articles in several disciplines (this can easily be verified with a Google search on the Internet by punching "Optimizing the Fairness of Student Evaluations" into Google on your computer). There have been three new citations in the last two years, proving the article is still being read and used by serious scholars and researchers.

"Optimizing the Fairness of Student Evaluations," which was blind reviewed by several reviewers at major universities several times over two years before it was finally published, is by far the most influential article I researched, wrote, and published in my career as a university professor.

This article contains a new metric I (Richard) invented for evaluating teachers: The composite indicator of teaching productivity (CITP), which is a ranking of ranks of teachers for instructor excellence, study production, learning production, and relative expected grades scores on student evaluations.

Teaching evaluations are the cause of untold frustration, conflict, Games, and injustice among teachers and administrators. Effective teachers want to be recognized and rewarded with merit raises, promotions, and tenure based on their relative teaching productivity, just like effective people in all fields want to be recognized and rewarded based on their relative productivity. How to prove teachers are good teachers (or better or worse than that) for merit raises, promotion, and tenure is not a simple problem.

Student evaluations and the data they collect do more good than harm, in my opinion, since teachers and administrators can see what all students in classes thought. Otherwise, teachers are at the mercy of Gamey hearsay picked up by administrators in hallways, offices, and faculty lounges in one-on-one furtive and often secret transactions.

I recommend that the CITP be used in all educational institutions to provide relevant and fair feedback to teachers; to enable administrators and faculty committees to make fair and rational merit raise, promotion, and tenure decisions; and to provide teachers with relevant data and information to show how well they taught, which they can use as defending evidence should they be unfairly accused (as is likely) on a Drama Triangle of being poor teachers by Game-playing Persecutor students, fellow teachers, parents, administrators, and politicians. The CITP measures the relative productivity of a teacher based on defining *teaching* as causing *learning* to occur in students, not disseminating facts, information, techniques, and fairy tales in pleasant ways for standardized tests, to get high instructor excellence scores on student evaluations to get high merit raises.

To read a PDF copy of "Optimizing the Fairness of Student Evaluations," click the following web address if you are reading this from an e-book or copy the address into Google or any search device on the Internet if you are reading from a print copy.

I was Professor S in the study. The article is not an easy read. It contains data, charts, graphs, and statistical difference tests. It takes about seven seconds to download the article onto a computer.

Cheers.

http://www.sagepub.com/holt/articles/Stapleton.pdf

About the Author

Richard John Stapleton, named Richard Coston Stapleton on his birth certificate by his parents Richard Gathright Maury Stapleton and Ida Belle Coston Stapleton, called Rick as a child, was born November 3, 1940 in Corpus Christi, Texas.

Rick's father, called Dick, worked at a Naval base in Corpus Christi as an itinerant carpenter for a few months, soon moving his family to Louisiana and then to Oklahoma for new government jobs in the Great Depression. After three years Dick had saved enough money to make a down payment on a farm near Lubbock, Texas, which he sold after a year or so and joined the Seabees, working on construction projects during World War II on the island of Okinawa. Dick returned to the town of Wolfforth ten miles southwest of Lubbock when World War II ended, where he became a successful contractor, businessman, banker, farmer, and rancher. Ida was the bookkeeper of the various enterprises Dick started.

Rick was generally considered a smart little boy but he was not comfortable or effective dealing with most people. Shy and introverted, kids teased him about his full name and his manners. He was a mediocre student in grade, junior, and high school, with anomalies in high school physics and plane geometry, in which he made A's. He also scored highly on achievement and aptitude tests administered by the county. On the other hand he was an outstanding athlete in football and basketball. According to the *Lubbock*

Avalanche-Journal in 1954 he was probably the youngest and smallest Class A high school starting quarterback in the United States, at age thirteen, five feet three inches tall, and one hundred ten pounds. He played college basketball two years on an athletic scholarship.

After experiencing more problems than most people adjusting to adult life and figuring out what he wanted to do for a living, the author got a doctor's degree and became a college professor. He legally changed his middle name from Coston to John in 1978 after a TA mentor told him this might psychologically help him violate some of his script injunctions.

Genealogical research in recent years revealed that one of the author's great great grandfathers Thomas Sanford Gathright was the first president of Texas A & M University and one of his great grandfathers many times removed the Reverend Doctor James Maury taught four US presidents—Washington, Jefferson, Madison and Monroe.

All four of the author's grandparents had ancestors living in Virginia at the time of the US Revolutionary War, with several fighting in that war. Several of his great grandfathers in the US before the Civil War were cotton farmers and several were slave owners in Virginia, North Carolina, Tennessee, South Carolina, Georgia, Alabama, and Mississippi.

Some of his ancestors were foot soldiers in the US Civil War, but one was a general and one was a commodore, both West Point graduates. All fought for the South.

According to Ancestry. com DNA analysis, many of Stapleton's ancestors in Europe were members of English, Scottish, Irish, and French nobility, including Braveheart and Richard the Lionheart.

This family history is not something to be blamed or praised, having been accidentally and inevitably caused, but it is relevant given the purposes and context of this book, focusing as it does on Parent, Adult, and Child ego states and family scripts.

While this family script conferred certain advantages on family members, the cumulative experiences of ancestors caused this family script and personality profile to be overly austere, reclusive, exclusive, and unemotional through the generations, causing psychological and social problems for various members of the family in various situations.

CPSIA information can be obtained
at www.ICGtesting.com
Printed in the USA
BVHW03s0731230918
528265BV00001B/149/P